THE
MIDDLE EASTERN
KITCHEN

GHILLIE BAŞAN

THE MIDDLE EASTERN KITCHEN

GHILLIE BAŞAN

WITH SPECIAL PHOTOGRAPHY BY
JONATHAN BAŞAN

This book is dedicated to our friend
Monica von Habsburg, who has
a passionate appetite for life

Previous page: View of the Bosphorus from the Süleymaniye mosque, Istanbul, Turkey
Right: The Friday mosque, Isfahan, Iran

Published in North America by Hippocrene Books, 2004.

For more information address:
HIPPOCRENE BOOKS, INC.
171 Madison Avenue
New York, NY 10016
www.hippocrenebooks.com

First published in Great Britain in 2001 by Kyle Cathie Limited, 122 Arlington Road, London NW1 7HP

ISBN 0-7818-1023-X

Cataloging-in-Publication Data available from the Library of Congress.
Printed and bound in Singapore by Kyodo Printing Co.

CONTENTS

INTRODUCTION

There's something incredibly sumptuous about the food of the Middle East. It is steeped in history and mystery, teasing the palate with exotic and tantalizing flavors. Delicate and spicy, aromatic and fragrant, scented and syrupy—these are some of the words that come to mind. The tastes are rich and pleasing, the images romantic, airy, and ancient. Rose petals and orange blossom, tamarind and dates, figs and apricots, mulberries and melons, saffron and orchid root, almonds and pistachios, olives, coriander and cumin—a myriad of flavors and dishes that are intricately entwined in the fascinating history of this vast, diverse, and exciting region.

Every village, town, valley, or hillside tells a story. There are the ancient Pyramids of Egypt and the Hanging Gardens of Babylon; the last route walked by Christ and the tomb of the Virgin Mary; the desert where John the Baptist survived on locusts, and King Herod's fortress where the dancing Salome was given a gift of the unfortunate John's head. There is the place where Cleopatra bathed and the site where Alexander the Great sought the Oracle's advice; the Mount of Olives, the Temple of Artemis, and the Gate of Hercules; the desert where Lawrence of Arabia was based during the Great Arab Revolt; Roman amphitheatres and the castles built by the Crusaders. There are the ancient cities, the holy cities, the ghostly, ruined cities, the desert cities, the towering mud cities, and the exquisite Nabataean fortress city carved out of sandstone; the Bedouin camps, the troglodite cave dwellings, and the reed huts in the marshes; the Black Sea, the Red Sea, and the Dead Sea. There are early Christian and Byzantine churches, Jewish synagogues, and magnificent domed, tiled mosques. And there is the splendid Topkapı Palace, from where the Ottomans ruled for almost five centuries and held lavish feasts. The history of the region drips like rain off every branch of the trees, it flows through the meandering rivers and breathes through the pores of the land. As a visitor you can't fail to be impressed, tripping over relics of antiquity like the raised roots of a wizened old olive tree. For the peoples who live there, the history has had a profound effect on their lives, shaping their beliefs, their customs, and their culinary traditions.

Historically, the lands of the Middle East have always been turbulent. They have seen civilizations and empires come and go. It is where Africa, Europe, and Asia have always met, traded, and fused. It is the birthplace of the three principal monotheistic religions—Christianity, Judaism, and Islam. So, for centuries, it has witnessed clashes between cultures and religions, forcing peoples and their traditions to merge or move. This is particularly evident in the culinary cultures of the region, where ingredients have been adopted and dishes have been adapted with the movement of peoples, the conquering of territories, and the might of religion. In the minds of many in the West, the Middle East strikes a discordant note. It is often regarded as one land, full of rich Arabs with multiple wives concealed behind veils and as a breeder of Islamic fundamentalism and fanaticism. This, of course, is not true. Beneath the simmering surface of this ancient region inhabited by Arabs, Turks, Persians, Assyrians, Armenians, Kurds, Muslims, Jews, and Christians there is a gentler side too, a world where they are all clearly united in two things—their hospitality and food.

For this book, I have selected loose boundaries, based on the modern definition of the Middle East, to

Herding goats in the mountains around Petra, Jordan

include Iran, Turkey, Iraq, Syria, Lebanon, and the Palestinian Territories, Jordan, Egypt, Yemen, Qatar, Kuwait, Oman, Saudi Arabia, and the United Arab Emirates. It is a difficult region to tie together for a book on food. There are so many blurred areas, where one culture claims a dish over another, so the pieces of the jigsaw don't always slot neatly into place, at times requiring a great deal more explanation than is permitted here. But if there is a single, modern Middle Eastern culinary tradition to be identified, it is one that has been influenced and united by the Persian, Islamic, and Ottoman empires, with a sprinkling of the Byzantine and Roman empires thrown in. Like the spices of a dish, these influences can be added with a light or heavy hand, for the

cooking of the Middle East is not academic. Two families living next door to each other might cook the same dish in different ways. A devout Muslim might reserve the dish for a religious feast, a Christian might eat it for supper with a glass of wine. Whatever the culture or faith, the culinary traditions are based on custom and lore passed down from mother to daughter. As a vociferous champion of Middle Eastern food and a grateful recipient of all the hospitality I have ever received, I hope this book will go some way toward making this monumental movable feast both accessible and enjoyable. But first, in order to get an understanding of the cooking of the Middle East today, we need to disentangle some of the elements of its fascinating culinary history.

A BRIEF HISTORY

Through the discoveries of archaeologists, we now know that as early as 12,000 BC, agriculture was first practiced by the earliest organized societies in the valley of the Nile and later, around 8,000 BC, in the Fertile Crescent of Mesopotamia (ancient Iraq). Known as the "Cradle of Civilization," Mesopotamia could also be considered the birthplace of Middle Eastern food. The meat of domestic and wild animals was roasted whole over an open flame. Wheat and barley were the principal grains. Vegetables were stewed with herbs or meat. Honey and date juice were used as sweeteners. Milk was turned into cheese and butter, which was clarified so that it kept. Archeological evidence suggests that there were about three hundred kinds of bread, some of them baked in a clay oven. Apart from the early desert inhabitants, who probably ate much the same food as the Bedouin today, little is known about the other ancient peoples of the Middle East, like the Syrians,

Cappadocians, and Babylonians. As they invaded and conquered, the Persian, Greek, and Roman empires would have contributed to the character of the region's food.

Around the twelfth century BC it was the Phoenicians, the intrepid seafarers and craftsmen who inhabited the eastern Mediterranean coast, who influenced the region with their articles of trade. Their ships carried shrubs, herbs, dried fish, and fruit, nuts, exotic spices, and perfumes. The lucrative spice trade was almost entirely controlled by the Phoenicians, until Alexander the Great set up his own entrepôt at the mouth of the Nile. The Persian Empire of 558–330 BC, which stretched from Russia to Egypt and from Greece to India, wielded a strong influence on the culinary practices of the region. Believers in pleasing the eye as well as the palate, the Persians spread their skills and their own produce, such as pomegranates and saffron. With the ancient Silk Route from China to Syria traveling through its northern regions and the trade routes in the south, the location of Persia in the ancient world meant that it served as a conduit for many products, such as lemons and eggplants, coming from the east. The Romans, whose sea power enabled them to send ships directly to India, took over from the Greeks and, at the same time, the Silk Routes across Central Asia, linking China and Rome, were regulated by Han emperors, who, in their drive to secure their borders, displaced the Mongol and Central Asian pastoral tribes, forcing them to invade

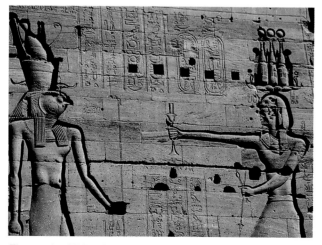

The temple of Philae, Egypt

new territories. This led to the severing of overland routes and, eventually, to the fall of the Roman Empire in the fifth century, but the sea trade routes survived.

With the split of the Roman Empire in AD 395, the eastern half became the Byzantine Empire, which governed Greater Syria until the early seventh century. During the reign of Justinian I and the empress Theodora in the sixth century, great feasts, comprising dishes from India, Armenia, Persia, Greece, Cyprus, and Syria, were held at the Byzantine court. Soups and vegetable stews were popular. Meatballs, grilled fish, duck, or whole baby lamb appeared as main courses, and roast suckling pig, cold hams, and spicy pork sausages were also consumed. However, the most sophisticated and lavish cuisine at this period came from the other great power, the Sassanids, a dynasty that ruled Persia from the third to the seventh centuries. With the decline of the Byzantine Empire and the influence of India, for Alexander the Great and his successors had made parts of India and Persia Hellenic strongholds, there was an exciting mix of well-developed culinary traditions and philosophies. In the early seventh century, when Byzantium was defeated and Alexandria, Jerusalem, Antioch, and Damascus were conquered by Persian generals, King Khusrow II, renowned for his cruelty and greed, held extravagant banquets. These often consisted of hot and cold meats, rice gelatin, stuffed vine leaves, sweet date puree, the meat of young camels, buffaloes, and wild donkeys, and game dishes prepared with hare and gazelle. Meat was sometimes marinated in yogurt and spices, fruit was often paired with meat, and nuts were ground to thicken sauces or fill pastries. Fruit jams and preserves were popular, and dates were stuffed with almonds. The influence of this

Arab trading ship

distinguished Persian cuisine, peppered with Byzantine and Indian traditions, is still evident in many of the dishes throughout the Middle East today.

The spread of Islam, following the death of the Prophet Muhammad in AD 632, changed the face of the Middle East for ever more. With revolutionary fervor, the Bedouin Arabs from the Arabian Peninsula swept into Greater Syria and Persia, conquering one territory after another, converting them to Islam, until they had established a vast Islamic Empire spreading right across Asia and North Africa and into Sicily and Spain. Wherever they went, the Arabs took their own culinary traditions and adopted those of the conquered territories along the way, so that a myriad of dishes and flavors permeated the empire. However, there were a few tiny communities, such as the Christians who entrenched themselves in the mountains of Lebanon, who held on to their ancient cultural beliefs, which have remained unchanged to

Camping in the desert, Wadi Umm al Hayat, Oman

this day. During its first century, the new Islamic Empire was governed from Damascus by the Umayyad dynasty of caliphs, but it was during the Abassid period, from the late eighth to the twelfth centuries, that cooking really flourished. With Mecca as its religious center and Baghdad as its capital, the Golden Age of Islam began. Arab ships sailed to China for silk and porcelain, to the East Indies for spices, and to Zanzibar and East Africa for ivory and gold. It was a time of intellectual and cultural awakening and a rich period for culinary creativity. During the reign of Harun-al-Rashid (786–809) culinary literature attained the status of an art, in the areas of both pleasure and health. The banquets held at the royal courts of the caliphs of Baghdad are legendary for their extravagance. Lavish dishes were invented, poems praising the food were recited, and diners ate to the sound of music and singing.

Prior to the Islamic Empire, the food of the Arabs, particularly the nomads, was basic. Their daily diet consisted of dates and the milk of camels, sheep, and goats, which was curdled or churned into butter and clarified for storing. Meat was a luxury, the usual kind being mutton; occasionally gazelle, hares, or ibex were hunted. The nomads supplemented their diet with wild plants, including desert truffles, and the Bedouin consumed grasshoppers, lizards, and mice. The settled communities cultivated vegetables and fruit, and they made bread from barley or wheat. The dishes were simple, containing few ingredients. Particularly popular were *tharid*, a bread-based meat and vegetable broth, and *hays*, a blend of dates, butter, and milk, which were also the Prophet's favorite dishes. Following the conquest, however, Arab cooking was transformed. With the newly acquired lifestyles and culinary techniques of the conquered peoples and the trade routes beyond the empire, a new distinctive cuisine emerged. There came olive oil from Syria, dates from Iraq, and coffee from Arabia. Chefs came from Egypt and spices were brought back from India,

Africa, and China. But the overwhelming influence came from Persia. The caliphs of Baghdad adopted the Sassanids' cult of gastronomy, resulting in a food vocabulary filled with Persian words: for example, *turshi* (pickles), *sanbusak* (small, triangular meat pie), *shurba* (soup), *kufta* (meatballs), and even the term *mezze*.

In the thirteenth century a number of Arab culinary books were written, of which only a few have survived. Some were compilations of recipes from the court cuisine, others were concerned with etiquette, diet, and health. The *Kitab al-tabikh al-Warraq*, the earliest surviving book, gives detailed accounts of the recipes, ingredients, utensils, table manners, and health properties of Abassid cuisine. The *Kitab al-tabikh al-Baghdadi*, in which the author refers to food as the noblest of human pleasures and to cooking as an art for which the cook should be intelligent and have a natural flair, is a collection of sophisticated and peasant recipes from the period. And the *Kitab al-Wulsa Ila'L-Habib Ibn al-'Adim*, often referred to as the *Wulsa*, was written by an aristocrat who was well acquainted with court cuisine and covers all aspects of food preparation, including distilling, and the perfuming of

The camel train from Constantinople to the Black Sea

the body and breath. Some of the recipes and instructions recorded in these manuals could have been written today, so strong are the bonds of culinary tradition.

Thousands of miles further east, in the eleventh century, the first important literary document of the Turks was being composed by Mahmud al-Kashgari. This Turkish–Arabic dictionary recorded aspects of the cuisine and cooking methods of the nomadic Turks, such as the thin flat breads, *yufka*; a fondness for yogurt; and the clay oven, *tandır*. As the Turks moved further westward through Central Asia these fierce warriors and skilled horsemen came into contact with the sophisticated culture and cuisine of the Iranians, but unlike the caliphs of Bagdhad, who were proud to cook elaborate Persian dishes, they preferred to stick to their ancient culinary tradition of roast meat on skewers and *mantı*, a kind of pasta dish with yogurt. Around the time that Mahmud al-Kashgari was busy on his dictionary, the Seljuk Turks settled in Konya, from where they ruled Greater Syria for most of the twelfth century. Scholars, poets, and mystics from different regions of the Islamic world flocked to Konya as it grew into a brilliant center of culture and cosmopolitan cuisine. The works of the great mystic and poet Mevlâna Jalal-al Din Rumi provide records of the vegetables, pulses, nuts, pickles, fruits, breads, pastries, milk products, and kitchen order of the time, and the tomb of his cook, Atesbazi-Veli, has become a shrine for gastronomic pilgrims.

In 1258 the Abassid caliphate fell at the hands of the Mongols. The Mongols were then driven out by the Mamluks, a soldier-slave caste of Turks founded by the military leader Saladin, who had also seized Egypt from the Ayyubid dynasty. The Mamluks were soon in

The Blue Mosque, Istanbul, Turkey

control of the Islamic realm, ruling Egypt, Syria, Palestine, and western Arabia for nearly three hundred years (1250–1517). Also in 1258 the chief of a pagan tribe of Turks had a son called Osman who converted to Islam and later established the Ottoman (*Osmanlı*) Empire, which was to determine the destinies of the Balkans, the Mediterranean region, and the Arab world for the next five centuries. By the middle of the fifteenth century, when Mehmet II conquered Constantinople, the Turks had assimilated the culinary traditions of their varied subjects and developed a sophisticated cuisine of their own. Chefs, who were brought from Bolu, specialized in a single culinary method—there was the maker of sweet, syrupy pastries, the *baklavacı*, and the maker of savory ones, the *börekçi*—which marked the beginning of the celebrated Palace cooking. At the great feasts held in the Topkapı Palace during the reign of Mehmet the Conqueror and Suleyman the Magnificent, the sultan's table displayed all the indulgent extravagance and glamour of an Abassid banquet. Once more, cooking was regarded as an art and a pleasure, enabling an already sophisticated cuisine to reach new heights

with lavish, sensuously named dishes such as *kız memesi*, young girls' breasts; *kadın göbeği*, ladies' navels; and *kadın buduğu*, ladies' thighs.

In the sixteenth century the Ottomans came to an agreement with their rivals, the Spaniards, so that goods en route from the New World to Spain were transported via the North African coast and Egypt directly to Constantinople. In this way, ingredients such as chili peppers, corn, eggplants, tomatoes, and sunflowers reached the territories of the Ottoman Empire much earlier than parts of Europe. In addition to the introduction of new ingredients and the expansion of the empire, the variety and sophistication of Ottoman cuisine were influenced by the fashionable urban life of Constantinople and the unique, dedicated slave system within the palace. Members of the ruling class became slaves to the sultans, the more able being trained and turned into courtiers and grand viziers. The sultan's wives and members of the household were all slaves, often captured in battle, purchased from pirates, or given as gifts. With so many blue-eyed, fair-complexioned followers of the Christian faith, bringing diverse culinary traditions, the Muslim pool was diluted and the cuisine was greatly enhanced. Food was so important to the Ottomans that the insignia of the Janissary force was a pot and spoon, and their titles of rank were drawn from the camp kitchen. After four hundred years of complete rule, the Ottoman Empire finally collapsed with the defeat of Turkey in World War I, but it left a glorious culinary legacy, which is still evident on the tables of all its conquered territories, including a large chunk of the Middle East, parts of North Africa, Bulgaria, Hungary, Romania, and Serbia, and parts of Russia, Greece, and Cyprus.

THE MIDDLE EAST TODAY

After World War I, the French and the British divided up the Ottoman Empire, with France controlling Syria and Lebanon, and Britain administering Palestine, Transjordan, Iraq, and Egypt. The French language and cuisine influenced the culinary life of Lebanon in particular and, for the next three decades, Beirut became an international playground and a paradise for food connoisseurs. Stripped of its Arab provinces, the Ottoman Empire was overthrown and the Republic of Turkey was declared under the leadership of Mustafa Kemal, known as Atatürk, in 1923. The cuisine of Turkey is mirrored in its history, which reflects the splendid

sophistication of the Ottoman legacy, seasoned with the diverse culinary traditions of eastern Anatolia—an area that remained relatively untouched during Ottoman rule. The population is predominantly Sunni Muslim, with a minority of Shi'ites, Kurds, Jews, and Armenians. At the same time as Turkey was declared a republic, Reza Khan of Persia overthrew the Ghajar dynasty and crowned himself shah. In 1934 he changed the name of the country from Persia to Iran. The majority of Iranians are Shi'ite Muslims, with a tiny percentage of Sunni Muslims, Jews, Armenians, and Assyrians. The cuisine, which is still often referred to as Persian, has changed relatively little since ancient times

Beit Jabri, Damascus, Syria

and is similar to that of Turkey and the neighboring
Arab countries, although it can be distinguished by its
unique rice dishes, the preference for a distinct sweet-
sour taste, and the combinations of meat and fruit.

After World War II, when the British withdrew
from Palestine, the United Nations divided it into
Arab and Jewish states. In 1948 the Jews, who had
spread far and wide since biblical times, flocked to this
new state they called Israel, which is still not
recognized by many neighboring Arabs. With them
they brought different food customs, to some extent
shaped by Jewish dietary laws, and drew from the
surrounding cultures. The division of the Jews into
Sephardi and Ashkenazi is reflected in their food.
The Sephardi Jews, who speak Hebrew, are split into
two streams, one that spread westward to Spain,
England, and the New World, and one that remained
in parts of the Middle East and North Africa; they
are sometimes referred to as oriental Jews. Those
who resided in Islamic-occupied Spain and Portugal
came under the same culinary influences as their
counterparts in the Arab lands. The Ashkenazi Jews,
some of whom still speak Yiddish, settled in the
Rhine Valley and to the east of it, from Alsace to the
Black Sea, so their culinary culture was influenced by
the Slavic and Germanic cuisines. The population of
the ancient Holy Land is not entirely Jewish, of
course, for there are the Palestinians, the Christian
Arabs, a small community of nomadic Bedouin, and
minority groups such as the Druze, Armenians,
Circassians, and Samaritans. As a result, the food is an
amalgamation of both Jewish branches, with a heavy
Arab influence, based on dairy products, wheat, lentils,
fava beans, fruit and nuts, raw vegetables, flat breads,
and lamb.

Dusk over the sandstone façades, Petra, Jordan

The Old City of Jerusalem, which can be traversed
in twenty minutes, is the center of the three most
important monotheistic religions. It is where the Way
of Sorrow, from Gethsemane, where Christ was
arrested, to Calvary, where he was crucified, is located.
It is the site of the third holiest shrine in the Muslim
world, the Dome of the Rock mosque, which is built
over the rock from which the Prophet Muhammad is
said to have ascended to heaven. Below the mosque is
the Wailing Wall, believed to be a retaining wall of the
Second Jewish Temple, which was destroyed by the
Romans in AD 70; and situated between the Dome of
the Rock and the Al-Aqsa Mosque is the Temple
Mount, the most sacred site for the Jews. The
proximity of such sacred sites has been perilous for
both resident Muslims and Jews, resulting in a series of
Arab–Israeli conflicts, including the Six Day War of
1967, which left Palestinian Arabs refugees. Those who
remained in Gaza and the West Bank came under
occupation; others fled to neighboring Arab countries.

Jordan, like other countries in the Fertile Crescent
and the Arabian Peninsula, is a new state in an old
territory. Its population is largely Sunni Muslim, with
more than 60 percent of it from Palestine. Jordan
missed out on oil deposits, so it relies heavily on

tourism. It is where King Herod's fortress was built and where the Nabataean Bedouins carved a fortress city from rose-red sandstone. Lawrence of Arabia was based at Wadi Rum during the Great Arab Revolt and eight centuries before that the Crusaders built their castles there. As a huge portion of Jordan is barren desert, the food production relies on three micro-climates: the fertile Jordan Valley, where citrus fruits, bananas, and vegetables are grown; the high plateau, which yields cereals, pulses, olives, and fruit that can be dried; and the desert, where sheep and goats survive. Until recently, the main food culture was that of the villages in the desert and of the nomadic Bedouin, but with such a large Palestinian population and its proximity to Lebanon and Syria, new culinary traditions have been introduced, resulting in a rich and diverse cuisine. It shares with Iraq, Saudi Arabia, and Syria the national dish *mansaf*, a whole sheep or camel presented on a bed of rice.

Crac des Chevaliers, Syria

Both Lebanon and Syria, neighbors on the eastern coast of the Mediterranean, enjoy a favorable temperate climate. Lebanon is tiny with high mountains and a long coastline, at one time famous as a country where one could ski in the morning and swim in the afternoon. Syria, on the other hand, is a vast country with large desert areas and a short coastline. The location of these two countries made the land prey to invasions by the Phoenicians, the Egyptians, the Persians, the Greeks, the Romans (who merged all the states between the Taurus mountains and the Sinai desert into one province called Syria), the Crusaders, the Ottomans, and finally the French, each leaving its mark on the culinary culture. The Ottoman influence is the most obvious, as it is throughout the eastern Mediterranean, but the French influence is evident in the refinement of Lebanese food. The two countries share ingredients and dishes, with an emphasis on fresh herbs, vegetables, fruit, bulgur, nuts, olives, yogurt, tahini, spices, lamb, and fish; and, with utter conviction, they both claim hummus, a garlicky puree of chickpeas and sesame paste; tabbouleh, a bulgur salad with onions and parsley; and *kibbeh*, pounded meat and bulgur balls. Given their history, both countries draw from the same pool of dishes but the preparation may differ. The Lebanese use fat and spices sparingly and produce more vegetarian dishes, partly because of the Lenten restrictions of its large Christian community, whereas the Syrians opt for stong flavors with their olive oil and hot Aleppo pepper, and they love their sweet dishes and syrupy pastries.

Iraq reflects the same agricultural and culinary divisions as ancient Mesopotamia, with the arid north (Al-Jazirah) and the marshlands in the south (Al Iraq).

Wheat and crops that require winter chill, such as apples, grow in the north while rice and dates grow in the south. Today, Iraq is the world's largest producer of dates. Generally, the food of Iraq is a spicier version of the cuisine of Lebanon and Syria. It is also influenced by its neighbor Iran in its dishes combining meat and fruit and in some of its food vocabulary, drawn from medieval texts rather than Arabic. That is apart from the south of Iraq, which relies on its own culinary culture, based on rice, fish, and dates, and its own food language, such as *timman* for rice. Relying heavily on grain, Iraqis often combine meat with wheat in dishes such as *kubba*, similar to the *kibbeh* of Lebanon and Syria; *harissa*, a porridge-like soup that is a staple dish for the mountain Kurds; *kashki*, a dish from Mosul that is flavored and colored with dried lime, cumin,

turmeric, and tomato; and *uruq*, also called *ghug*, which consists of meat cut into small pieces and fried, then mixed with onions and celery leaf in a leavened dough, and baked like bread. The Marsh Arabs of the south call the same dish *khubz lahm*, meaning "meat bread." The meat from cattle and water buffalo is used more frequently than anywhere else in the Arab world, and meat cooked on a skewer is called *tikka*, a term that is adopted in the Gulf, but, is known as *kebab* (kabob) elsewhere.

The rivers of Iraq provide freshwater fish, such as carp and catfish, which are cooked in the national dish *samak masquf*, or *simach mazguf* in the south, which involves suspending the gutted fish on stakes around a fire until they are cooked and then sprinkling them with spices, onions, tomatoes, and lemon juice. There

Pilgrims and scholars at the shrine of Imam Ali, Najaf, Iraq

are two minority groups in the northeast of Iraq: the non-Arab Muslim Kurds, who speak a language related to Persian, and the Christian Assyrians, who speak a modern dialect of Aramaic. Both cook the heavy meat, grain, and vegetable stews suited to their cold winters. The Kurds are known for their syrupy preserves, and the Assyrian women are reputed to make the best syrupy pastries and a yogurt soup flavored with dill, called "Assyrian soup," throughout Iraq.

Neighboring Iraq to the south and east are found the member countries of the Gulf Cooperation Council. They include Saudi Arabia, Kuwait, Bahrain, Qatar, the United Arab Emirates, and the Sultanate of Oman—a total population of about 25 million. The terrain of this vast area is varied, with extensive desert and a long coastline, the majority of the land receiving occasional rainfall. The food of the whole area is often referred to under the collective banner "Arabian," or "Gulf" when excluding Saudi Arabia. Perhaps more than any other region of the Middle East, the food of the United Arab Emirates and Oman has been influenced by distant culinary cultures—Ottoman to the north, Horn of Africa to the west, Iran and India to the east—resulting in an incredibly diverse and vibrant cuisine in the main population centers. Oman has a long history of trade with India and East Africa, resulting in a mixed population of different ethnic groups and, with the proximity of its northern tip to Iran, separated only by the Strait of Hormuz, there is a substantial population of Persian ancestry too. Dubbed the "playground of the Gulf," the United Arab Emirates, which was formed as recently as 1971, is a loose federation of seven tiny sheikhdoms. Interestingly from a culinary point of view, 85 percent of the population of almost 2 million is expatriate,

from Pakistan, India, Sri Lanka, the Philippines, North Africa, Europe, and America, and this has a huge impact on the cuisine. The largest and most populous of the Emirates is Abu Dhabi, the second largest being Dubai. Until the 1960s, when commercial exploitation of oil began, both were little more than sand. In Dubai the population was largely nomadic, subsisting on a diet of fish, bread, honey, and dates; now there are international restaurants and futuristic shopping malls selling alcohol and pork, and a ruler who has spent a fortune turning the desert green, so much so that strawberries from Dubai are exported to Europe.

Aside from the external influences, the core food of the Gulf region of Arabia is traditionally Arab, similar to that of Syria and Lebanon. The national dish is *khouzi*, a roast or baked whole lamb stuffed with chicken, eggs, onions, rice, spices, and saffron and served on a bed of rice, garnished with almonds and ghee. Saltwater fish such as *hammour* (grouper) and *zubaidi* (silver pomfret) are popular grilled, and the big Gulf shrimp are often cooked with rice and herbs in a dish called *machbous*. Lamb and chicken are roasted on spits in *shawarma* stalls, the Gulf equivalent of the Turkish *döner kabob*, or *gyro*. The markets are stacked with all the usual vegetables and herbs, including purslane, rocket, melokhia, fenugreek, cilantro, and dandelion. Dates are the main fruit, used in sweet dishes and pressed for their molasses, but bananas, mangoes, oranges, and watermelons are also common in the Gulf. Coffee is the main drink, sometimes flavored with cardamom, and tea is drunk black and sweet. Honey is used for sweetening dishes, and the combination of Indian spices, the Arab spice mixture *baharat*, and the dried Omani limes, *loomi*, give the food its distinctive character.

Landscape and terraces of the Qadilia Valley, Lebanon

Saudi Arabia, on the other hand, takes itself very seriously. The kingdom is the cradle of Islam and the Arabic language. It is home to the two most sacred Islamic sites—Mecca, the birthplace of the Prophet Muhammad, and Medina, the place of his burial. Mecca, the site to which Muslims bow in prayer five times a day, is also the location of the Ka'bah, the shrine that is said to have been built by Abraham, the father of the Arab race. The unexpected death of the Prophet in the year 632 left a crisis in the Islamic world, as there were no heirs. Followers of his widow, A'isha, eventually became known as Sunni and make up approximately 85 percent of the Islamic world. The majority of Saudis are Sunni Muslims, as are the Turks, the Jordanians, and the Islamic population of the United Arab Emirates. They believe the first four caliphs were the rightful heirs and don't require the

spiritual leader to be a member of the Prophet's family, whereas Shi'a Islam rejects the first three caliphs and regards Ali, the Prophet's cousin and son-in-law, as the original caliph. They insist that their imam must be a descendant of Ali and his wife. Most Shi'ite populations are found in Iran, Iraq, Lebanon, Yemen, and Azerbaijan, with minorities in Kuwait, the Emirates, and Saudi Arabia. The Sunni Muslims of Saudi Arabia are followers of the Wahhabi sect of Islam, the most orthodox of all.

In an area of approximately 757,000 square miles, most of which is desert, the bulk of Saudi Arabia's population is centered around Jeddah and Riyadh. The Empty Quarter, the largest sand desert in the world, traversed on foot by the indefatigable explorer Wilfred Thesiger, takes up roughly half the country. After fourteen centuries of receiving Muslim pilgrims from all over the world, on their Hajj to Mecca, and an influx of expatriates involved in oil, Saudi Arabia has quite a diverse population and cuisine. Only the people of Najd in the Saudi heartland remain homogeneous in their pure Bedouin ancestry, which is reflected in their culinary traditions.

The Bedouin, who have a strong but basic food culture, were nomadic herdsmen who lived in the deserts of Arabia and North Africa. They depended on their flocks of sheep and goats to provide milk and meat, using their dried hides to make water and food carriers and for churning milk. Their camels provided transport and dung for fuel. Surplus bull calves would be slaughtered for their meat, hide, and hair. Dates grew in all the oases and were easy to carry with them, and, in the encampments, flat breads would be cooked on a sheet of metal over a fire. With basic needs and animals that could survive in arid conditions, the Bedouin were able to penetrate vast tracts of merciless desert in which others would perish. The Bedouin rules of hospitality, which are still upheld in Bedouin camps and traditional Arab households today, included the provision of accommodation and protection for three days and three nights, and a beast would be slaughtered in the guest's honor to demonstrate the host's wealth. While the beast was being prepared by the women, the men would offer the guest coffee and dates. The slaughtered sheep or camel would be served in the traditional dish, *mansaf*, now the principal hospitality dish of the whole of Arabia and Jordan, and the guest would eat first, followed by the men. The women and children would eat separately after the men had finished.

Today the numbers of nomadic Bedouin are in decline, but their culinary traditions, such as *mansaf*,

have influenced the sedentary populations of the Arab world.

The most arable spot on the Arabian Peninsula is Yemen. It is also the most populous, made up of strong tribal units, all of whom trace their ancestry to Qatan, son of Prophet Hud, who was descended from Noah. Islam is the principal religion but there is a Jewish minority. The northern part of Yemen includes the highest part of the Arabian plateau, where heavy rain falls at the time of the summer monsoon, allowing sorghum, coffee, wheat, and corn to grow on the terraced slopes. The oases towns were once on the Spice Road leading to the Mediterranean. In ancient times, frankincense and myrrh grew on the coast of the Gulf of Aden in the southern part of Yemen (formerly the British colony of Aden), which lies on the rim of the Indian Ocean. With its proximity to North Africa and the trade routes with India, there has been a degree of intermarriage between different ethnic groups, which is strongly reflected in the culinary culture. Chilies are used more than anywhere else in the Middle East, and fenugreek could be seen as the culinary symbol of Yemen. The national dish, *salta*, is a fiery, spicy stew containing pulses and lamb, and the peasants live on a sorghum porridge of

Muslim farmers herding goats, Yemen

ancient origin, which is served with spicy clarified butter. Clarified butter is the principal cooking fat and it is often served with honey to dip bread into. Most Yemenis eat with their right hand, using the bread as a scoop.

"The Mother of the World," the birthplace of one of the greatest civilizations, is linked to the body of the Middle East by Sinai, where Moses received the Ten Commandments on the Mount. Egypt is the most populous country in the Arab world, with most of its people centered in bloated Cairo and the fertile Nile Valley, with Bedouin communities in Sinai. Like Saudi Arabia across the Red Sea, Egypt is a vast country but most of it is desert or marsh. The majority of Egyptians are Muslim, the rest being mainly Coptic Christian, but racially they can be divided into three groups: the Hamito-Semitic race (this includes the Berbers), which has populated the Nile for millennia,

the Bedouin Arab nomads, and the Nubians. Egypt's recorded history is so ancient, surviving in written documents, wall paintings, and tombs, that it reveals a great deal about the food of the early civilizations. Ancient cooking methods, such as lighting a fire inside a concave pottery hearth, outside or on the flat roofs, are still practiced today. The Arab and Turkish conquests and the dominant influence of Islam are evident in the haute cuisine of Egypt, but the peasant communities still cook the simple dishes of their forebears in pharaonic times. The national dishes, such as *ful medames*, brown beans with cumin and parsley, and *melokhia*, a soup made with the mucilaginous mallow plant, are of peasant origin. Pigeons are an Egyptian specialty, and grilled meat and chicken are standard fare, but the tradition of *mezze*, which is such a fabulous feature of Lebanese, Syrian, and Turkish cooking, has almost been lost.

Sailing on the Nile, Egypt

THE PRODUCE

Market stall in Ankara, Turkey

Geographically, the Middle East is extremely varied, with lush, wooded coastlines, high, arid mountains, extensive flat plains, steep, rocky outcrops, marshlands, and endless deserts providing different growing conditions for a vast range of plants and crops. Rice grows around the Caspian Sea and in the marshlands of southern Iraq, date palms thrive in the desert areas of Jordan, Iraq, and Saudi Arabia, pistachio and olive trees grow where nothing else will, and the lush plains of the Fertile Crescent and Anatolia produce an abundance of fruit and vegetables. On the whole, the produce is rich and plentiful, and the people are generous with it.

Fruit and vegetables are sold fresh and dried. The juicy fruits, such as the honey-sweet melons, oozing purple figs, dripping peaches and apricots, black mulberries, grapes, and the tart, green plums that are dipped in salt are generally consumed fresh in season. Some of the fresh fruit, such as apples, plums, and quinces, are stuffed and cooked, while others, such as figs, dates, and apricots, are dried and cooked with meat and vegetables, used in stuffings, or poached in syrup. The white mulberries, originally from China and cultivated in Turkey for the silkworms, are dried and eaten as a snack, rather like raisins. Fresh vegetables, such as the mammoth leeks, giant cabbages, carrots, zucchini, fat bulbous eggplants as well as long, slender ones, knobbly plum tomatoes, and scaly globe artichokes, are generally used raw in salads, stewed with meat or pulses, stuffed with rice, or cooked with olive oil and served cold. Some vegetables, such as eggplants, peppers, and okra, are dried and hung on strings, like chunky necklaces. Pulses, which were once regarded as a staple of the poor, are enjoyed in many dishes right across the social divide. And wheat is the preferred grain, although rice features highly in the food of Iran and is the staple of southern Iraq.

Beef and the meat of water buffalo, camel, and goat are all eaten, but the preferred meat is lamb. Chicken is almost as popular as lamb, and turkey, duck, and pigeon are consumed too. Because of Islamic dietary law, pork is rarely eaten, even by the Christians. Islam also prohibits wine, which might be why so many of the meat dishes are given a sweet or sour flavoring for extra interest. Milk is rarely consumed fresh but is made into yogurt, clarified butter, clotted cream, and cheese. Surrounded by seas and carved up by some of the world's major rivers, such as the Euphrates and the Nile, there is a wide choice of fresh and saltwater fish.

An Egyptian spread: pigeon stuffed with rice, peas and bread

Herbs, flavorings, and spices have been used throughout the Middle East since antiquity, but it was during the early Abassid period that spices began to be extensively employed in the region's cuisine. They came from the Arab domains such as southern Arabia, Syria, Persia, and central Asia, and from East Africa, India, and China. Top-quality spices were expensive and the ability to purchase them was a mark of status. Spices and herbs were essential to the medieval Arab kitchen, valued for their alleged medicinal and aphrodisiac properties. Flavorings such as rose water and orange-flower water have also been used since medieval times. More recently, since the end of the nineteenth century, an unusual flavoring has been extracted from *bois de Panama*, the dried inner bark of the American tree *Quillaja saponaria*. The pale bark has a bitter-sweet taste, with a hint of almond, but it is employed more for its foaming qualities than for its flavor. Boiled and simmered, then strained and whisked, it produces a brilliant white foam, which is combined with sugar to make *naatiffee*, a mousse-like cream that is served with *ma'amoul*, the sweet pastries favored by Christians at Easter and by Muslims during Ramadan.

The fresh herbs are glorious, piled high in the markets and sold like large bouquets of flowers. They are so popular in the Middle East, they are used liberally and with abandon, often served on their own as a nibble or to freshen the palate. Dried herbs and spices are often sold in the markets, alongside each other, in large sacks bursting at the seams. The air around them can be quite heady with the pungent aroma of fragrant herbs, warm spices, and hot chili. *Bahar* is the Arabic for spice, *baharat* being the collective word used for the various spice blends. In

Iranian women picnicking on *lavash*, jams and teas

medieval times, one of the spice blends contained distinct echoes of India in its use of betel nut, nutmeg, mace, cardamom, cloves, rosebuds, the fruit of the ash tree, and ginger, flavors that still feature in Oman and the Gulf region.

Salt, particularly rock salt, was also an ingredient in medieval Arab cuisine. Several recipes called for scented salt, such as the lemon salt still used in Iran. And salt flavored with spices, sour pomegranate seeds, or toasted sesame seeds was, and still is, popular, like the spice mixture *zaatar*. During the Ottoman era salt formed a lucrative branch of commerce. Great quantities of it were gathered from inland saline lakes, which dry up in the summers and leave an encrustation of high-quality coarse salt. Salt has also been a symbol of hospitality since ancient times—to eat bread and salt with someone is to enter into a covenant of brotherhood. There is a medieval Arab saying, "Salt is as necessary in food as grammar is in speech."

Honey, along with the molasses of some pressed fruits, such as mulberries, grapes, and dates, is an ancient and vital sweetener. The oldest written reference to the use of honey dates back to Egypt, around 5500 BC, when Lower Egypt was called Bee Land and Upper Egypt was known as Reed Land. Honey is also mentioned on Babylonian tablets for its medicinal uses and it has long been believed to sweeten life and ward off sadness. Today it is mainly used to sweeten syrupy pastries and is poured over wild duck roasted with almonds and eaten daily with fresh bread or yogurt. One of the joys of honey is its immense range of colors and flavors. Whether it is in comb form or pressed, each one has its own distinct fragrance and taste and with such an enormous variety of scented blossoms, the villages and markets of the Middle East provide an astounding choice. The most unusual I have ever tasted is the dark *deli bal*, meaning "crazy honey," which comes from eastern Anatolia, where the bees extract the pollen from the wild opium poppies. Needless to say, it is mildly hallucinatory with an unexpected fiery kick.

MEZZE

The tradition of *mezze* is one of the most enjoyable and relaxing features of Middle Eastern food. The savoring of freshly roasted pistachios, fleshy green olives, juicy melon, delicately flavored pastries, garlicky eggplant dips, pink-tinged pickled turnips, cubes of white cheese, strips of salted cucumber, and thin slices of perfumed quince can be a sensual, mystical experience. It is an ancient tradition, enjoyed by the Greeks, Romans, Persians, medieval Arabs, and Ottomans. Traditionally, the *mezze* table was laid out to accompany *araq* (*rakı*) or wine, with the aim of achieving a "pleasant head" to delight the palate, not to fill the belly. Originally, it was a custom enjoyed only by men—traders and travelers, kings, sultans, and noble men—but in the less restricted parts of the Middle East it can be a family affair. The word *mezze* has come to mean a "pleasant taste," probably derived from the Persian word *maza*, meaning "taste" or "relish." In Syria and Lebanon the word is *mazza* and in Turkey it is *meze*.

The wonderful thing about *mezze* is that there are no rules. The *mezze* table can be the start of a meal, or completely separate from it. There is no set time or place, just the unspoken understanding that the food should be served in small quantities to be shared and savored at a leisurely pace and that one should rise from the table feeling contented and comfortable, not stuffed. Generally, though, the partaking of *mezze* tends to be an evening activity, partly because for many it would be unthinkable without *araq*. In some Muslim communities, where the prohibition of alcohol is strictly adhered to, the *mezze* tradition has either been lost or the dishes are accompanied with tea, coffee, or sherbet drinks instead. Throughout the Middle East, the Lebanese and the Turks are renowned for their delightful *mezze* spreads.

Ramadan tent at El Hussein mosque in Old Cairo, Egypt

THE QUR'AN AND RAMADAN

Islam is the predominant religion in the Middle East, so it exerts the most influence on the customs, traditions, and culinary cultures of the region. The book of Islam is the Qur'an (Koran), which is a collection of revelations or commands from Allah (God) received by the Prophet Muhammad through the Angel Gabriel. As a gift from Allah, food is mentioned throughout the Qur'an, especially what is permitted and what is not. Of particular importance are the restrictions on the slaughtering and preparation of meat (p 68) and the prohibition of alcohol. However, in the modern world, these laws are observed with varying degrees of laxity. Outside the Christian communities, it is extremely rare for people to eat pork, but the drinking of, or cooking with, alcohol is quite common, although this is a matter of personal preference rather than a national characteristic.

Ramadan is the ninth month of the Muslim calendar, when the Prophet experienced the revelation of the Qur'an. Since the Muslim calendar is a lunar one, Ramadan falls eleven days earlier in each successive year of the Western calendar. During the month of Ramadan, every devout Muslim must abstain from food and drink between sunrise and sunset. Nothing must pass his or her lips. This act of self-discipline and faith is deemed necessary to submit completely to the will of Allah and to engender a sense of compassion for the poor, who are always hungry. When Ramadan occurs in the summer, the month of fasting can be difficult because of the heat and the longer wait to sunset. *Suhur* is the meal taken before sunrise and *iftar* is served to break the fast at sunset. When the new moon is in sight, Ramadan ends and the new month begins with 'Id al-Fitr (the Feast of the Breaking of the Fast), a three-day holiday of celebration, sumptuous feasting, and exchanging of gifts.

LANGUAGE AND HERITAGE

Arabic is the principal language of the Middle East. The other main languages are Farsi, Hebrew, and Turkish. The term "Arab" really applies to the original nomadic Arabs, distinguished by their language, and the inhabitants of the conquered provinces who adopted Arabic. As the majority of the Arabs live in the Fertile Crescent, renowned for its food produce and culinary delights, I have based a large portion of this book there, under the loose banner "Arab food," noting the obvious Turkish and Persian influences and dishes. Also, to keep it simple, the ingredients are listed in Arabic and the recipes in their language of origin, or in the language of the country in which I have tasted them. As there is so much fission and fusion between the countries, a huge number of dishes cross all borders and religious divides. The references to some dishes from Iran as "Persian" is intentional when they are of ancient origin and are relatively unchanged.

BASIC FOODS

BREAD

(KHUBZ)

Bread is a gift from God. Traditionally it is broken by hand. To cut it with a knife would be to lift up a sword against God's blessing. If a bit of bread falls on the ground, it is picked up and held to the lips and forehead as a gesture of atonement and respect before it is put aside. And it is never thrown away. Instead, stale bread is used in a variety of traditional ways, such as in *fattush* (p181) and the ancient *tharid*.

The first cereal crops are believed to have been grown in Anatolia, Persia, and Syria before 7000 BC. So important was the skill of bread-making in ancient times, there are records of full-time bakers among the Egyptians, the Phoenicians, and the Cappadocians. In Rome, a bakers' guild was set up around 150 BC. In medieval times bread was primarily made of wheat, although the poor used barley and millet, and it was often flavored with spices or stuffed with sweet, scented fillings. During the Ottoman period more sophisticated breads emerged and experimentation began with thin flat breads as a pastry dough in savory and sweet, layered dishes such as baklava (p137). Today, there are hundreds of varieties of bread, some savory, others sweet. Bread is used to break the fast during Ramadan and it is broken and blessed in the meal-taking of Orthodox Jews. It is eaten with every meal and some people simply cannot enjoy their food without it.

THE PRODUCTION

First the harvested grains have to be ground into flour, which was traditionally done between two heavy, flat grinding stones. All cereal flours, particularly wheat, consist of starch and protein, which react with water to form gluten. As the dough is kneaded, the gluten molecules form strands and absorb water which results in a smooth, elastic dough. For flat bread, all that is needed is water but, to produce a risen loaf, some kind of leaven is required. The first leavened loaves are attributed to the ancient Egyptians, who may have accidentally discovered yeast on a batch of dough infected with wild spores. The Israelites left their leaven behind when they fled from Egypt in the Exodus and had to exist on unleavened bread. The Romans introduced ale-barm (brewer's yeast), which had more predictable results. The first breads in tribal encampments would have been cooked on flat stones or metal sheets directly over the fire, much as it is in some villages today. The next developments were to make a freestanding clay cylinder, called a *tinuru*, used for unleavened bread, and a hollow, beehive-shaped

Assorted leavened and unleavened breads

32

A baker removing loaves from the oven, Yemen

outdoor oven, known as a *tannur*, which produced better risen loaves. This was the precursor to the outdoor clay oven (*tandoor* in Arabic, *tandır* in Turkish), used to bake flat breads throughout the Middle East. Leavened loaves are often baked in a hot, communal oven, called a *furn* (Arabic) or *fırın* (Turkish), which can also be used for unleavened breads by sticking the flat dough to the inside hot walls or on the outside. The most traditional of all the flat breads is as wide as an arm-length and as thin as fine cloth. It takes years of practice and great skill to shift a small ball of dough from hand to hand, and then arm to arm, carefully stretching it and keeping it taut and circular, until it resembles a thin sheet of paper.

APPEARANCE AND TASTE

There are hundreds of different kinds of leavened and unleavened breads, from the round rings scattered with seeds, such as *semit*, to the paper-thin sheets, called *phyllo* in Arabic and *yufka* in Turkish, which come in different grades for savory and sweet pastries. All have their own unique taste from the flour or the oven used,

from the baker or the hand that made them. One thing is sure, they all taste and smell delicious. There is the ubiquitous pita bread, known in Arabic as *khubz* or *eish shami*, which is a round or oval flat bread made with refined wheat flour, with a hollow pocket demanding to be filled. The Egyptian *eish baladi* is a whole-wheat version, often flavored or sprinkled with the spice mixture *dukkah* (p163). There are many other flat breads, each with its own characteristic, such as the whole-wheat *nan-e lavash* and *nan-e tâftoon* of Iran, and the thick *pide* of Turkey. There is village bread, sometimes made from barley or corn, Armenian bread padded like a quilt, Jewish bread made with egg doughs, olive bread, sweet breads, and savory, spicy, or herb breads.

BUYING AND STORING

In the Middle East, bread-making is such a part of daily life that people often bake their own or send their dough along to the communal oven. Almost every village has a baker, who bakes batches of fresh bread once or twice a day. If you don't bake your own, you will have to look for Middle Eastern-style loaves

and flat breads, such as pita and *fila*, which are now readily available in supermarkets and specialty stores, or look for the real thing in Middle Eastern stores. As bread goes stale quickly and fresh bread is so easily attainable in the Middle East, storing is not a problem. Fresh bread is eaten immediately and stale bread has many uses. If *phyllo* is sealed in an airtight bag, it will keep for a few weeks in the refrigerator or for two to three months in the freezer.

CULINARY USES

Leavened and unleavened bread is eaten with food at every meal. It is a scoop, a mop, a palate cleanser, and an essential part of the overall enjoyment. Warm fresh bread is usually eaten for breakfast with cheese, olives, dates, and honey. A choice of buns, dried breads, and the savory bracelets called *kahk* (p163) are eaten as a snack. Toasted or stale bread is used in village vegetable soups and the Syrian peasant dish *fattush* (p181), a lovely, crunchy, herb-laden salad made with broken flat bread. Stale bread is also soaked in a syrup made from poached fresh fruit topped with the strained fruit and served with clotted cream. Hollow breads are often filled with grilled meatballs or falafel (p113)

with parsley, onions, tomatoes, and a squeeze of lemon or yogurt. Some flat-bread doughs are filled with eggs or ground meat (p188)– such as *lahma bi ajeen*—or with a sweet *tahini* paste before being baked. A particular characteristic of Middle Eastern food is to use the flat bread as a base for other ingredients: the Turkish dish *Iskender kabobı* consists of grilled meat, a tomato sauce, and yogurt, layered over thick *pide*. Similarly, there are the Arab *fatta* dishes (*fatut* in Yemen), which involve breaking toasted or stale bread and soaking it in a broth or stock with vegetables or meat before topping it with yogurt. This dish, which was known as *tharid* in Arabia, was the favorite dish of the Prophet Muhammad, who praised his favorite wife in this way: "A'isha surpasses other women as *tharid* surpasses other dishes." In ancient times this dish was made plain with bread sopped in broth or stew, but some modern versions alternate layers of stew and flat bread. The thin sheets of flat bread, known as *phyllo*, are used for a variety of savory and sweet pastries. In Turkey, the *yufka* is used to make different-shaped filled pastries called *börek*, and the thin sheets of dough are layered with nuts and soaked in syrup to make some sweet pastries. In Egypt, *om Ali* (p133), a popular syrupy dessert, is made with nuts, cinnamon, and crumpled sheets of phyllo.

Bread airing after the heat of the oven in a bakery in Giza, Cairo

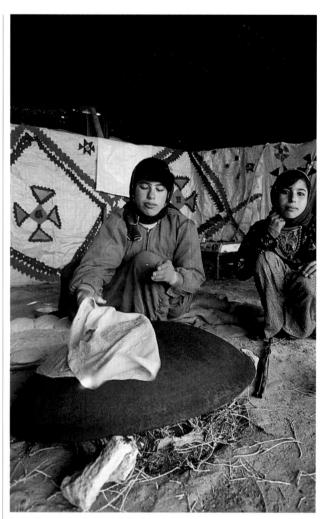

Bedouin women making phyllo bread, Syria

Fatta dishes are wholesome family meals that are popular throughout the Arab world. The word *fatta* describes the crumbling or breaking of the bread into pieces and the dish probably originated as a method of using up stale bread. All *fatta* dishes have a bed of toasted bread soaked in stock or cooking broth, followed by a layer of ground meat, chicken, chickpeas, or vegetables, topped with a layer of thick, creamy yogurt, over which toasted pine nuts or Middle Eastern red pepper is sprinkled. Pita breads, lightly toasted or crisped in a hot oven, are the best breads to use for *fatta*.

FATTET HUMMUS
(CHICKPEAS WITH TOASTED BREAD AND YOGURT)

Serves 4
Preparation time 5 minutes (+ at least 6 hours' soaking)
Cooking time roughly 1·hour 20 minutes

½ cup chickpeas, soaked for at least 6 hours or overnight
2–3 dried bay leaves
1 tablespoon olive oil and a little butter
1 onion, chopped
½ teaspoon cumin seeds
1 scant teaspoon ground coriander
Juice of ½ lemon
2¼ cups thick, creamy yogurt
2–3 cloves garlic, crushed
2–3 large pita breads
A small handful pine nuts
Salt and freshly ground black pepper

Simmer the chickpeas with the bay leaves in plenty of water for at least 1 hour, until they are very tender. Drain them and reserve some of the cooking liquid. Remove any loose skins from the chickpeas and heat the reserved cooking liquid with a little salt.

Heat the oil and butter in a skillet and stir in the onion and cumin seeds. Once the onions begin to brown, stir in the coriander and the chickpeas. Toss them about until they are well mixed, then add the lemon juice and season to taste with salt and black pepper.

In a bowl, beat the yogurt with the garlic and season to taste. Then open out the pita breads and pop them in a hot oven for a few minutes, until they are crisp and brown. Meanwhile, heat a small heavy-based pan, toss in the pine nuts, and roast them until they look nicely browned and oily.
Break up the toasted breads with your hands and lay them in a serving dish.

Spoon some of the heated cooking liquid over them, making sure they are well soaked, then spoon the chickpeas on top, followed by the yogurt and a sprinkling of roast pine nuts. Serve immediately.

Generally known as *khubz* in Arabic and *eish shami* in Egypt, these flat breads with a hollow pocket just begging to be filled are known outside the Middle East as pita bread. The same bread made with whole-wheat flour is called *baladi*, and olives or spices can be added to the dough. In Turkey a similar, thicker bread, *pide*, is often filled or used as the base for many kabob dishes. In Iraq, the same bread dough is mixed with ground meat to make the special *khubz abbas*, while the plain *khubz* was traditionally distributed to the poor with melted butter and sugar on top.

Selling assorted sweet and plain bread on the street, Turkey

KHUBZ
(PITA BREAD)

Serves 6–8
Preparation time approximately
   3½ hours
Cooking time 6–10 minutes

1 cake compressed fresh yeast or
  1 scant tablespoon active dry
  yeast
½ teaspoon sugar
Roughly 1¼ cups lukewarm water
4 cups all-purpose flour
½ teaspoon salt
Sunflower oil

Dissolve the yeast with the sugar in a little of the water and leave in a warm place for 15 minutes,

until it bubbles and froths.

Sift the flour with the salt into a large bowl. Make a well in the center and pour in the yeast and most of the water. Using your hands, draw in the flour and knead the dough, adding more water if necessary, until it forms a pliable ball. Place it on a floured surface and knead for about 15 minutes, until it is smooth and elastic. Pour a drop or two of oil into the bottom of the bowl, roll the dough in it, cover the bowl with a damp cloth and leave the dough to rise in a warm place for at least 2 hours, until it has doubled in size.

Punch down the dough and knead it briefly. Divide the dough into lumps—the size of a pomegranate for large pita breads, the size of an apricot for small ones—and flatten them with the palm of your hand, or a rolling pin, on a floured surface, until they are roughly ¼ inch thick. Lay a clean cloth on a flat surface and dust it with flour. Place the flat doughs on top, with a gap for expansion between them, and sprinkle with flour. Dust another clean cloth with flour, lay it over them, and leave them for about 1 hour, until they have expanded.

Preheat the oven to 450°F (or even hotter, if you can). Lightly grease two baking sheets and place them in the hot oven for 10 minutes, just before baking. Quickly pop the flat doughs onto the hot baking sheets, sprinkle a little cold water over them to prevent them from browning, and bake for about 8 minutes. As soon as they are ready, slip them off the baking sheets onto a wire rack and leave to cool—if your oven is hot enough, the bread should be soft and white with a hollow pouch. They firm up on cooling, so if you want them to remain soft, put them into a plastic bag until you are ready to use them.

COFFEE

(KAHWA) Coffea arabica

Ground coffee

The coffee plant is thought to have originated in Ethiopia, where it grows wild. The discovery of the plant in Arabia is interwoven with myths of dancing goats and sleepy monks. The berries would have been eaten first and the fermented pulp then made into a kind of wine. The earliest record of coffee as a drink was in the writing of Rhazes, an Arabian physician in the tenth century, but the practice of roasting the beans didn't begin until the thirteenth century. According to legend, coffee became popular among the Sufis of Yemen, as they believed that it helped them perform their religious ceremonies, bringing on mystical raptures and prolonging the hours of prayer. By the end of the thirteenth century in Yemen, the drink was known as *qahwah*, probably because of its stimulant qualities, as the word was originally a poetic name for wine. The dervishes and Muslim pilgrims contributed to the spread of coffee throughout the Middle East, and by the end of the fifteenth century cultivation had begun in Yemen with plants transported from Ethiopia. The Ottoman Turks refined the art of coffee-making and spread it throughout their empire in the sixteenth century, giving the name of Turkish coffee to a drink that was originally of Arab origin.

SOCIAL ROLE

Coffee is the main drink in the Arab world, particularly in Saudi Arabia, Yemen, Jordan, Syria and Lebanon. It is part of the social life. The Bedouin are reputed to drink so much of it, they would almost collapse without it, although tea is drunk just as often. In the rural parts of Turkey and Iran, coffee is reserved mainly for ceremonial occasions, tea being the common drink. In Iran it is served at funerals, and in Turkey it plays a traditional role in the selection of a bride: a young girl must serve coffee to her prospective mother-in-law so that the older woman can inspect her beauty and grace.

Throughout the Middle East the serving and drinking of coffee are entrenched in tradition and ceremony. As a mark of hospitality, it is the first thing a host prepares for visitors and it is rude to refuse. In the serving of coffee, strict rules of etiquette must be observed—a person of high rank, or the father of the household, must be served first, followed by the older guests or relatives, and men are always served before women. Among the Europeanized communities of the large cities, such as Amman, Beirut, and Istanbul, these rules have been waived and women are generally served first.

In the Arab countries, coffee is the principal social drink for men. They spend hours drinking in the coffee houses, talking, joking, and playing backgammon, sometimes soaking up the coffee with a sweet, syrupy pastry, or a piece of *lokum* (Turkish Delight). At one time Islam seemed to be under threat as attendance at the mosque slackened while the coffee houses filled. In the Arab communities, business in the marketplace, in the office, or in the home is always conducted with a small cup of coffee, whereas tea would usually be served in those situations in Turkey and Iran, unless it was immediately after a meal.

A Bedouin man brewing coffee over an open fire in Wadi Umm al Hayat,

PREPARATION AND PRESENTATION

In the Middle East, two types of coffee are made: Arabic coffee, which is drunk solely in Arab communities, particularly in Saudi Arabia, Yemen, and by the Bedouin; and Turkish coffee, which is fashionable in the cities, especially in the ones influenced by the Ottoman Empire, and in Turkey. Arabic coffee is made in two pots (*dallahs*)—brewed in the first and poured into the second—always without sugar. Turkish coffee is brewed in small, long handled, tin-lined brass pots (called *kanaka, rakwi* or *ibrik* in Arabic and *cezve* in Turkish).

The coffee beans are always freshly roasted and then pounded or ground to a very fine powder, which is added to the water in the pot. As the coffee is sweetened during the preparation, guests are always asked whether they would like theirs sweet (*helou* or *hilweh* in Arabic, *şekerli* in Turkish), medium (*mazbout* or *wassat* in Arabic, *orta* in Turkish), or plain (*murra* in Arabic, *sade* in Turkish), hence the need for several coffee pots in each household. However, at happy, festive occasions, the coffee is often made sweet for everyone, whereas at sombre occasions such as funerals, it is a solemn drink, black and unsweetened. Milk is never added to coffee, although there is a drink in Lebanon and Syria called "white coffee" which, in fact, has nothing to do with coffee but is made with orange-flower water. In the Arab countries such as Yemen, Saudi Arabia and Jordan, a cardamom pod is often added to the coffee pot for flavoring. Cardamom is also added to coffee in Iran, but it rarely features in the coffee of Turkey, and ground ginger is often added to the coffee in Yemen.

The coffee cups are small and cylindrical and, in some societies or social circles, they are delicate with no handles, so as to slot into ornate metal holders, matching the patterned or inscribed serving tray, usually made of brass or silver. When the coffee has been drunk, it is customary to turn the cup upside down on the saucer to let the sediment dribble down the sides of the cup. Once the cup has cooled, it is lifted up and the pattern of coffee-grain rivulets formed on the inside is read to determine the individual's fortune. The saucer is then held up and read too.

BUYING AND STORING

To make authentic Arabic or Turkish coffee, any arabica bean can be used. Mocha from Yemen is popular but beans from Brazil and Kenya are used too. The beans must be ground to a very fine powder, otherwise the coffee will be too gritty and you won't get the creamed, foamy effect. Cans and packages of Turkish coffee are available in Middle Eastern stores and some specialty stores.

Arabic coffee pot and cup

Kahve, **Turkish coffee**

The Turks have been promoting their coffee for a long time. The first British coffee house was opened in Oxford by a Turkish Jew in 1650. A little later, in 1688–9, the Turkish Ambassador to France encouraged the Parisian élite who attended his lavish parties to drink Turkish coffee. Dressed in decorative oriental costumes, his black slaves served hot, fragrant Mocha coffee in tiny porcelain cups on gold or silver saucers.

KAHVE
(TURKISH COFFEE)

Serves 2
Preparation time –
Cooking time 2–3 minutes (with practice)

All you need is a *cezve* that holds 2 coffee cups of cold water, to which you add 2 coffee spoons of finely, ground coffee and the required sugar on top. Using a teaspoon, carefully stir the sugar and coffee into the surface of the water, making sure the spoon doesn't go anywhere near the bottom of the *cezve*. This little stir gives the froth a kick-start.

Place the *cezve* over a medium flame and heat the water up, gradually stirring the outer surface edges into the middle to create an island of froth.

Pour about a third of the coffee into each cup to warm it, return the *cezve* to the heat, and continue to gather the froth in the middle. Just as it is about to bubble up, take the *cezve* off the heat and pour the hot coffee into the warmed cups (some people spoon a little of the froth into the cup before pouring in the coffee).

Serve the coffee immediately, while it is hot and frothy, but, before you drink it, leave it to stand for a minute to let the coffee grains sink to the bottom of the cup.

TEA

(CHAI)

Linden tea

Hibiscus tea

Although coffee, surrounded by tradition and ritual, is the king of drinks in the Middle East, tea occupies an important place in Iran and Turkey, where it is the drink of the masses. In Iran coffee is mainly reserved for funerals, and in rural Turke, it is drunk only on ceremonial occasions, so tea is the everyday beverage.

It wasn't always the case, though. Tea, thought to have first arrived in Iran with the early Persian caravans, didn't make an impact until comparatively recently. Instead, coffee was the

most popular drink. Brought from Arabia in the ninth century, it was blessed by Islam and drunk at religious ceremonies, making coffee houses the focal point of communities throughout the Middle East. But in Iran, between the seventeenth and twentieth centuries, the coffee houses were suspected of fostering political and religious dissent, as well as encouraging acts of vice, much the same as the evils attributed to the drinking of alcohol. In the 1920s coffee was finally banned in Iran and new types of tea, imported from China,

A group of men taking refuge from the heat with tea, Yemen

took its place and filtered through to Turkey. Now where there are packed coffee houses in the rest of the Middle East, there are busy tea houses and tea gardens dotted around the towns and villages of Iran and Turkey. In both these countries, it is often the first drink to be offered to a guest in a home, or when conducting business in an office or the bazaar. It is also the first drink of the day and the last, with many in between. It seems to be served endlessly throughout the day until your bladder is ready to burst.

Tea is also a popular beverage in Syria, Lebanon, and Jordan, where, according to legend, it was originally introduced by the Circassians. The Bedouin, who have a reputation for drinking gallons of coffee, are equally keen on tea. No Bedouin camp or compound can be visited without the customary partaking of tea. In these regions, the tea is prepared and drunk much the same way as in Iran and Turkey, although it is often flavored with spices like cinnamon and aniseed, or with fresh spearmint leaves. Aromatic infusions, or herbal teas, drunk for pleasure or medicinal purposes, are also popular throughout the Middle East. Rose petals are recommended for colds, and mallow or lime flowers for coughs. Dried pomegranate flowers are believed to relieve intestinal complaints, mint and aniseed to aid digestion, and infusions of dried thyme are reputed to cure a number of ailments, as well as acting as an aphrodisiac.

Sage tea

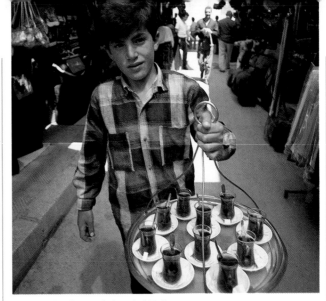

A boy delivering tea in Istanbul, Turkey

BUYING AND STORING

In Turkey tea is grown in the damp hills at the eastern end of the Black Sea, and in Iran it grows in the Caspian littoral and very little is exported. Some Middle Eastern stores may stock it, otherwise you will have to use a loose tea of your choice, preferably organic. I tend to use the fragrant Darjeeling or a mixture, in equal proportions, of Assam and Earl Grey. All loose teas should be kept in an airtight container in a cool place, otherwise they lose their aroma and flavor quite quickly.

PREPARATION AND PRESENTATION

Traditionally, tea is prepared in a samovar, originally imported from Russia. Often an elaborate brass vessel, the early samovars consisted of a compartment at the bottom for burning coals to heat the water in the "kettle" section, on top of which sat a small teapot in which the tea brewed all day and was continually topped up with fresh water and tea. Some households and tea houses still use the old samovars, but many people have converted to a lighter, more practical version made out of tin or enamel. Although less impressive to behold, the principle is the same: placed on the stove, the larger pot acts as the kettle while the tea brews in the smaller pot placed on top. In theory, by constantly replenishing the tea leaves and water, tea is available throughout the day.

Tea is served in glasses. In Turkey, these glasses are shaped like tulips, a legacy of the "Tulip Period" during the reign of Ahmet III (1703–30). The glasses usually rest on glass or silver saucers and are presented on a tray. Sugar lumps are offered with the tea, but rather than stir them in, it is customary to place them on the tongue and sip the tea through them.

Two-pot tea system

CHAI
(A POT OF TEA)

To make a light, fragrant, amber-colored tea, select tea leaves of your choice and use one teaspoon per pot. Add a sprinkling of sugar (and of herb or spice, if you like) and a splash of water to moisten the leaves. Fill the larger kettle pot with water, place it on the stove or flame, and put the teapot on top.

When the water has boiled in the kettle pot, fill the teapot and pour some water into the tea glasses to warm them. Top up the water in the kettle pot and place it back on the heat with the teapot on top.

Wait for the water in the kettle pot to boil again, allowing the tea to brew gently, then tip the water out of the glasses and pour in the tea, about two-thirds of the way up. Top up each glass with the boiled water and serve with sugar cubes.

Add some more tea leaves to the pot, top it up with water, top the kettle up, and start all over again.

Tea served in a tulip-shaped glass

APPEARANCE AND TASTE

The sour taste associated with yogurt comes from the lactic acid, produced by bacteria during fermentation. Sometimes, the bacteria are joined by yeasts, which make the yogurt taste fizzy and slightly alcoholic, a feature of many rural yogurts in the Middle East. It is made from the milk of cows, sheep, goats, water buffalo and, occasionally, camels—all of which lend a distinctive texture and flavor. All yogurt should be creamy and tangy, not watery and tasteless. Cow's-milk yogurt, which is the mildest and thinnest, curdles easily, so it needs to be stabilized (p 42) if used in cooking. Sheep-milk yogurt, which is thick and creamy, and the strong-tasting goat-milk yogurt are both good for cooking, as they tend not to curdle. The yogurt made from water buffalo and camel milk is extremely rich and thick, but slightly sweeter than the others, and can be used in cooking too. When yogurt is strained through a suspended piece of cheesecloth, it loses its whey and reduces in quantity, intensifying the flavor and creaminess. If it is mixed with a little salt and left to drain for a long time, one to two days, it gets thicker and firmer until it is the consistency of dense cream cheese. Often referred to as "yogurt cheese," this is known as *labna* in Arabic.

YOGURT

(LABAN)

Yogurt has been a basic food in the Middle East since the earliest nomadic and pastoral tribes. As with cheese, the discovery of it probably came about by accident when a batch of fermenting milk was invaded by bacteria. Ancient methods of curdling milk to make yogurt are still used in the Middle East. In eastern Anatolia some nomads use crushed ants' eggs as a yogurt culture, mountain shepherds use a specific herb, and in the Mediterranean regions villagers often use a fig branch, as the sap produces a chemical reaction that turns the lactose in milk into lactic acid. Referred to as "Persian milk" in medieval manuals, yogurt is known as *laban* in Arab countries, *laban zabadi* in Egypt, *mâst* in Iran, and, in Turkey, *yoğurt*, from which the English word derives. The very same word was used by the ancestors of the Turks, who roamed Central Asia and valued yogurt so highly they offered it to the gods, the sun, and the moon. The Turks add yogurt to practically everything and get through one million tons a year.

A tub of strained yogurt

BUYING AND STORING

Yogurt is always in constant supply in the Middle East. In rural areas it is still made in the home and stored in tin-lined copper urns, but practically everywhere else freshly made yogurt is sold by street sellers, in the markets, and in local stores. Making it yourself is very easy but nowadays we're spoiled for choice in most big supermarkets, whole-food stores and Middle Eastern and Asian stores. Look for live, organic yogurt, with nothing added. Strain it yourself through a piece of cheesecloth or buy a Greek brand of ready-strained yogurt. All yogurt needs to be kept covered in the refrigerator and used by the sell-by date. If you make it yourself, it should last for two weeks.

MEDICINAL USES

The lactose found in milk is converted to lactic acid during the fermentation process, making yogurt much more digestible than milk and more suitable for people who suffer from lactose intolerance—a common condition in the Middle East. Containing significant amounts of calcium, yogurt has long been regarded as a nutritional, health-giving, and healing substance. It is rich in minerals and vitamins, it soothes skin conditions such as rashes and sunburn, it contains antibiotic properties, it aids the digestion, and it contributes to longevity.

A traditional tin-lined copper yogurt urn from Trabzon, Turkey

CULINARY USES

Yogurt

In the Middle East, yogurt has multiple uses. It is like a staple food. It is eaten for breakfast with honey; it is eaten as a snack, often sprinkled with powdered sugar; it is diluted to make the refreshing drink *ayran*; it accompanies most meals; and is an integral part of many dishes. The one thing it is rarely served with is fish. It is often served with meat dishes, such as kabobs, or it is spooned over them, as in the Turkish specialty *yoğurtlu paça* (p51), which consists of poached sheep's feet on a bed of toasted flat bread, topped with yogurt and melted butter, and is served at the Islamic festival Kurban Bayramı. In Iran this everyday yogurt is used to marinate meat, and it is mixed with egg yolk and saffron to form the crunchy bottom of the famous Persian rice dishes. In Turkey it is mixed with crushed garlic and used as a sauce for grilled and fried vegetables, for egg dishes, such as *çılbır*, and for *mantı*, an ancient dish of pasta parcels filled with ground meat, chickpeas, or nuts. A similar pasta dish, *shish barak*, which is a specialty of Syria and Lebanon, is

prepared with a hot yogurt sauce. Also in Lebanon there is *immos*, meaning "his mother's milk," which is a rather morbid dish that calls for the meat of a young lamb to be cooked in yogurt made from its mother's milk. Owing to their dietary laws, this dish is prohibited among Jews. In Iran, Lebanon, Syria, and Turkey, a number of dishes involve cooking meat in yogurt, or adding yogurt to soups and stews to impart a creamy, lemony flavor. Yogurt is also used in a number of refreshing salads with cucumbers, lamb's lettuce, beets, peppers, zucchini, and eggplants. Strained yogurt is ideal for the sumptuous, creamy *mezze* dishes made with cooked vegetables that have been chopped or pulped, like spinach and smoked eggplant, known as *ezme* in Turkey and *boorâni* in Iran. And the thick, creamy strained yogurt, *laban* (*süzme* in Turkish), is often served on its own or mixed with white cheese and flavored with garlic or herbs like mint and dill as a dip for bread.

In the Middle East, some recipes call for yogurt to be used as the cooking liquid. It is often made in batches and stored in the refrigerator to be used in a variety of dishes during the week. Yogurt made from sheep and goat milk tends to not to

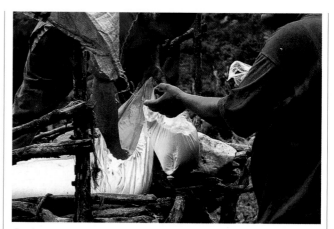

Fresh yogurt, strained through cloth, Iran

curdle, but cow's-milk yogurt does, so it needs to be stabilized by using egg white or cornstarch. To stabilize four and a half of yogurt, beat it in a pan until it is liquid, then stir in one egg white or a tablespoon of cornstarch made into a paste with a little water or milk, and a scant teaspoon of salt. Slowly bring the liquid to a boil, stirring all the time in one direction, and then leave it to simmer over a very low heat for about ten minutes, until it looks thick and creamy. Use it immediately in a dish or leave it to cool and store in the refrigerator.

Yogurt cheese

Labna is often eaten as a *mezze* dish on its own, drizzled with oil and sprinkled with fresh herbs or Middle Eastern red pepper, and it is used in thick *mezze* dips and in some desserts. It is also served as a healthy, sweet snack with a dribble of honey and a dusting of cinnamon. *Labna* is also used to make *labna bi zayt*, which are balls of yogurt cheese marinated in olive oil and served as a *mezze* or snack with bread and herbs.

An ancient product using *labna* is a dried curd, particularly popular in Jordan and among the Bedouin. Balls of yogurt cheese are dried in the sun until they become hard, then they are crumbled and rubbed with the fingers, or grated, until they resemble fine bread crumbs, before being dissolved in water to make a nourishing drink for journeys. Sometimes the freshly strained *labna* is mixed with flour and left in the sun to dry into hard cakes (the Bedouin do this on top of their tents). These are called *jameed* in Jordan, where they are used to make a sauce that is poured over the country's national dish, *mansaf*, and in a lentil and rice dish, *reshuf (rajuf)*. Similarly, in Turkey, the yogurt cheese is left to ferment and dry in the sun and is then rubbed into pellets to be used to thicken soups and stews. Or it is mixed with cracked wheat and pulped vegetables, fermented, dried, and crumbled, and called *tarhana*. The soup made with it is called by the same name. These crumbled pellets are also used to make a kind of peasant porridge, or they are mixed with crumbled cheese and eaten for breakfast. Occasionally, *tarhana* is chewed as a snack. The Arabs make a fermented product with yogurt and bulgur, called *kishk* (p125), which derives from the Persian tradition known as *kashk*, meaning crushed wheat or barley. In modern Iran, *kashk* tends to refer to dried whey or buttermilk, which is employed in the popular creamy, sour-tasting eggplant dish *kashk-e bâdenjân*.

Known as *doogh* in Iran, *laban* in parts of the Arab world, and *ayran* in Turkey and Lebanon, this refreshing drink was enjoyed by Persian kings and the ancient ancestors of the Turks, who also called it *ayran*. It is a popular drink in the Middle East, usually flavored with fresh mint, although basil is used in Iraq, and it is served chilled or with ice. It is prepared in homes, cafés, and kabob houses, and by street vendors to quench the thirst in hot weather. Traditionally, it is drunk as an accompaniment to meat dishes, especially lamb kabobs.

AYRAN
(YOGURT DRINK WITH MINT)

Serves 3–4
Preparation time 2 minutes
Cooking time –

2½ cups chilled thick, creamy yogurt
2½ cups cold water
A pinch of salt
A few coarsely chopped fresh mint leaves, or 2 pinches dried mint

Beat the yogurt in a bowl and gradually add the water, until it is well blended. Alternatively, whiz them together in a blender.

Season it to your taste —a little salt just lifts it—then pour it into tall glasses, with ice if you like, and sprinkle it with the mint

Yogurt soups are popular throughout the Middle East. In Turkey and Iran, cold yogurt soups, made with cucumber and mint, are refreshing in the hot summer months. In Egypt, the traditional yogurt soup, *labaneya*, is made with spinach or beet and served hot. The Iranians also make a hot yogurt soup, *eshkeneh Shirazi*, which is flavored with walnuts and fresh fenugreek; the Armenians add noodles to the traditional yogurt soup, *tutmaj*. The following recipe is for the Turkish yogurt soup, made hearty with the addition of chickpeas and rice and usually flavored with dried mint or safflower. If you prepare the chickpeas in advance, it doesn't take long to make.

YOĞURT ÇORBASI
(YOGURT SOUP)

Serves 4
Preparation time 5 minutes (+ at least 6 hours' soaking of chickpeas)
Cooking time 35 minutes (+ 50 minutes' simmering)

Roughly 2 tablespoons chickpeas, soaked for at least 6 hours
1 onion, finely chopped
1 tablespoon clarified butter or ordinary butter
1–2 tablespoons all-purpose flour
2½ cups well-flavored lamb or beef stock
⅓ cup long-grain rice, rinsed
2 cups thick, creamy yogurt
Salt and ground black pepper
Dried mint for serving

Simmer the chickpeas in plenty of water for about 50 minutes, until they are tender.

In a deep saucepan, soften the onion in the butter. Remove from the heat, quickly stir in the flour, and pour in the stock. Return to the heat, bring to a boil, stir in the rice and the cooked chickpeas, cover the pan, and leave the soup to simmer for about 20 minutes, until the rice is cooked. Then season.

Beat the yogurt in a bowl and add it gradually to the soup, stirring all the time, making sure you only heat it through and don't boil it, as it would curdle. Serve immediately with dried mint sprinkled on top.

Ayran

CHEESE

(GEBNA)

kaşar peynir

Cheese dates back to the earliest pastoral societies. Once there were herds, there was milk and the act of cheese-making may have come about by accident from the fermented products. The ancient Egyptians are known to have made cheese; traces of it were found in a tomb dating back to 3000 BC. It was a staple food of the ancient Greeks and Romans, and Abraham gave milk from his cattle to the poor when he first migrated to the land of Canaan. However, milk is rarely consumed fresh in the Middle East. According to Islamic custom, it should have ceased flowing before it is consumed, so it is used for milk puddings and made into cheese, yogurt, butter, and clotted cream. Medieval Arab sources reveal that a variety of cheeses was produced throughout the Islamic Empire and that Jerusalem was famous for its milk and cheese. More sophisticated blocks of white cheeses were made during the time of the Ottomans, when the milk of sheep and goats and, in some parts, buffalo, was treated with rennet. Today the cheese is made following the traditional ways using the milk of the same animals. In the rural villages and Bedouin camps, cheese is made in goatskins to make it easy to carry.

Cheese stored in sheep's stomach

APPEARANCE AND TASTE

A whey cheese, similar to ricotta, with a creamy texture and a mild flavor is popular in most parts of the Middle East, often eaten with honey or sugar. A firm, crumbly white cheese, in the style of feta, made from sheep or goat milk, is salted and preserved in brine. This is the most common, everyday cheese with a slightly salty, lemony taste, delicious with olives. *Hallum* is a salty, semi-hard cheese made from sheep milk. It is matured in whey and often sprinkled with nigella seeds. Lebanon and Cyprus are known for their *hallum* (*haloumi* in Cyprus). Of the many village cheeses, some are buried underground in clay pots and left for months to mature, and there is a special cheese made in the spring from the milk of nursing ewes. There is also a hard, yellowish cheese with a tangy flavor, encased in a rind. It too is made from sheep milk and is called *kashkawan* in Arabic (*kaşar* in Turkish). And there is a curious stringy, white cheese, *jibna majdula* or *dil peyniri*, that looks a bit like a plastic block of compressed thin layers—these peel off in strips.

Blocks of white cheese kept fresh in brine at a market, Turkey

A *mezze* spread including hummus, yogurt dips and slices of white cheese, Lebanon

BUYING AND STORING

There is a large selection of cheeses to choose from in the Middle East, the only difference sometimes being the village they come from. However, outside the region, only a handful are available. The crumbly white cheese, sometimes called "Turkish feta" is sold in Middle Eastern stores; this can easily be replaced by Greek feta in the recipes. *Kaşar* is sold in some Middle Eastern stores and can be substituted with a dry, tangy cheddar or Pecorino. *Haloumi* from Cyprus also may be available in Middle Eastern or other specialty stores. All cheeses need to be stored in the refrigerator.

CULINARY USES

Fresh white cheese is often eaten as a snack with a hunk of bread or for breakfast with olives, dates, and honey. A classic Turkish breakfast will include freshly baked bread, thin slices of white cheese, a choice of the local black and green olives, honey or rose petal jam, slices of ripe tomatoes and cucumber, and fresh figs. White cheese is also a popular *mezze*, either with a little olive oil drizzled over it, sprinkled with dried oregano and flaked Middle Eastern red pepper (p152), or served with cubes of juicy, honey-sweet melon. It is used as a filling for savory pastries, such as the ubiquitous *börek*, and it is mixed with vegetables in patties and in

the Turkish dish of ground-turkey balls, *gelik köftesi*. The soft ricotta-style whey cheese and a denser, creamier cheese are often eaten with honey for breakfast, or used in sweet pastries and semolina desserts. The soft and crumbly white cheeses are often mixed with herbs or strained yogurt to make a dip for bread, such as the Iranian *poloor* (p176). These cheeses and dips are sometimes sprinkled with *zaatar* (p196) or nigella seeds and they are occasionally combined with ground walnuts and red pepper paste in the delicious *mezze*, *muhammara* (p136). The same white cheeses are used in Turkey to make *peynir tatlısı*, small sponge puddings bathed in syrup, and in Syria and Lebanon they are used in a cheese-flavored version of the

semolina pudding, *ma'mounia*. The hard sheep cheese *kaşar* is eaten on its own with bread, or is used as a filling in savory pastries and in dishes that require melted cheese. Baked cheese-filled eggplants are a popular Jewish dish and *haloumi* and *kashkawan* are sometimes dredged in flour and deep-fried as an appetizer, served with

Beyaz peynir stored in water to reduce the salt content

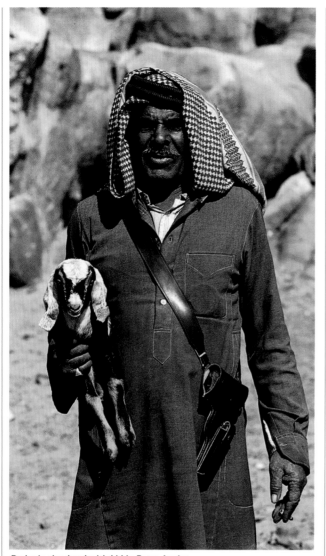

Bedouin shepherd with kid in Petra, Jordan

BEĞENDİ

(SMOKED EGGPLANT PUREE
IN A CHEESE SAUCE)

Serves 4
Preparation time 15 minutes
Cooking time 10 minutes

2 big eggplants
Roughly 2 tablespoons butter
1–2 tablespoons all-purpose flour
2½ cups milk
¾ cup grated kaşar or other
   cheese
Salt and ground black pepper

Place the whole eggplants directly over a gas flame, on a charcoal grill, or in the embers of a fire. Leave them to smoke, turning them from time to time, until they feel soft when pressed. Split them open with a knife to spoon out the flesh, or hold them under running cold water to remove the skin. Chop the flesh into a pulp.

Melt the butter in a saucepan and, off the heat, stir in the flour to make a roux. Place the pan back over the heat and pour in the milk, stirring all the time, until the sauce begins to thicken.

Gradually stir in the grated cheese, then beat in the pulped eggplant. Make sure it is mixed together well, season to taste. Serve with bread to mop it up.

Konafa (called *künefe* or *kadayif* in Turkish) is a specialty of Antakya, in the southern-most region of Turkey where the atmosphere is Arab in character, and it is one of the most popular desserts in Jordan, particularly among the Palestinian community. It is also popular in Lebanon, where some people eat it for breakfast, sandwiched inside sesame bread. Made with the famous pastry that looks like shredded wheat, sometimes called *kadaif*, it is not practical to make from scratch at home—the batter needs to be tossed through a strainer onto a metal sheet over a fire; then, as soon as it sets, it has to be scraped off quickly before it cooks. The good news is that ready-made packages of the shredded pastry can be bought in the same specialty stores that make *börek* and *yufka* or phyllo and, outside the Middle East, they are sold in Middle Eastern and Greek stores. Although the shredded pastry can be filled with chopped nuts, it is the cheese filling that makes *konafa* so unusual and delectable. Each region uses its own white cheese, including the stringy *dil peyniri*, for which mozzarella is the best substitute.

lemon. They are also fried with peppers, *çökelekli*, or with eggs, *beid bi gebna maqlia*. The stringy white cheese is a popular snack with adults and children alike—it is such a delight to peel off the layers and eat them with pickles. And it has one major culinary role as a filling in the delectable syrupy desert *konafa*, which is made with thin strands of pastry that look like shredded wheat.

There is a Turkish dish called *Hünkâr beğendi*, meaning "Sultan's Delight": it obviously pleased one of the great Ottoman rulers. Traditionally, the dish is made with meatballs cooked in a tomato sauce, or a meat and tomato stew, served on a pureed bed of smoked eggplant in a cheese sauce— the *beğendi*. The following recipe is for the puree, which is delicious on its own or served with meatballs or roast meats. In Turkey the cheese used is *kaşar*, the hard, tangy sheep cheese, but one could substitute a strong-tasting hard cheese such as mature cheddar or Parmesan.

Sheep lined up for sale, Syria

KONAFA

(SYRUPY SHREDDED PASTRY WITH A CHEESE FILLING)

Serves 6
Preparation time 20–25 minutes
Cooking time 1¼ hours

1 cup sugar
⅓ cup water
Juice of ½ lemon
½ pound ready-made shredded pastry
½ cup clarified butter (ghee), melted
12 ounces mozzarella, sliced (you can use other cheeses, such as ricotta)

Preheat the oven to 325°F.

Prepare the syrup: Put the sugar and water into a pan and bring it to a boil, stirring all the time. Add the lemon juice, then reduce the heat and leave to simmer until the syrup thickens a little and coats the back of a spoon. Leave to cool, then place the syrup in the refrigerator.

Put the shredded pastry into a bowl and separate the strands as much as possible. Pour the melted clarified butter over them and, using your fingers, rub it into the strands to make sure they are well coated. Put half the pastry into an ovenproof dish or individual dishes and lay the slices of mozzarella over the top. Cover the cheese with the rest of the pastry, tucking it down the sides of the dish to seal in the cheese, and flatten the top with the palm of your hand. Pop the dish, or dishes, into the oven and bake for about 1 hour, then turn up the oven to 425°F for about 15 minutes, until the *konafa* turns golden brown. Take the *konafa* out of the oven and pour the cold syrup over it. Serve immediately, as *konafa* is best eaten warm.

Konafa

COOKING FATS

SHEEP TAIL FAT
(ALYA)

The flavorsome rendered fat from the tail of Awassi sheep, a long-fleeced Asian breed with enormous, podgy, bulbous tails, has been used in the cooking of the Middle East since the time of the early nomadic and pastoral tribes. These sheep don't need lush pastures and can survive in hot, arid temperatures as, similar to the hump of a camel, the fat stored in their tails provides them with all the sustenance they need. Marco Polo was one of the first Europeans to write about his encounter with the sheep, which he described as being as big as a donkey with a thick fat tail, weighing thirty pounds or more. He also noted that they were delicious to eat. The fat was put to good use in many medieval Arab recipes, which began with instructions to melt or fry the tail.

Nowadays, this heavy, strong-tasting fat is really used only in rural areas, such as the mountainous regions of eastern Turkey and northern Iraq. Sheep tail fat is known as *alya* or *aliya* in Arabic, *kuyrukyağı* in Turkish, and *roghan-e donbeh* in Farsi.

CLARIFIED AND ORDINARY BUTTER
(SAMNA)

Butter replaced sheep tail fat. It was made from the milk of sheep, goats, or buffalo, which gave it a strong, distinctive, almost rancid smell and taste. Among the Bedouin and peasant communities, it fell to the women to churn it, in goatskins suspended on sticks. The nomads carried the butter in the goatskins to supply the towns. The kitchens of Aleppo and al-Karak (now in Jordan) were famous for their lavish use of butter. In order to preserve it, the butter was melted over boiling water and then strained through dampened cheesecloth to clarify it, a process that still used in most rural communities. Clarified butter or ghee (*samna* in Arabic) is rich and strong, with a slight nutty taste, and only a small amount is required for a dish. It is easy to make at home by melting butter in a pan until it froths, then straining it through a piece of cheesecloth to remove the impurities. Pour the clarified butter into a jar or container, leave it to cool and solidify, then cover it and store in a cool place.

Clarified butter

OLIVE OIL AND OTHERS
(ZEIT ZAYTUN)

Olive oil is the principal cooking oil of Turkey, Syria, Lebanon, and Jordan, where it has been produced for thousands of years. The ancient Romans spread its cultivation throughout their empire as a fuel for oil-burning lamps as well as for cooking. The ancient Hebrews used it for anointing and in temple offerings. In the Middle Ages, Syrian olive oil was regarded highly in the Islamic world. Traditionally, many Christians in the Middle East cook only with olive oil during their religious fasts. The Jews use it to deep-fry morsels at Hanukkah, in commemoration of the miraculous oil that features in the story of Judas Maccabaeus' victory. Olive oil didn't make an impact on Turkey until the late seventeenth century, when it was employed in the famous Ottoman Palace dishes, which involved gently poaching vegetables, balanced with "warming" or "cooling" herbs and then leaving them to cool in the oil before serving. Priorto that in Turkey, olive oil had been used only as a lighting fuel in the mosques.

The olives used to make olive oil need to be gathered when they are quite ripe and undamaged. The flesh then has to be crushed without breaking the stones and pressed to

Olive oil

extract the oil. The fluid that is extracted is left to settle so that it separates naturally into oil and a bitter watery substance (this is removed from olives for eating by soaking them in a lye solution). Olive oil is extremely healthful, containing no cholesterol, and it has long been used for its medicinal properties, to nourish dry skin, to soothe sprains and earaches, and as a laxative. In fact, an ancient Roman prescription for longevity involved drinking wine and cooking with olive oil. Early and medieval Arab recipes used a variety of other oils, including pistachio, walnut, sesame, safflower, cotton seed, sunflower, and corn, some of which are still used today.

BUYING AND STORING

Unless you know a breeder of Awassi sheep or go to a Middle Eastern store supplied with its own butcher, I would imagine sheep tail fat is impossible to find in the West. Clarified butter, however, is readily available in Indian and Middle Eastern stores and some supermarkets, often sold in cans as ghee from India. It keeps for a long time in a cool place and doesn't have to be stored in the refrigerator. The choice of olive oils in the stores is growing all the time but it is rare to find one from a Middle Eastern country. This is partly because the olive-growing regions don't produce enough and, until recently, it wasn't sufficiently refined for export. This is changing now and Turkey, in particular, is beginning to export a satisfying, comparable product, but, alas, in the name of progress all the depth and character of the crude, pungent, virgin oils made in the villages have virtually disappeared. Sunflower, sesame, walnut, and corn oils are all available in supermarkets. All oils need to be kept in a cool dark place.

Olive oil factory

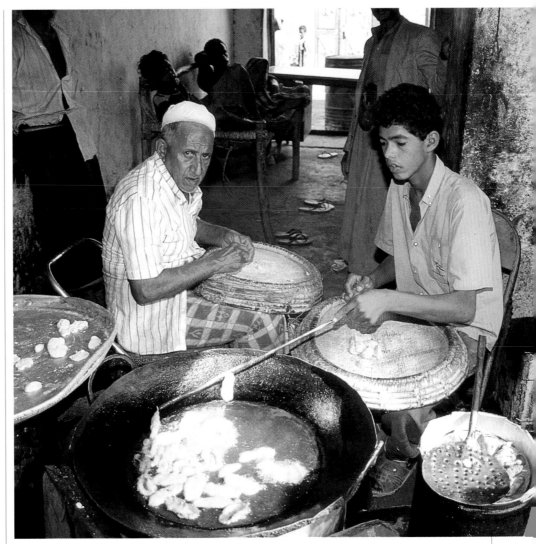

Frying sweet pastries in the Bayt Al Faqih market, Yemen

CULINARY USES

In Turkey, the whole sheep tail is boiled and consumed with bread during the feast of Kurban Bayramı, which marks the near-sacrifice of Isma'il (p 69). In the rural parts of the Middle East, the flabby tails of the Awassi sheep are burned to release the fat to use in meat and grain dishes. Its distinct flavor is unique to a number of peasant dishes.

Clarified butter is popular throughout the Middle East in savory dishes that are cooked and eaten hot, particularly meat stews and soups, and in grain dishes. It also gives a distinct characteristic to some sweet pastries and sweetmeats, which keep moist for months without tasting rancid. In urban areas though, ordinary butter, made from the milk of cows or sheep, is often used.

The mellow, fruity flavor of olive oil is favored for vegetable dishes, fish, and in dishes that are served cold, such as the numerous delectable *mezze* dishes. It plays a principal role in the special Ottoman-inspired olive oil dishes (*zeytinyağlı*), coating vegetables such as artichokes, fava beans, celery root, leeks, stuffed peppers, and stuffed eggplants. It is also used as a preserving oil for olives, prepared vegetables such as roast pimento peppers, and for the balls of yogurt cheese.

In areas where olive oil is expensive or difficult to obtain, a cheaper oil such as sunflower or safflower might be used for most dishes. Otherwise, the completely tasteless and lighter sunflower oil is reserved for frying and deep-frying. Sesame and walnut oils tend to be used only in cold dishes involving sesame seeds or walnuts, such as Circassian chicken, *Çerkez tavuğu* (p 62).

This is a Turkish specialty, a legacy of the Ottomans. It is called *İmam bayıldı*, meaning "the Imam fainted," as it is believed that the quantity of olive oil used in this tender and delicious dish caused him to keel over. Whether he fainted from shock or pleasure, no one knows.

İMAM BAYILDI
(STUFFED EGGPLANTS IN OLIVE OIL)

Serves 4–6
Preparation time 20–25 minutes
Cooking time 1 hour

1 large onion, finely sliced
3 large tomatoes, skinned and chopped
4 cloves garlic, finely chopped
A bunch of fresh parsley and dill, chopped
1 teaspoon salt
⅔ cup olive oil
2–3 long eggplants, partially peeled in zebra-stripes and soaked in salted water for 5 minutes
¼ cup water
1 tablespoon sugar
1 lemon, cut into wedges, to serve

In a bowl, mix the onion, tomatoes, garlic, and herbs with the salt and a little of the olive oil. In a skillet, heat enough oil to just cover the base. Pat the eggplants dry and pop them into the pan to soften them quickly on all sides.

Place the eggplants on a board and, carefully, slit them open from top to bottom, making sure you create a deep pocket to fill. Pack the onion and tomato filling into the pockets and place the eggplants, side by side, in a deep pan.

Mix together the remaining olive oil and water and pour it over the filled eggplants. Sprinkle with sugar and cover with the lid.

İmam bayıldı

Buying and selling sheep, Kuwait

Cook the eggplants gently for about 1 hour, basting them from time to time, until they are soft and tender and only the olive oil is left in the bottom of the pan. Leave them to cool and serve cold with a little of the oil spooned over them and lemon wedges to squeeze.

At the Islamic festival Eid-el-Kurban (Kurban Bayramı in Turkish), a day that marks the near-sacrifice of Isma'il (p 69), a sheep is slaughtered and almost every part of it is cooked in the fat from the tail. In Turkey, the following is made with the feet.

YOĞURTLU PAÇA
(SHEEP FEET IN YOGURT)

Serves 4
Preparation time 15 minutes
Cooking time approximately 4¾ hours

6–8 sheep feet, scrubbed clean in salted water

For the stock:
Juice of 1 lemon
1 onion, quartered
3–4 cloves garlic, smashed
2 dried bay leaves
1 teaspoon coriander seeds
A few peppercorns
4 pita breads or 6–8 slices day-old brea, crusts removed

2–3 tablespoons sheep tail fat
1¼ cups thick, creamy yogurt
2 cloves garlic, crushed
1 tablespoon clarified butter
1 teaspoon Middle Eastern red pepper (p152)
Salt

Preheat the oven to 350°F.

Blanch the sheep feet in boiling water for about 5 minutes, then drain. Put them into a large pan with the stock ingredients and cover with water. Bring to a boil, then simmer gently for 3–4 hours. Drain the feet, reserving the stock, and take the meat off the bone. Reduce the stock and season it to taste.

Heat the sheep tail fat in a wide pan, fry the bread until crisp, then lay the pieces in a shallow, ovenproof dish. Arrange the meat on top, moisten with a little of the stock, cover with foil, and place the dish in the oven for about 10–15 minutes.

Meanwhile, beat the yogurt with the garlic and season it to taste. Melt the butter in a pan and stir in the red pepper. Take the meat out of the oven, spoon the yogurt onto it, and pour the butter over the top. Serve immediately.

green olives

OLIVES

(ZAYTUN) *Olea europaea*

Olive trees outside Nazareth

HOW THEY GROW

APPEARANCE AND TASTE

Known as the "sultan of the table," olives appear at almost every meal. A handful of olives and a lump of white goat cheese have sustained peasants and nomads since ancient times. Wild olives originated in the eastern Mediterranean, where the small, bitter fruit was gathered by Neolithic peoples. The tree was first cultivated in Syria or Palestine, long before 3000 BC, and gradually spread west to Crete and Greece, and north and east into Anatolia and parts of Central Asia. The ancient Greeks claimed the first olive tree was given to humans by the goddess Athena. Along with the Romans, the Greeks held the fruit in high esteem, the olive branch being a symbol of peace. It was regarded as a sacrilegious act to destroy an enemy's olive tree. Olive motifs feature on some ancient Egyptian artifacts, and the polished stones of the fruit are used throughout the Islamic world as prayer beads, flicked between thumb and finger. Today, Syria, Lebanon, Jordan, and Turkey are all producers of olives and olive oil.

Wild olive trees (*Oleaster*) still grow in their regions of origin but the bitter fruit contains more stone than flesh. The cultivated olive tree produces larger, fleshier fruit, which are delicious on the table and ideal for pressing to extract the oil. Olive trees are evergreen, with silvery-green leaves and deep roots. They are slow to mature, but can live for a long time in poor, stony soil, up hillsides, and on uneven ground. There is an old Arab saying that the olive tree remains a strong and useful wife, in spite of neglect and hardship. Some trees live for hundreds of years and still produce a crop of fruit. The tree flowers in spring, and the fruit is harvested, by shaking the tree and gathering up the fallen fruit in late autumn and on into winter.

In spite of their bitter and almost soapy taste, the green wild olive fruits are prized by some people as a table olive. All other olives are fleshy, round or oval, and come in a variety of colors: shades of green, sometimes tinged with red or pink, red wine, violet, deep purplish-black like some eggplants, muddy brown, and jet black. The only difference between them all is in the ripeness, the black ones being fully ripe and the oiliest. The

A huge variety of olives on sale at market, Turkey

Ripe black olives

green ones, picked immature, must first be soaked in a lye solution to remove the glucoside, which makes the fruit very bitter, before they are preserved in brine. The sweeter black olives, which have been left to ripen on the tree, can be picked and put into brine immediately. Generally olives are cured whole, but to speed up the process, some olive growers make small incisions in the flesh, or crack them by striking them gently with a mallet. Not all olives are cured in brine; some are repeatedly rinsed in water, others are soaked or rubbed in oil, and the ripe black olives are often sprinkled and turned in salt, which crinkles the skin and softens the flesh, turning it brown.

Black olives left to ripen on the tree

BUYING AND STORING

Most supermarkets, delicatessens, Italian, Greek, and Middle Eastern stores have a wide selection of olives. If you can, buy them in brine, rinse them well, and marinate and flavor them yourself. They keep well in olive oil in a sealed jar in a cool, dry place, away from the light.

CULINARY USES

All table olives are enjoyed as they are. No *mezze* table is complete without a bowl of the shiny green ones, bathed in oil and flavored with coriander seeds, or the crinkled black ones tossed in oil and fresh mint. The most common marinade is a combination of olive oil and lemon juice, to which a variety of spices or herbs can be added, the favorite being dried marjoram, oregano or thyme, fresh mint, flaked Middle Eastern red pepper,

coriander seeds, and crushed garlic. Olives are also popular for breakfast, eaten with white cheese and bread.

Green olives are crushed with garlic and coriander seeds to make a tasty paste for bread known as *çakiste* in northern Cyprus and southern Turkey. In Egypt and other parts of North Africa, green olives are sometimes cooked with chicken, duck, or pigeon. In the Mediterranean regions, black olives are added to bread doughs, cold fish dishes and bean salads, such as the Turkish *fasulya piyaze*. Black olives are also used for garnishing many dishes and in some coastal regions they are added to a delicious potato dish with tomatoes or cooked with squid in a wine and tomato stew, Greek and Italian style.

The Egyptians are fond of pigeon, stuffed, baked, grilled, roasted, or stewed. Along with quails and chickens, some

families even raise them in their gardens for the pot. Qasr Al Nil, the road that leads to the pyramids, is lined with restaurants serving grilled pigeon, refreshed with lemon juice and chopped herbs. The pigeons in Egypt are different from the ones in the West, but this spicy recipe, with its tart bursts of lemon juice and olives, works well with wood pigeon too. If you have already made up the Arab spice mixture *baharat* (p 162), you can use 1–2 teaspoons of that instead of the spices listed.

HAMAM BIL ZAYTUN
(SPICY PIGEON WITH OLIVES)

Serves 2
Preparation time 10 minutes
Cooking time approximately 1¼ hours

2 teaspoons tomato paste
½ teaspoon paprika
½ teaspoon ground cinnamon

½ teaspoon ground ginger
¼ teaspoon ground cloves
A little grated nutmeg
A sprinkling of sugar
1–2 tablespoons clarified butter (ghee)
2 pigeons, cleaned and split in half lengthwise
2–3 dried bay leaves
Juice of ½ lemon
Roughly 16 green olives
Salt and freshly ground black pepper

Mix together the tomato paste, spices, and a sprinkling of sugar.

Heat the clarified butter in a heavy-based pan and add the pigeons and bay leaves. Brown the pigeons and then stir in the spicy paste, the lemon juice, and roughly 1 cup water. Cover the pan and simmer gently for about 1 hour, until the pigeons are tender.

Add the olives and simmer with the lid off for 15 minutes. Season and serve with bread to mop up the sauce.

Çakiste

This olive paste is a popular *meze* dip in southern Turkey and northern Cyprus, where it is often pepped up with hot red pepper. It is always made with tart green olives, although crushed black olives make a delicious paste too, and is served along with other *meze* dishes (p 28) such as cubes of white cheese bathed in olive oil, cubes of honey-sweet melon, and pickled vegetables.

ÇAKİSTE
(GREEN OLIVE AND CORIANDER DIP)

Serves 4 as part of meze spread
Preparation time 15–20 minutes
Cooking time –

Roughly ⅓ cup green olives
2–3 cloves garlic
1 teaspoon coriander seeds
A squeeze of lemon juice
Salt
A sprinkling of Middle Eastern red pepper (p152) or chopped red chili

Pit the olives.

Using a mortar and pestle, crush the garlic and coriander seeds to a smooth paste. Add the olives and pound it to a coarse paste. Stir in a little lemon juice and season with salt, if necessary.

Tip the paste into a bowl, sprinkle the red pepper or chili over the top and serve with toasted flat bread.

Olives spiced with chilies and thyme make a delicious *mezze* dish in Syria, Lebanon, Turkey, and Jordan. They are often served with cubes of firm, salted white cheese that is either drizzled with olive oil or fried. *Hallum* is particularly good for this.

ZAYTUN MSABBAH
(OLIVES SPICED WITH CHILIES AND THYME)

Serves 4–6 as mezze
Preparation time 2–3 hours
Cooking time –

1⅓ cups fresh green olives, soaked in water for 1–2 days
1 fresh, hot chili, chopped or 1 teaspoon Middle Eastern red pepper (p152)
1 teaspoon dried thyme
Roughly ½ cup olive oil
Juice of ½ lemon

Drain the olives and cut 3 or 4 slits in each one. Put them into a bowl, pour in the olive oil, and mix well. Add the chili and thyme, and leave to marinate for a few hours.

When ready to eat, squeeze a little lemon juice over them, sprinkle with a little salt if you like, and serve with cubes of white cheese and bread to mop up the chili oil.

Pickled eggplant rolls

PICKLES

(MEKHALEL)

Fruit and vegetables are an important part of the Middle Eastern diet. In order to enjoy the abundant supply of freshly harvested fruit and vegetables throughout the year, some of them have to be preserved. In season they are tasty and cheap, so every traditional household reserves a quantity for drying, poaching in syrup, pressing into molasses, or for pickling in vinegar—delectable delights that will nourish the soul and brighten up the cold winter.

The medieval Arabs adopted their food preservation methods from the Greeks, the Romans, and the Persians. The most common method of all was pickling, which was applied to fruit, vegetables, nuts, chicken, eggs, small fish, birds, and even lamb and goat. Today the method has not changed but, with the year-round availability of imported produce and refrigeration, some of the ingredients have. Tongue and brains are still pickled, and fish is still popular (in fact, the Turks of the Black Sea don't believe a fish is worth eating if it can't be pickled), but, on the whole, most pickles consist of fruit and vegetables. They are so popular, there are stores and street-vendors dedicated to them. The arrays of jars containing colorful pickles, stacked in store windows or in the bustling bazaars, have a dazzling and enticing effect on passersby, who can't resist stopping for a quick pickle snack. And in the hot weather the pickling juice is often drunk to quench the thirst.

APPEARANCE AND TASTE

The majority of Middle Eastern pickles are made with a combination of vinegar and salt; a few are made with brine. The vinegar is commonly made from dates, grapes, or apples, although other fruit can be used. Nuts, garlic, and a wide variety of spices, seeds, and herbs, such as nigella, tarragon, angelica seeds, spearmint, and cinnamon, are added for flavoring, but nothing else. And Middle Eastern pickles are always sour, never sweet. The fruit and vegetables are often picked immature and raw, so that they retain a delightful crunch throughout the pickling process, or they are lightly poached. Green walnuts are pickled, as are the unripe almonds still in their furry green skins. Immature apricots and watermelons are popular, and baby eggplants are often stuffed and wrapped in celery or vine leaves. Grapes, beans, peas, garlic, cauliflower, peppers, chilies, carrots, lemons, chickpeas, pears, melons, tomatoes, cucumbers, artichoke hearts, turnips, and cabbage are all pickled. Fruits, nuts, and vegetables are pickled individually or mixed together in a variety of personal combinations. The ratio of vinegar to salt varies too, according to personal taste. And some people like to throw in a few slices of beet to give a pink hue, or use red cabbage for its purple tint.

Pickled vegetables, including chilies, cabbages, and stuffed eggplants stacked in a store window, Istanbul, Turkey

Pickled olives, gerkins, stuffes pepper, beet and cabbage

TORSHI LEFT
(PICKLED WHITE TURNIPS)

Makes 2 big jars
Preparation time 20 minutes
Cooking time –

2¼ pounds small white turnips,
  peeled and cut into quarters
1 beet (or 2 if you want a strong
  pink), peeled and sliced
A few celery leaves
Roughly 3½ tablespoons salt
3 ¾ cups water
1¼ cups white wine vinegar

Pack the turnips into sterilized jars, interspersing them with the beet slices and celery leaves.

Stir the salt in the water until it has dissolved, then mix in the vinegar. Pour the pickling juice over the turnips and seal the jars tightly. Leave the pickles to sit for 2 weeks before tucking into them.

The vegetables, herbs,, and their quantities can be altered according to taste—just make sure they are all well washed and patted dry before using.

Pickled vegetable stall, Turkey

BUYING AND STORING

In the Middle East, if you don't make your own pickles, then you go to the pickle store. It's quite simple. Elsewhere, you will have to look for them in Middle Eastern and Asian stores. The vinegar-based pickles are designed to keep for a year, but if they are unopened and stored in a cool place, away from direct light, they keep for a couple of years.

CULINARY USES

Pickles are often served as *mezze*, or as an accompaniment to some main courses, particularly grilled meat dishes. In Turkey, they are eaten with slices of *pastırma* (p198) and *sucuk* (p166) as a snack, and they are often served with the popular late-night stomach filler, or early-morning hangover cure, *işkembe çorbası* (p 208), tripe soup. In other parts of the Middle East, pickles are often

tucked into pita bread with hummus or falafel (p113), and they are always served with bowls of *ful medames* (p116), the Egyptian brown beans. Invariably, pickles are eaten as a snack with cheese and with bread to mop up all the vinegary juice.

The following recipe is for pickled turnips, a great favorite in Egypt, Syria, and Lebanon. The small white turnips are traditionally colored pale or bright pink by adding slices of raw beets to the jar.

TORSHI-YE LEETEH
(PICKLED VEGETABLE RELISH)

Makes roughly 4 pounds relish
Preparation time approximately
  1 hour
Cooking time –

¾ cup peeled and chopped
  carrots
1⅓ cups chopped white cabbage
1 onion, peeled and chopped
2 celery ribs, chopped
1 leek, chopped
1 zucchini, chopped
1 green pepper, chopped roughly
6 cloves garlic, peeled
1 eggplant, cut into cubes
Roughly 2½ cups white wine or
  cider vinegar
A large bunch parsley and
  cilantro, chopped

A small bunch mint and dill,
  chopped
Roughly 2 tablespoons salt
½ tablespoon nigella seeds
½ tablespoon coriander seeds
A few peppercorns

Put all the chopped vegetables
except the eggplant into a bowl
with the garlic. Put the eggplant
cubes into a shallow pan. Pour
in enough of the vinegar to just
cover and bring it to a boil for
just under 1 minute. Tip the
eggplant and vinegar into the
bowl of vegetables and mix
thoroughly with the herbs,
spices and salt.

Push the vegetable mixture
through the large hole of a
meat grinder, then spoon it into

sterilized jars, leaving a gap
(roughly the depth of a
thumbnail) at the top. Pour the
remaining vinegar into the gaps,
then seal the jars. Leave the
relish to sit for about 2 weeks
before opening.

Pickled hot or sweet peppers
are popular throughout the
Middle East, often served with
cheese as a *mezze* dish. They
are also popular with kabobs,
meatballs, and falafel (p113).
The following recipe is for the
long, slender, perfumed green
peppers, which can sometimes
be a bit sharp.

Torshi felfel

TORSHI FELFEL
(PICKLED GREEN PEPPERS)

Makes 2 big jars
Preparation time 5 minutes
Cooking time –

1 pound long, green peppers
2½ cups water
1¼ cups white wine vinegar
1 tablespoon salt

Pack the peppers into a jar. Mix
the water and vinegar with the
salt and pour it over the
peppers. Seal the jar tightly and
store in a cool place for 2
weeks before opening.

MEAT & FISH

Goose and chicken seller, Egypt

CHICKEN

(DJAAJ) *Gallus domesticus*

The wild ancestors of the chicken are thought to have been native to the Indian subcontinent, but they have been domesticated in the Middle East since the ancient Romans bred them for meat. Poultry was so highly regarded in the medieval Arab kitchen that numerous recipes for chicken were recorded in the *Wusla*. Some of these included rhubarb and mulberries, quince and pomegranates, walnuts and almonds, rose water and musk, echoes of which exist in many of the recipes of today. During the Ottoman period the markets were full of feathered creatures, such as chickens, turkeys, geese, and ducks, and there was an abundance of game birds, including some exotic species. Game birds such as partridge and

pheasant still feature on the tables of the Middle East, particularly in the hunting areas. Pigeons are eaten in Egypt, and duck is favored in Iran and Iraq, but none of these is used as frequently as chicken, which is almost as popular as lamb. If a festive occasion doesn't call for the slaughtering of a sheep, chicken will often be served instead. Among Jewish communities, chicken is the traditional food eaten before Yom Kippur, the Day of Atonement, which is a day of fasting and prayer. On the eve of the fast, a light chicken soup is served, and to break the fast, a number of chicken dishes are prepared, such as stuffed roast chicken, elaborate chicken stews, and thick chicken and vegetable soup.

Egg and potato stall at the Bayt Al Faqih market, Yemen

BUYING AND STORING

Chickens and other poultry are often bought live in the markets in the Middle East. They cluck, cackle, and squawk in caged crates, while the buyers poke and prod them as they haggle over the price. The purchased bird is either killed and plucked on the spot, or carried home alive and squawking, held upside down by its feet, to meet its fate in the kitchen. In the rural areas, hens are free-range, fed on a diet of corn, and the meat is beautifully lean and tasty. With the emphasis on mass production in the West, the only way to acquire a tasty bird is to raise it yourself, or to buy the more expensive, certified organic, free-range chickens. However, with the rising population in the Middle East, there has been an increased demand for poultry and egg production in the last few decades, resulting in hens reared industrially on imported feed. Fresh chickens should be eaten within three or four days, but they can be stored in a freezer for about three months.

CULINARY USES

Often small chickens and other small birds are split down the backbone, flattened out, marinated in spices, and grilled over charcoal. The tender, tasty meat is then eaten with fruit-based sauces, such as sour cherry or pomegranate, or stuffed into pita bread with onions, parsley, lemon, and yogurt. This is a particularly popular way of eating chicken outdoors, and the smell emanating from the chicken being grilled in the streets or in the open country air is quite irresistible. Chicken kabobs are also popular in small rural kabob houses and gardens, as well as in sophisticated urban meat restaurants. For festive occasions, large chickens are often boiled first to obtain a stock for soup, and the meat is then served with rice. Large chickens are also cooked with vegetables, such as okra, spinach, and eggplant, or added to rice with saffron, nuts, vegetables, or fruit, to make a substantial meal.

The Iranians, who specialize in dishes using fruit, make a delicious stew with chicken and

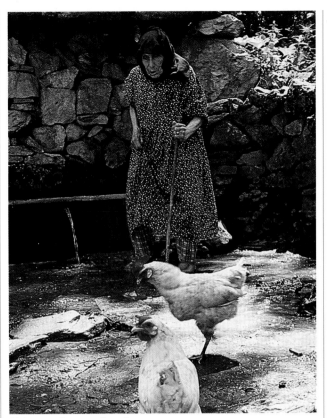

Free-range hens, northern Iran

oranges, *khoresht-e naranj*, and they are responsible for the famous *fesenján*, which can be made with chicken, duck, or fish, combined with walnuts in a pomegranate sauce. The Iranians also make a splendid baked rice and chicken dish, called *tahcheen-o morg*, which is served inverted so that the crusty bottom is on top. In Egypt, chicken is served with rice and the special *melokhia* soup, which is spooned over like a sauce. Also in Egypt, chicken is cooked with a calf's foot, eggs, and wheat grains in a medieval dish called *ferique*. In Jordan and Lebanon, the Palestinian dish *musakhan* (p189) is popular. It consists of sautéed chicken, richly flavored with sumac (p188) and spices, and served inside pita bread with lots of thick yogurt. And in Turkey, *Çerkez tavuğu*, a dish of Circassian origin, is favored as a *meze* dish in restaurants or as a meal in the home.

Throughout the Middle East, all birds, large and small, are stuffed. Quails and pigeons are often stuffed with bulgur, while chickens, ducks, and turkeys are usually stuffed with rice, which might be flavored with saffron, herbs, and spices, and contain meat, fruit, or nuts. The most impressive of all stuffed chicken dishes must be the Iranian *koofteh tabrizi*, which is a huge dumpling made from rice, yellow split peas, and ground lamb, inside which a whole, boned chicken stuffed with apricots and walnuts is concealed. Chicken livers and kidneys are often popped into stock or included in stuffings and, in Turkey, they are used in an extremely tasty rice dish, *iç pilavı* (p161). The most unusual of all the dishes using chicken has to be the chicken breast pudding, *tavuk göğsü*, a fabulous creation of the Ottoman palace kitchens.

Chicks dyed bright colors for sale at festivals, Abu Dhabi

Although pigeon, quail, duck, and pheasant are eaten in other parts of the Middle East, the Turks rarely sway from chicken and *Çerkez tavuğu* is one dish that they have put their stamp on. Having said that, the dish is originally Circassian and the heavy use of walnuts is echoed in a number of classic Persian dishes. Moreover, a true *Çerkez tavuğu* is said to be flavored with cilantro, an herb that features little in Turkish cooking. But although the dish has moved away from its origins, it is still delicious, served with the characteristic Turkish topping of melted butter and red pepper.

ÇERKEZ TAVUĞU
(CIRCASSIAN CHICKEN)

Serves 6
Preparation time approximately 35 minutes
Cooking time 1 hour

1 whole medium-size, free-range chicken

For the stock:
2 onions, quartered
4 cloves
4–6 allspice berries
4 black peppercorns
3 bay leaves
1 teaspoon coriander seeds
Salt

3 slices day-old white bread, with crusts removed
⅔ cup milk
1⅓ cup walnuts
3–4 cloves garlic, crushed
Roughly 2 tablespoons butter
1 scant teaspoon Middle Eastern red pepper (p152)
Salt and freshly ground black pepper

Remove any excess fat from the chicken and place it in a large pan with all the stock ingredients. Pour in enough water to just cover the chicken and bring it to a boil. Lower the heat and leave the chicken to simmer for about 1 hour.

Remove the chicken from the pan and leave to cool a little before taking the meat off the bone. Discard the skin, tear the meat into thin strips, and put it into a bowl. Meanwhile boil the stock for about 15 minutes to reduce it. Season it with salt and strain it.

Soak the bread in the milk. Grind the walnuts and garlic to a paste and beat in with the soaked bread (or blend them together in a food processor). Add the mixture to the chicken and bind with spoonfuls of the seasoned stock. Keep adding stock until the mixture is light and creamy.

Season to taste, then spoon the mixture onto a serving dish. Melt the butter, stir in the flaked red pepper, and spoon it over the top.

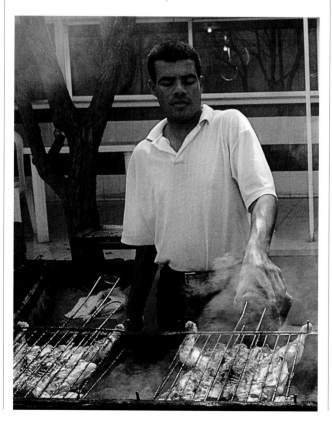

"Eat sweet, talk sweet," say the Turks, who are fond of their milk puddings and syrupy pastries. And, of all the puddings they will insist you try, *tavuk göğsu* is the one in which they take most pride. Probably originally a dish of the Romans, adopted by the Turks who migrated to Anatolia, once the hub of the Eastern Roman Empire, *tavuk göğsu* reached its pinnacle of sophistication during the height of the Ottoman Empire. Regarded as an Ottoman pudding, it is one of the most delectable creations of the Topkapı Palace kitchens.

TAVUK GÖĞSU KAZANDIBI
(CHICKEN BREAST PUDDING)

Serves 6
Preparation time 15 minutes
Cooking time approximately 45 minutes

1 chicken breast
5 tablespoons rice flour
3¾ cups milk
1¼ cups light cream
¼ teaspoon salt
¾ cup sugar

Place the chicken breast in a pan with a little water. Bring it to a boil, reduce the heat, and simmer until the meat is cooked. Drain and tear the breast into very fine threads.

Mix the rice flour to a loose paste with a little of the milk. Put the rest of the milk into a saucepan with the cream, salt, and sugar, and bring to a boil.

Add a few spoonfuls of the hot liquid to the rice-flour paste, mix well, pour it into the pan, and beat vigorously. Reduce the heat and keep stirring until the mixture begins to thicken. Beat in the fine threads of chicken and continue to cook the mixture until it is very thick.

Tip the thick mixture into a heavy-based skillet and place it over the heat for 5–10 minutes to burn the bottom of the pudding. Don't stir, but move the pan around over the heat so that the bottom is burned evenly.

Leave the pudding to cool and become firm in the pan, then cut it into rectangles. Using a spatula, lift the pieces out of the pan and place them on a plate or flat surface. Roll each piece into a log and place on a serving dish.

Serve chilled or at room temperature, sprinkled with a little cinnamon, if you like.

Left: Cooking chicken outdoors in the Bekaa Valley, Lebanon

Right: *Tavuk göğsu kazandibi*

FISH AND SHELLFISH

(SAMAK)

With the Black Sea, the Aegean, the Mediterranean, the Red Sea, and the Arabian Sea, the Middle East is not short of fresh seafood. Only Iraq and Jordan are without extensive coastlines. The varieties of fish include sole (*samak Moussa*), named after Moses (it is said to be so thin because it was cut in half when he separated the Red Sea); red mullet (*Sultan Ibrahim*), the favored fish of the Romans; gray mullet, sea bass, grouper, red snapper, porgy, anchovies, swordfish, flounder, mackerel, and tuna, along with shrimp, squid, and mussels. Of the freshwater varieties found in the lakes and rivers of the Middle East, the most common are trout, different species of carp, and barbel. One of Iran's crowning glories is the sturgeon of the inland Caspian Sea, from which the finest caviar is produced.

In former times, the fish was often salted and dried so it could be transported inland or taken on long journeys, but nowadays only a few fish, such as mackerel and anchovies, are preserved this way as a matter of preference.

A common feature in the recipes of the Middle East, in both the early cooking manuals and those of the present day, is that the fish to be used is not specified. Generally, people cook the fish of their region or the fish they like. When grilling and frying, almost any fish will do, but there are dishes where the size, oiliness, or flavor of a certain fish means it works better than others. Another feature of cooking fish in the Middle East is that yogurt and milk are almost never used. I say almost never, as al-Baghdadi had a recipe for fish cooked with milk in his medieval culinary manual, and I have eaten grilled fish with a yogurt sauce in the home of an Armenian family. But the belief that the combination of fish and milk could be harmful is fairly widespread.

The shape of a fish is also significant in the Middle East. Carved in early tombs and in metal, it has traditionally been a symbol of Christianity, but among many communities it is also believed to ward off the evil eye. At New Year, the Iranians eat fish to cleanse their bodies of evil and the Jews display a fish head in the center of the table to indicate that they will always be at the "head."

Selling fish at Karaköy on the Bosphorous, Istanbul, Turkey

Fresh anchovies displayed in market, Lebanon

CULINARY USES

All fresh fish is delicious grilled over charcoal; known as *samak meshwi*, the fish is whole or in chunks that have been marinated. Red mullet is particularly delicious grilled, so very often that is the only way it is cooked. Lemons and limes are served to refresh the fish, and sumac (p188) is often sprinkled over it while it is cooking. Ingredients used in the marinade could include allspice, coriander, fenugreek, cumin, chilies, garlic, and onion juice, and the preferred fresh herbs to serve with fish are parsley, cilantro, and dill. Generally, grilled or fried fish is popular served with a garlicky *tarator* sauce, usually made with crushed walnuts, pine nuts, and almonds, or a tahini sauce.

Another popular way of eating fish is with rice, as in the Arab dish *sayyadiah*, which is often colored and flavored with saffron, and garnished with fresh herbs or nuts. On the Black Sea coast, where the anchovy is king, the rice dish *hamsili pilav* is famous and served at every opportunity. Filets of fish are combined with bulgur to make light *kibbeh* in Syria and Lebanon. Similarly, in Turkey they are combined with spices and bread crumbs to make *köfte*.

The Turks also specialize in fish, particularly mackerel, cooked in olive oil and served cold. In all regions, fish is baked with vegetables, such as tomatoes, celery root, carrots, and onions, and it is baked in sauces made with tahini or crushed nuts. In the northern provinces of Iran, whole fish are stuffed with apricots, prunes, and walnuts, bound with sour pomegranate syrup, and then baked. In the southern provinces the stuffing for a whole, baked fish is fruity and spicy with tamarind, turmeric, chili, and fenugreek. Medieval Arab culinary manuals call for fish to be baked with a walnut stuffing, a combination put to best effect in the resplendent stuffed mackerel dish *uskumru dolmasi*, a legacy of the lavish feasts of the Ottomans.

Fish also features in a variety of soups and stews. Most of the hearty fish soups of the Mediterranean region, which are more akin to a stew than a soup, have been inherited from the Phoenicians, Greeks, and Romans. They are often packed with vegetables and flavorings as well as the day's catch and are mopped up with lots of fresh bread. In Iran there is a fish *fesenjân*, cooked with walnuts and pomegranate paste, just like the duck equivalent. Also in Iran, there is a delicious fish stew, *ghaliyeh mâhi*, with tamarind, turmeric, fenugreek, chili, and

BUYING AND STORING

The fish markets of the Middle East are busy and noisy, with stalls of the gleaming live or gutted catch. In ports and seaside resorts, fish are often sold from the boats, sometimes cooked there and then as a snack. And along the rivers, small makeshift stalls are set up for the day's catch. One thing is sure: the fish is always fresh. At the end of a day, the stalls are empty and washed down with water in preparation for the next day. There really is only one golden rule with fish—buy it fresh and eat it that day. It is not meant to be stored, unless you freeze it immediately, salt and dry it, or marinate it in vinegar.

Drawn from the very same waters and on a par with the better-known Russian caviar, Iranian caviar is now available in specialty stores and some supermarkets.

Drying sardines on the beach, United Arab Emirates

garlic—the distinctive Indian flavors of the Persian Gulf. A similar stew, *ghaliyeh maygoo*, is made with shrimp.

Shrimp and octopus are often grilled or pan-fried and served as salads. Shrimp also feature in some stews, particularly in the Arabian Gulf. In most of the coastal regions, scallops, mussels, and shrimp are sautéed with rice. In Turkey, squid and mussels are popular coated in a beer batter and deep-fried, then served with a *tarator* sauce—a dish that is served in high-class restaurants and as snacking fodder in the streets. Squid are also stuffed with bulgur or rice and baked, and mussels are stuffed with an aromatic rice in the Turkish delicacy *midye dolması* (p183).

In the Middle East, fish is often grilled over charcoal for the lovely smoky aroma it lends to the flesh. In rural communities, the fish is rubbed with onion juice or clarified butter and spices before being threaded onto a stick and set above the glowing coals. This recipe, popular in Arabia and among the Marsh Arabs in southern Iraq, is particularly delicious, as the fish is rubbed with pureed dates. In these regions, a freshwater fish, such as carp or barbel, would be used, but a firm-fleshed fish, such as trout or red mullet, works well too. If possible, cook the fish on a barbecue: It tastes so much better.

SAMAK MASHWI
(GRILLED FISH WITH DATES)

Serves 4
Preparation time approximately 1 hour
Cooking time 10 minutes

1¼ cups dried, pitted dates
2 onions, grated
2 cloves garlic, crushed
1 teaspoon turmeric
1 teaspoon baharat *spice mixture (p162)*
1 good-size trout or 4 medium-size red mullet, with scales on but gutted and cleaned
Salt

Soak the dates in water until they are soft—if the dried dates are moist, this won't take long—then rub them through a strainer or puree them in a food processor.

Mix together the onions, garlic, salt, and spices. Rub the mixture around the inside of the fish and close the cavity with a skewer or stick, piercing the skin. Push a long stick or skewer through the mouth and stand it in a tall pitcher or in the ground so that the fish is supported freely, upside down.

Rub the date puree all over the fish and leave for about 15 minutes.

When the charcoal is glowing, hold the fish above it and cook each side for about 5 minutes (less if using red mullet).

Serve immediately, removing the skin before you eat the fish.

The morning's catch at a fish market, Lebanon

Sayyadiah

This popular Arab dish, found all over the Middle East, varies from region to region. Some people bake it in a mold and turn it out with the whole fish on top, some fry a whole fish and add it to the rice, and others add fish filets to the rice. The following is an Egyptian version that works well with most firm-fleshed fish, such as sea bass, porgy, turbot, haddock, or halibut.

SAYYADIAH

(FISH WITH RICE)

Serves 4–6
Preparation time 15 minutes (+ 1 hour for making the stock)
Cooking time 45 minutes

2 pounds fish filets (keep the bones and head for stock), cut diagonally into 2–3 pieces
2½ cups long-grain rice, well rinsed
2 onions, sliced or chopped
2–3 tablespoons clarified butter or olive oil
1 teaspoon cumin seeds
A handful pine nuts, lightly roasted
Salt and pepper

For the stock:
1 onion, quartered
1 carrot, roughly chopped
1 celery rib and leaves, roughly chopped
A few peppercorns
A few saffron threads
Salt and black pepper

Preheat the oven to 300°F.

Put the fish head and bones into a pot with the stock ingredients, cover with water, and bring to a boil. Reduce the heat and simmer for about 1 hour. Drain the stock and season it.

Pour about 2½ cups of the stock into a pan and bring it to a boil. Throw in the rice and boil vigorously for 1 minute, then reduce the heat and simmer until almost all the liquid has been absorbed. Turn off the heat, cover the pan with a clean dish towel, followed by the lid, and leave the rice to steam for about 15 minutes.

Meanwhile, fry the onions and cumin in the butter or oil. When the onions begin to color, add the fish, tossing it gently in the pan. Season with salt and pepper and turn off the heat.

Tip the rice into a baking dish and carefully toss in the fish and onions. Pour a little of the extra stock over the top to keep it moist, or melt 1 tablespoon of clarified butter and pour that over it instead.

Sprinkle with the pine nuts and place in the oven for about 20 minutes, then serve immediately.

LAMB

(QOUZI)

Historically, the only food products to rival the date and the olive in the diet of the Middle East are those from livestock. Throughout the region, the preferred meat has traditionally been mutton or lamb. The most highly prized meat comes from the fat-tailed sheep, which are thought to have originated in the Middle East around 3000 BC. Like the hump of a camel, the tail stores the fat, which acts as an emergency supply in arid climates and periods of drought. Ever since the early nomads herded their sheep for sale into the villages and towns, the meat has been added to the daily diet of bread, bulgur, rice, or beans. Regarded as a high-status food, enjoyed with regularity by the wealthy but a rarity for most, it had to be used sparingly and imaginatively, cut into small pieces or ground, to make a little go far. One custom that dates back to the early pastoral nomads was to fry pieces of mutton in the melted fat from the carcasses and tail, which were then packed into earthenware jars, sealed with clay, and stored in a cool place or underground. This method of preserving meat, called *qawarma* in Arabic and *kavurma* in Turkish, still practiced in some rural communities today, enabled the nomads and villagers to impart a meaty flavor to their winter soups and stews.

Medieval recipes just state "meat" without specifying what kind because, apart from the occasional kid, camel, rabbit, or gazelle, and the occasional wild boar among the Christian communities, only lamb and

General sheep market, Kuwait

mutton were consumed. Beef was seldom eaten, as the cows and oxen were valued for their milk and labor in the fields. Nowadays, lean beef or veal is often substituted for lamb in stews and meatballs, particularly in Iraq; water buffalo is popular in Egypt; and goat is often roasted whole for rural festivities. Nevertheless, lamb and mutton still reign supreme at ritual slaughters, which occur at births, funerals, and weddings, the blessing of a new house, the well-wishing or thanksgiving at the start or end of a long journey, the honoring of an important guest, and religious festivals and ceremonies.

The sacrifice of Isaac (Isma'il in the Qur'an)

The Jews recall Abraham's near-sacrifice of Isaac at Rosh Hashanah (the New Year) with the tradition of baking a sheep's head in the oven, signifying the ram that Abraham saw and sacrificed to God instead. In many modern households it's now quite common to substitute brains or tongue for the sheep's head. In the Qur'an, Ibrahim (Abraham) offers Isaac's brother, Isma'il, for scarifce. Throughout the Islamic world, Muslims mark this near-sacrifice at the festival called Eid-el-Kurban in Arabic, or Kurban Bayram› in Turkish, held on the tenth day of the last month of the Muhammadan year. The sheep are paraded for sale through the streets and villages, and every family that can afford to, buys one and takes it home to sacrifice, first turning its head toward Mecca and then uttering the words "In the name of Allah" as its throat is slit. Some families rub the carcasses with onion juice, herbs, and spices before roasting it whole over an open fire, while others carve up the carcasses to distribute meat to the poor, reserving a little for themselves. A local butcher may be invited to do the carving to ensure that every bit of the animal is used. The tenderloin is cut into small pieces and threaded onto skewers, often alternated with pieces of sheep tail fat. Other cuts of meat will be cooked in soups and stews, or fried in fat from the carcasses. The tail is boiled and eaten with bread; the intestines are used for soup or are stuffed with other variety meats and spices; and the liver and kidneys are mixed with rice and spices and used as stuffing, or are grilled or fried. The sheep's head, complete with eyes, is used to flavor soup; the brains may be boiled separately and eaten cold as a delicacy; and the feet are either used in soup or boiled and served with yogurt on bread.

Whole carcasses hanging in a butcher's shop, Egypt

Dietary laws

For Muslims and Jews, there are certain restrictions regarding meat. The Qur'an forbids an animal to be slaughtered in any other manner than by cutting its throat; it forbids the consumption of an animal's blood; it forbids the consumption of an animal slaughtered for any other god; and it forbids any form of pork. Traditionally, all Jews adhered to the dietary laws of *kashrut*, which were revealed to Moses on Mount Sinai. Detailed and strict, they formed the basis of what was *kasher* (kosher, or permitted) and what was *terefah* (forbidden). Today, many of the archaic laws, such as Jews being forbidden to eat in the home of a non-Jew, have been dropped in most communities, but some of the laws regarding the slaughtering and cooking of animals remain. Basically, only those animals that "chew the cud" and have cloven hooves may be eaten. They must be slaughtered by cutting the throat and draining the blood. The consumption of blood is forbidden, so all traces of it must be removed to render the meat kosher. First, the meat has to be soaked in cold water for half an hour. It is then sprinkled with salt and left to sit for an hour to draw out the bloody juices, before being washed three times in cold water. And meat and milk must be kept completely separate.

BUYING AND STORING

There are a variety of sheep breeds in the Middle East, but, as has been said, the most popular is the fat-tailed. As all the fat is stored in the tail, the meat is very lean and tasty, and in traditional and rural dishes the tail fat is used as a cooking fat. Although fat-tailed sheep are bred outside the Middle East, the meat may be difficult to find. There is no substitute for the tail fat, but organic breeds of sheep can yield lean, tasty meat. You are best advised to contact organic breeders or ask your butcher. Fresh lamb keeps in the refrigerator for a week, but it can be frozen for at least three months.

CULINARY USES

In the Middle East, every part of the sheep has a culinary use. The head, eyes, brains, tongue, lungs, intestines, feet, tail, and even the testicles are all considered delicacies, and, as a mark of respect or hospitality, it is these parts that are often offered to guests—every Westerner's nightmare! The whole animal or cuts of meat are generally roasted over open fires, grilled on skewers, stewed with vegetables and fruit, stuffed and roasted, or baked. The ground meat is layered with vegetables and baked, as in *mousakka*, pounded with herbs and spices into meatballs, *kofta* (*köfte* in Turkish), or pounded with bulgur to make *kibbeh* (p126), which in turn are sometimes filled with ground lamb and spices. Ground meat is also combined with rice and spices and used as a filling for vegetables, poultry, and fruit.

Slicing meat for a gyro, or *döner kabob*, Turkey

Kabobs

The ubiquitous lamb kabob, meaning chunks of lamb grilled on a skewer, served with rice, has become almost synonymous with parts of the Middle East. Tourists visiting Turkey and Iran often think it is the national dish. Kabobs, however, cover a wide range of grilled or roast meat, from the primitive method of grilling cuts of meat over a fire, called *meshwi* in Arabic, to the long sheaths of ground meat grilled on swords in open ovens and deposited on the table with a flourish. The portable, outdoor grill (*mangal* in Turkish, *manqal* in Farsi) provides one of the simplest and most effective means of cooking kabobs. It can be set up on balconies, on verandas, in the street, and in the countryside. The aroma of meat cooking in the open air is mouth-watering. Almost all kabobs have one thing in common—the skewer. Made of metal, which conducts heat, skewers of different widths are used for livers, kidneys, chicken, chunks of lamb and beef, and ground meat. Ground meat kabobs, such as the fiery *Adana kabobı*, require a great deal of pounding and kneading so that the mixture holds together.

The *şiş kabob* from Turkey is perhaps the best known of all kabobs. It is reputed to have been created during the Ottoman Empire by the Turkish soldiers who, forced to camp out for months on end, threaded chunks of meat onto their swords and grilled them over the open fires. The same kabob is called *lahma mashwi* in Arabic. Another common type of kabob is the *shawarma* of the Arab world, *döner* to the Turks, and gyro to us, which involves threading slices of marinated lamb onto a vertical spit (sometimes alternated with sheep tail fat, onions, and peppers) to form a huge cone shape, which is trimmed and grilled by slowly rotating the spit in front of a tiered charcoal fire. The meat is skillfully cut off the sides as it cooks, and is eaten inside or on top of pita bread with sliced onions, tomatoes, parsley, pickles, tahini, or yogurt.

Another interesting kabob in Turkey is *çöp şiş*, literally meaning "rubbish kabob," as it is made with tiny scraps of meat. Marinated in onion juice and flavored with cumin, the meat is grilled on thin skewers then pushed onto a thin, pliable flat bread, topped with onions, flat-leaf parsley, and a squeeze of lemon The flat bread is then folded or rolled up and eaten just like that.

Roast and stuffed meat

A traditional Bedouin dish, *mansaf*, meaning "large tray," is a communal feast served to honor guests or to celebrate special occasions. The huge tin-lined copper or silver tray is covered with flat bread, topped with a mound of rice, on top of which sit chunks of boiled lamb or a whole roast lamb. Over all this is poured a sauce, *jameed*, made with the juices of the cooked meat and dried sheep-milk yogurt. It has become the national dish of Jordan, served at weddings and state banquets, which can call for such astounding proportions of *mansaf* that one is reputed to have included a whole baby camel that had been stuffed with several sheep, inside which were turkeys that had been stuffed with chickens—just like a Russian doll.

Stuffing cavities, such as hollowed-out vegetables and fruit, is a popular activity in the Middle East. It is put to its most flamboyant in the stuffing of whole lambs or kids, which are then roasted over a fire and served with a huge dish of rice. At one time, this way of serving meat was practiced by the wealthy and the imperial courts, but now it is a special dish prepared for communal festivities. Examples of this way of roasting are found in the *çebiç* of Turkey, the *barreh tu por* of Iran, and the *qouzi* or *kharouf mahshi* of Saudi Arabia. The shoulder of lamb is also often stuffed with a mixture containing nuts and dried fruit, such as apricots. The Persian-inspired Arab dish *dala' mahshi* is probably the most delicious example of this—the breast of lamb is stuffed with rice, ground beef, pine nuts, and raisins, and served with stewed apricots, apples, quince, or black cherries.

Kabob skewers

Street-seller grilling _kokoreç_—stuffed intestines

Meatballs and dumplings

Meatballs are popular all over the Middle East. Whatever the dish, all meatballs have to be kneaded and pounded well to make them light and hold together. They can be made with grains, pulses, or vegetables such as eggplant or zucchini. In Iran, the ordinary meatballs are called _cottlet_, whereas the _koofteh_ are more like dumplings, blended with rice or pulses and cooked in stock—an elaborate example being the mammoth _koofteh Tabrizi_, which consists of a whole, boned chicken, stuffed with walnuts and dried apricots, encased in a dumpling mixture of ground beef or lamb pounded with rice and yellow split peas, and cooked in a tomato-based stock. In Turkey, the _köfte_ are generally made with meat and onions, sometimes flavored with spices and herbs, and grilled or fried. Only a few Turkish meatballs are pounded with bulgur or rice, such as the Ottoman favorite _kadın buduğu_, meaning "ladies' thighs." Sometimes meat is the filling, as in _içli köfte_, meaning mother-in-law's _köfte_, and the stuffed potato balls of both Iran and Turkey. Also in Turkey there is a fabulous dish of meatballs or ground meat served on a bed of smoked eggplant and yogurt puree called _ali nazik_, and

another dish inherited from the Ottomans called _Hünkâr beğendi_, which consists of meatballs served with a hot smoked eggplant and cheese puree. Similarly the _kibbeh_ (p126) of Syria and Lebanon, called _kubba_ in Jordan and Iraq, are made with meat that is usually pounded with bulgur and grated onions until the mixture resembles a paste. Done by hand, this generally takes a long time, so the making of _kibbeh_ is often a communal activity for special occasions, such as the Christian feast day 'Id al-Salib, which marks the day Queen Helena, the mother of the Roman emperor Constantine, was said to have found the Crucifixion cross on a basil-covered hill in Jerusalem. _Kibbeh_ are extremely popular raw or cooked. Mixed with spices and eaten raw with lettuce leaves, they are known as _kibbeh naye_ in Arabic, a dish that is similar to the spicy _çiğ köfte_ of Turkey. Some stuffed _kibbeh_ are cooked in a tomato or yogurt sauce, as in the Arab dish _shish barak_, while others are molded and simply fried or baked. Small _kibbeh_ are sometimes added to stews and soups. All _kibbeh_ require practice and skill, and come under much scrutiny. Only some women are considered to have the knack.

Soups and stews

Jewish meat cookery is characterized by long, slow cooking in soups and stews, for kosher meat, which has not hung for very long and has been salted and washed, is generally tough. The Egyptian specialty _dfeena_ is a popular stew for the Jews on the Sabbath. It can be left to simmer from the Friday and consists of cubed meat, often beef, cooked with a calf's foot, eggs in their shells, and chickpeas or haricot beans. Lamb or mutton is used in a number of soups, often to celebrate a happy event, such as _düğün çorbası_, the cinnamon-flavored wedding soup of Turkey. Lamb or mutton is also combined with vegetables and pulses to make a substantial meal, such as the Iranian _âbgoosht_, which is served in two courses—the soup is strained and the broth is served as an appetizer, and the meat and pulses are served separately with bread.

This way of cooking meat in light vegetables stews is common daily fare in households throughout the Middle East. It is called _yakhnie_ in Syria and Lebanon, and _yahni_ in Turkey. Cooking meat with fruit is another popular method found in the Middle East, inspired by the old Persian fruit

and meat stews, _khoresht_, designed to be served as a sauce for rice. Meat from head and legs is used to make _fatta_ (p 34), a layered dish of bread soaked in a broth, usually flavored with lamb. The bones and cheaper cuts of meat are also used to impart flavor to the porridge-style dish known as _harissa_ in the Arab world, _keşkek_ in Turkey, and _haleem_ in Iran. The early cooking manuals called for meat to be cooked in milk or yogurt, a method that is still popular in parts of the Middle East and is best illustrated in the Lebanese dish _immos_, literally meaning "his mother's milk," as the lamb or kid must be cooked in its own mother's milk. Such dishes are contrary to Jewish dietary restrictions.

Variety meats

Throughout the Middle East variety meats are popular. There are street-sellers with their cooked specialties, and stores and restaurants devoted just to tripe, or brains, or one of the many spicy stuffed stomachs. Among Jewish communities, kosher meat was always expensive, reserved for the Sabbath and special occasions, so the cheaper variety meats, such as the brains, liver, intestines, and feet, became popular. Generally, liver is lightly fried in olive oil or clarified butter and flavored with red pepper,

Freshly cleaned variety meats hanging for sale

thyme, or mint. Brains are poached and served hot or cold, and the feet are often used to flavor soups. In Turkey, the feet are cooked and served on a bed of pita bread with lots of garlic-flavored yogurt in the Anatolian dish *yoğurtlu paça* (p 51).

Intestines are often used as a casing for the many spicy meat and variety-meat sausages, and they are stuffed with ground mutton and ingredients such as rice, chickpeas, onions, and spices in the popular specialties *kokoreç*, which is grilled, and *krush mahshiyya*, which is boiled. Tripe is particularly popular in soup, often served with pickles, as a pick-me-up late at night. It is also used like pasta in parts of Syria and Lebanon, where they cut the stomach into small squares, spoon a little spicy meat mixture onto each one, then fold them over and sew the edges together so that they can be boiled. Kidneys, sweetbreads, and ram's testicles are usually grilled and served with melted clarified butter, while in eastern Anatolia there is a preference for the much larger bull's testicles.

Bedouin woman spinning wool, Jordan

Whole lambs or kids are stuffed and roasted for festive and ceremonial occasions throughout the Middle East. It is a feast for the rich and the poor, although many of the poor can afford to eat meat only at Eid-el-Kurban. The following dish is a Saudi Arabian specialty. Traditionally, the whole kid or baby lamb is stuffed, roasted over charcoal in a pit, and served on a huge tray, surrounded by mounds of rice, sliced raw onion, hard-boiled eggs, and lots of fresh parsley.

At home, you can use a whole spring lamb, which a butcher can help you to prepare, and cook it on a barbecue or, as I have done in this recipe, in a conventional oven. If you prefer, you could use breast of lamb and reduce the quantities in the recipe.

KHAROUF MAHSHI
(ROASTED STUFFED LAMB)

Serves roughly 16 people
Preparation time approximately 40 minutes (if the butcher has prepared the lamb for you)
Cooking time almost 2 hours

Bedouin herding a flock of sheep through the desert

18 pound baby lamb, cleaned, with entrails and head (some people leave it on) removed
Juice of 3 onions, which have been grated and pressed
2–3 tablespoons ground coriander
1 tablespoon ground ginger
Salt and black pepper

For the stuffing
Roughly 5⅓ cups long-grain rice, well rinsed
2 pinches saffron threads
2 onions, chopped
2 tablespoons clarified butter (ghee)
1 cup coarsely chopped almonds
1 cup coarsely chopped pistachios
1 cup coarsely chopped walnuts
1 cup raisins
1 teaspoon ground coriander
1 teaspoon ground cumin
1 scant teaspoon ground fenugreek
A large bunch of flat-leaf parsley, coarsely chopped
Salt and freshly ground black pepper

Preheat the oven to 425°F.

Rinse the lamb inside and out, and wipe it dry. In a bowl, mix together the onion juice,

coriander, ginger, salt, and pepper, and rub all over the lamb, inside and out. Put the meat aside.

Put the rice into a pan and add just enough wate to cover. Bring it to a boil, stir in the saffron, and cook for about 10 minutes, until the rice is tender. In a wide pan, fry the onions in the clarified butter until they begin to color, then stir in the nuts, raisins, and spices. Tip in the rice, mix well, and season with salt and pepper.

Stuff the lamb with the rice, packing it in tightly, and sew up the opening with a strong thread. Place the stuffed lamb on a large baking sheet and pop it into the preheated oven. After 20 minutes, reduce the oven temperature to 325°F and roast the lamb for about 1½ hours (or more if you like your meat well done), basting it in its own juices. Serve the lamb on a large dish, or tray, with lots of fresh flat-leaf parsley and extra rice prepared in the same way as the stuffing.

Of all the kabobs in the Middle East, these are my favorite. Traditionally made with scraps of meat, hence the name "rubbish kabob," they can also be made with a lean, tender cut of meat. The key to these kabobs is to cut the meat into very small pieces so that they take only minutes to cook and can be wrapped up in the flat breads, which are made at the same time. For this recipe, which is designed for the barbecue, it is easier to have two cooks at the end, one to turn the meat on the skewers, the other to flip the flat breads.

ÇÖP ŞİŞ
(ANATOLIAN LAMB KABOBS)

Serves 6
Preparation time roughly 3–4
   hours
Cooking time 5 minutes

2 pound shoulder of lamb, cut into
   small bite-size pieces with most
   of the fat removed

For the marinade:
2 big onions, peeled
Roughly 1 tablespoon salt
2 cloves garlic, crushed
2–3 teaspoons crushed cumin
   seeds

For the flat breads:
2 cups strong white flour
½ cup whole-wheat flour
1 teaspoon salt
¾–1 cup lukewarm water

To serve:
2 red onions, finely sliced
A big bunch of flat-leaf parsley,
   roughly chopped
3–4 lemons, halved or quartered,
   ready to squeeze

Grate the onions into a bowl (or in a food processor) and sprinkle with a generous quantity of salt. Cover and leave to weep for about 10 minutes. Push the salted onion pulp through a strainer into another bowl, making sure you squeeze out all the juice. The liquid collected in the bowl is the onion juice for the marinade.

Stir in the garlic and cumin seeds and, using your hands, toss in the pieces of lamb until well coated. Cover the bowl and leave to marinate for at least 2–3 hours.

Meanwhile, sift the flours and salt into a bowl. Make a well in the center; add the water gradually, drawing the flour in from the sides, and knead into a firm dough. On a floured board, divide the dough into 24 pieces and roll each piece into a ball. Leave the balls to rest on the floured surface, covered with a damp cloth, for at least 30 minutes.

While your charcoal grill is heating up, roll out each ball of dough into a wide, thin circle. Keep the circles dusted with flour so they don't stick to one another, and keep them covered with a damp cloth at all times to prevent them from drying out.

Thread the meat onto skewers and place over the hot charcoal. While the meat is cooking, quickly flip the flat breads, one by one, onto a hot griddle or flat pan. Each side takes just seconds as they brown and buckle a little.

Push the cooked meat off each skewer onto the flat breads, throw on some onions and parsley, squeeze lemon juice on it, and roll it up so that you can hold and eat it.

Çöp şiş

FRUIT

BARBERRY

(ZERESHK) *Berberis vulgaris*

In medieval times, barberries were fashionable in England and Europe, often preserved in jams and jellies. In North America, the early settlers regarded them as "the poor man's red currant" and preserved them in syrup and vinegar. These tart, bright little berries are still popular in Iran.

HOW IT GROWS

Many species of the berberis shrub grow wild in temperate regions of Europe and Asia but it is the *B. vulgaris,* with its edible, sour berries, that grows in Iran.

APPEARANCE AND TASTE

The berries hang in clusters and look like bright red jewels, the size of a small red currant. They are really too tart to eat fresh, so they are dried in the sun and used in cooking for a burst of color and their refreshing, sour flavor.

BUYING AND STORING

Dried barberries are available in Iranian stores and Middle Eastern stores. They keep well in an airtight container, or in the freezer, and will need to be picked over for stalks and washed before using. Like currants, they spring back into shape when soaked in water or sautéed in oil.

A barberry dish such as *Khoresht-e zereshk* is often served at traditional weddings in Iran

CULINARY USES

Dried barberries add a sour punch to a number of Iranian and Persian-inspired dishes. They are sprinkled over stews and pilafs, added to stuffings and the Iranian herb omelet *kookoo-ye sabzi*, but they are best known for their role as a brilliant jewel in the stunning Persian rice dish *morasa' polow*, and in the wedding dish *khoresht-e zereshk*.

In Iran, most wedding dishes are sweet, designed to ensure happiness for the newlyweds. However, this tart dish is also traditionally served at weddings, to remind the newlyweds that there is sadness in life too.

KHORESHT-E ZERESHK

(BARBERRY AND NUT STEW)

Serves 4–6
Preparation time 25 minutes
Cooking time approximately 1 hour

2 tablespoons olive oil
2 onions, chopped
1 pound lean lamb, trimmed and cut into cubes
2 cups chopped or slivered blanched almonds
2 cups chopped or slivered pistachios
2 pinches saffron threads
2 tablespoons sugar
2 cups dried barberries
Salt and freshly ground black pepper

Heat the oil in a heavy-based pan and fry the onions until golden brown. Stir in the meat and brown it. Pour in enough water to cover the meat, put on the lid, and simmer for about 40 minutes. Stir in the nuts and simmer, with the lid off, for a further 15 minutes.

Meanwhile, using a mortar and pestle, grind the saffron threads with 1 teaspoon of sugar and pour in a little boiling water to extract the color.

Heat a splash of extra oil and toss the barberries in it, to plump them up. Sprinkle them with the remaining sugar and add to the stew with the saffron. Season the stew to taste and spoon it over plain rice.

Morasa' polow

This sumptuous rice dish is as beautiful to behold as it is to eat. It is a light saffron rice dotted with little barberries, which look like rubies among other dried fruits and nuts resembling precious stones and jewels. The fruits and nuts vary a little in the Gulf, Iraq, and Turkey; the dish is of Persian origin.

MORASA' POLOW
(JEWELLED RICE)

Serves 6
Preparation time 5 minutes (+ 20 minutes' soaking)
Cooking time 30 minutes

2½ cups basmati long-grain white rice
1½ cups dried barberries
⅓ cup dried sour cherries or cranberries
1–2 tablespoons slivers of bitter-orange peel
2–3 tablespoons olive oil with a little butter
2 pinches saffron threads
½ cup raisins or golden raisins
½ cup slivered dried apricots
1 cup slivered blanched almonds
1 cup chopped or slivered pistachios

Rinse the rice well and leave it to soak in water for 20 minutes.

Place the barberries, sour cherries, and bitter-orange peel in individual bowls, pour a little boiling water over them, and leave to soak for 10 minutes. Drain the rice, barberries, and sour cherries but reserve the bitter-orange soaking water.

Boil the rice in plenty of salted water for about 10 minutes, until it is al dente, then drain.

In a large, heavy-based pan, heat the oil and butter. Stir in the saffron, then tip the rice in with all the other ingredients and a sprinkling of salt. Carefully mix it all together, adding a little extra oil to coat it.

Cover the pan with a clean dishtowel, followed by the lid, and steam the rice over a very low heat for 15–20 minutes, until it is tender. Serve hot or at room temperature.

LIME

(LOOMİ) *Citrus aurantifolia*

Fresh limes

CULINARY USES

There are various kinds of lime but the *citrus aurantifolia*, which originated in Malaysia, is often referred to as "the true lime." It is thought to have traveled to the Middle East with the Arab traders in medieval times. Among the leading producers of this lime is Egypt, where it is known as *limun baladi*; it is also grown in Iran. The *Citrus limettoides*, a sweet and juicy lime, often referred to as the Palestine lime, is also popular in the Middle East and is known as *limun helou*, or *limun succari* in Egypt. What is interesting about limes in the Middle East is that they are often left in the sun to dry before use. In their dried form, they are known as *noumi basra* in Iraq, as *limoo amani* (Omani limes) in Iran, and in Oman itself, they are simply *loomi*.

Neither fresh nor dried limes are used much in the food of Turkey, Lebanon, and Syria—they feature more in the food of Egypt, the Gulf, Iraq, and Iran. Fresh limes are used much like lemons to lend a citrus flavor to a sauce, or to accompany fish in the lime-growing regions. Whole dried limes, on the other hand, are in demand for the musty, tangy flavor they lend to stews such as *gheimeh*, an Iranian vegetable stew. In the Arabian Gulf, they are often cooked with fish, particularly in *samak quwarmah*, a popular way of cooking fish with spices. The limes are also ground to a fine green powder to add to stews or stuffings, such as the Iraqi specialty *koubba helwa*, a dumpling filled with lime-flavored meat and cooked in a tomato sauce. Ground dried lime is also sprinkled over soups and stews for a splash of tartness. And a refreshing tea, *chai hamidh*, is made by breaking open the dried limes and pouring boiling water over them.

HOW IT GROWS

Most limes grow mainly in tropical climates, but some grow in milder climates. In the Middle East, they grow in the Arabian desert and in Egypt and Iran.

APPEARANCE AND TASTE

We tend to think of them as a green fruit, because they are picked before they are ripe. If they were left on the tree, they would turn orange, then yellow, and look rather like lemons. The *limun baladi* is quite tart to taste but the *limun succari* is sweet and juicy. The Omani limes are pale or dark, depending on how long they have been dried. In many places they are selected according to the color of the soup or stew that is being prepared, but in Iran the paler, more delicate-tasting limes are preferred. They sound hollow when tapped and give a distinct musty, tangy, sour flavor to a dish.

BUYING AND STORING

Fresh limes are available everywhere but the dried fruit are available only in Middle Eastern stores. Powdered dried lime is also available in packages in Middle Eastern stores. Both the dried limes and powder should keep for about a year.

Lime powder

The following recipe from the Arabian Gulf, where the flavors are often influenced by Indian cuisine, is an example of many such dishes involving fish, seafood, or chicken. The use of fresh ginger and dried limes is typical of this region.

Dried limes

SAMAK QUWARMAH
(SPICY FISH WITH GINGER AND LIME)

Serves 6
Preparation time 5–10 minutes
Cooking time approximately 40 minutes

A chestnut-sized piece of fresh ginger, peeled and chopped
2–3 cloves garlic
2 tablespoons clarified butter (ghee)
1½ pounds fish steaks (e.g. tuna, grouper, sea bass, trout)
2 onions, chopped
½ teaspoon hot chili pepper
1 teaspoon ground turmeric
1 teaspoon baharat (p162)
1 piece of cinnamon bark
4–5 tomatoes, peeled and chopped
1 teaspoon sugar
2 dried limes
Salt

Samak quwarmah

Using a mortar and pestle, grind the ginger with the garlic to form a paste.

Heat the clarified butter in a heavy-based pan and sear the fish steaks on both sides. Remove from the pan and stir in the onion.

Just as the onion begins to color, stir in the ginger and garlic paste, the spices, and the cinnamon bark.

Add the chopped tomatoes, sugar, and dried limes (pierced twice with a skewer). Pour in , roughly ⅔ cup of water, and simmer gently for about 15 minutes.

Season the sauce with salt and place the fish steaks in it. Cover the pan and simmer for a further 15 minutes, until the fish steaks are cooked.

Remove the cinnamon bark and dried limes, and serve with rice.

This unusual dish is an Iraqi specialty. Although, in essence it is really a filled *kibbeh*, it has one distinct characteristic—the sharp, musty flavor of the dried limes.

KOUBBA HELWA
(IRAQI DUMPLINGS)

Serves 4–6
Preparation time 40–50 minutes
Cooking time approximately 40 minutes

1¼ cups semolina
1 cup ground beef
1 onion, grated
1 dried lime, pounded to a powder in a mortar
Salt and freshly ground black pepper
A little all-purpose flour for dusting

For the sauce:
1 tablespoon clarified butter (ghee)
1 onion, chopped
2 cloves garlic, chopped
1 zucchini, thinly sliced
1½ tablespoons tomato paste
1 teaspoon sugar
A small bunch fresh parsley and cilantro, chopped
A squeeze of lemon juice

Put the semolina into a bowl with a little salt and pour in enough water to make a thick paste. Knead it with your hands to make it doughy.

In another bowl, mix together the ground meat, onion, and ground dried lime. Season it with salt and pepper, and knead with your hands to form a smooth paste.

After you've washed and dried your hands, dust them with flour, and take a chestnut-size lump of the semolina paste. Roll it into a ball, flatten it in your hand and place 1 heaping teaspoon of the meat filling in the center. Fold the semolina shell over the filling, pinching it together, and pat it back into a ball.

Repeat with the rest of the mixture, rolling each finished ball in a little flour so they don't stick together.

Heat the clarified butter in a wide, heavy-based pan and stir in the onion. When it begins to color, add the garlic and zucchini, and cook for 1–2 minutes. Stir in the tomato paste, sugar, herbs, and a squeeze of lemon juice.

Pour in enough water to just cover the dumplings and bring to a boil. Season with salt and pepper, then reduce the heat and gently drop in the dumplings.

Cover and cook gently for 25–30 minutes, until the semolina is soft and the dumplings begin to float. Scoop out the dumplings and keep them warm while you boil the sauce vigorously to reduce it. Serve the dumplings hot with the sauce and rice.

LEMON

(LAMOUN) *Citrus medica*

The lemon tree is thought to have originated in India and found its way to the Mediterranean at the end of the first century AD, when the Romans discovered they could reach India from the southern end of the Red Sea. Arab traders spread the lemon tree westward along the Mediterranean to North Africa and eastward to China.

While the lemon was still rare and expensive in Europe in the Middle Ages, the Arabs of the eastern Mediterranean were exploring its culinary uses, making lemon syrup and preserves, recipes that are still in use today. Before the arrival of lemons in the Middle East, the juice of sour pomegranates or sour grapes was used as a souring agent but nowadays it is lemons that grace practically every meal. In Iran, a classical Persian meal will always include lemon or a combination of lemon and saffron.

Fresh lemons

Buying fruit and vegetables in the market

HOW IT GROWS

Lemon trees grow in the coastal regions of the Mediterranean and in Iran. The fruit is usually harvested in September.

APPEARANCE AND TASTE

The lemons of the Middle East are small and round or oval, and yellow, sometimes with a tinge of green. They have thin skins and are very juicy, with a sharp, tart taste, as you would expect.

BUYING AND STORING

Lemons are readily available all year, but the best lemons are bought in season. Harvested in September, when they are juicy and fruity, they keep for weeks in a cool, dry place.

Ripened lemons ready for harvest

CULINARY USES

Fresh lemons serve as an accompaniment to fish, seafood or lamb. The juice enhances numerous savory dishes and makes a refreshing, clean-tasting dressing for salads and steamed vegetables. It also brings out the flavor of other fresh fruits, such as olives and melon. Lemon juice is a crucial ingredient in some strong-flavored sauces, such as *tarator*, a garlicky nut sauce served with fish and seafood in Lebanon, Syria, and Turkey, and tahini dressing for raw root salads in the same regions. It is combined with egg to make a slightly tart sauce for poached and steamed vegetables, and for

Lemon juice seller, Turkey

the Turkish dish of meatballs in lemon sauce, *terbiyeli köfte*. The popular Arab *mezze* dish of smoked eggplant puree with tahini and lemon, *baba ghanoush*, requires a lot more lemon juice than one thinks. The juice, pith, and seeds are a source of pectin for jam-making, and the peel, which contains all the oil and intensity of flavor, is ideal for desserts and baking. Fresh lemons are pressed for their juice to flavor thick syrups that are poured over sweet pastries and are used as the basis of a cooling sherbet drink. They are also dried, pickled, or preserved in salt or sugar.

Strongly flavored with lemon and garlic, this tangy chicken broth is favored by the Egyptians. Traditionally, it is served either as a sauce for

plain rice or, during a meal of several courses, first as a soup and then as a sauce for the rice. This recipe is for the basic broth, which is really like a well-flavored stock, to which other vegetables could be added.

HAMUD
(EGYPTIAN CHICKEN AND LEMON BROTH)

Serves 6–8
Preparation time 1 hour for stock
Cooking time 50 minutes

1 chicken carcass, giblets, and
  bones, cooked or uncooked
Celery leaves
1 tablespoon clarified butter
4 celery ribs, sliced
4 cloves garlic, sliced
Juice of 2 lemons
⅔ cup long-grain rice, washed
Salt and freshly ground black
  pepper

Put the carcass, giblets, and bones into a pan with the celery leaves and cover with water. Bring to a boil, simmer for 1 hour, then strain the stock. Pick the chicken off the bones and add to the stock. Reserve roughly 7½ cups.

Melt the clarified butter in a deep pan and stir in the celery. Cook for 1–2 minutes and add the garlic. Just before the celery and garlic begin to color, pour in the reserved stock and bring it to a boil.

Pour in most of the lemon juice, reduce the heat, and simmer for about 30 minutes.

Toss in the rice, bring the soup to a boil once more, then simmer for a further 20 minutes, until the rice is cooked but not mushy. Pour in the rest of the lemon juice and season to taste.

This creamy, tangy eggplant and tahini dip is an old favorite, almost as popular as the ubiquitous hummus. Also known as *moutabal*, the strong flavors are sharpened by what seems to be a lot of lemon juice, but it can stand it. The quantities vary according to personal taste, as some people like their *baba ghanoush* lemony, while others like the strong taste of the tahini. Usually, it is served as a *mezze* dish with lots of bread to scoop it up.

Baba ghanoush

BABA GHANOUSH
(SMOKED EGGPLANT DIP WITH TAHINI AND LEMON)

Serves 4–6
Preparation time 25 minutes
Cooking time –

2 eggplants
2–3 cloves garlic
Roughly ¼ cup tahini
Juice of 2 lemons
A small bunch of flat-leaf parsley, chopped
A few black olives
Salt

Place the eggplants directly on a gas flame, over charcoal, or in a grill, and cook them until they are soft and oozing. Hold them by the stem under running cold water, peel off the skin, and squeeze out the juices.

Using a fork, mash the eggplants in a bowl. Crush the garlic with a little salt and beat it into the eggplant until it is smooth and creamy. Add the tahini and lemon juice alternately, beating all the time, then season to taste.

Spoon the puree into a serving bowl, and garnish with chopped parsley and black olives.

Literally translated as "well behaved" *köfte*, these meatballs are also known as *ekşili* (sour) *köfte*. Served with, or cooked in a tart egg and lemon sauce, they are a specialty of Turkey.

TERBİYELİ KÖFTE
(MEATBALLS IN AN EGG AND LEMON SAUCE)

Serves 4–6
Preparation time 25 minutes
Cooking time 45 minutes

2 cups ground lamb or beef
1 onion, grated
1 tablespoon long-grain rice, washed and drained
A small bunch of fresh dill and parsley, finely chopped
2 egg yolks
Juice of 2 lemons
All-purpose flour
Salt and freshly ground black pepper

Put the ground meat, onion, rice, herbs, and seasoning in a bowl. Knead well and pound to form a paste. Take walnut-size portions in your fingers and shape them into balls. Roll in a little flour and put aside.

Bring roughly 4 cups of water to a boil. Drop the *köfte* into the water, cover the pan, and bring the water back to a boil. Reduce the heat and simmer for about 35 minutes, until the rice in the *köfte* has cooked.

Meanwhile, beat the egg yolks in a bowl until light. Beat in the lemon juice and a little of the hot cooking liquid from the pan. Make sure it is well blended and seasoned, then sit the bowl over a pan of water and gently heat the egg and lemon mixture until it is thick and hot, taking care not to curdle it.

Drain the *köfte* from the cooking liquid and pop them into the egg and lemon sauce. Serve hot with plain rice.

ORANGE

(NARANJ) *Citrus sinensis*

The sour orange (*C. aurantium*) traveled westward from China and India with the Arab traders, who probably introduced it to Sicily and Spain, but the sweet orange (*C. sinensis*) didn't appear in the Mediterranean region until the fifteenth century. The Arabic word for orange is *naranj*, which is said to come from an old Sanskrit term, *narunga*, meaning "fruit like elephants." The Persian word for bitter orange is the same as the Arabic, but the word for sweet orange is *portoghâl*, like the Turkish word, *portakal*, which reflects its origins in Portugal, where a superior sweet orange was cultivated shortly after the Portuguese explorer Vasco da Gama returned from his voyage around the Cape of Good Hope in 1498. The main oranges in the Middle East are Jaffa, which originated in Palestine in the mid-nineteenth century and is now grown in Cyprus and Turkey; the navel orange, which is thought to be the orange brought to Portugal from China, and now grown extensively in Turkey; and the bitter orange, grown in Iran for its peel.

Dried orange peel

HOW IT GROWS

Generally oranges thrive in subtropical climates. The Jaffa orange originated as a bud mutation on a Beladi tree near Jaffa. The navel orange, which matures early, is seedless and has to be propagated by cuttings. And the bitter-orange has grown in the Caspian region for 2,000 years.

APPEARANCE AND TASTE

Jaffa oranges are almost seedless with a fine, sweet flavor. Navel oranges are aptly named, as each fruit contains a "baby" or mini orange in its apex. They are large with quite thick skins, so they are easy to peel, and they are sweet, juicy, and seedless. The bitter oranges of Iran are similar to Seville oranges.

MANUFACTURING

In Adana, in southern Turkey, a sweet fragrant wine is made from the juice of pressed oranges, but it is not exported. And in Turkey and Iran the blossoms of the bitter-orange tree are distilled to make a fragrant essence, which in its diluted form is sold as orange-flower water.

BUYING AND STORING

Both Jaffa and navel oranges are available in most supermarkets. If Jaffa oranges are picked when they have fully ripened, they keep well and remain juicy. The bitter oranges from Iran may be available in Iranian and other Middle Eastern stores, but Seville oranges are a fine substitute. Packages of dried bitter-orange peel can be bought in Middle Eastern stores. Dried peel keeps well in an airtight container but if you are going to use it only very occasionally, the finely sliced peel of a fresh orange will work just as well. Orange-flower water is available in bottles in almost every Middle Eastern, oriental, and whole-food store.

CULINARY USES

In Iran, two wonderful syrupy conserves are made for spooning over creamy rice puddings: *morabbâ-ye khalâl-e nâranj* is made with wide strips of bitter-orange peel rolled into the shape of rosebuds and poached in syrup with cardamom seeds—it is a joy to look at and deliciously aromatic; *morabbâ-ye bâhar nâranj* is made

Fresh oranges

Piles of oranges at the market

Assorted candied orange segments, often used for decorative purposes

with the blossoms of the bitter orange, soaked in lime water and poached gently in a rose-flavored syrup—it is delicate in both appearance and flavor.

Throughout the orange-growing regions of the Middle East, oranges are preserved in syrup—they are peeled and poached whole or in thick slices in a sugar syrup, sometimes flavored with orange-flower water and orange peel. They are also boiled and pulped to make the light, moist orange and almond cakes for the Jewish Passover. Other light cakes flavored with orange peel are popular too, such as the Turkish semolina cake, *revani*, which is soaked in a lemon syrup. Fresh oranges or their juice is often added to raw root-vegetable salads, which echo the flavors of North Africa and are often served with spicy food in southern Turkey and Syria. In both Iran and Turkey, oranges are married with chicken and cinnamon in popular stews. The juice of fresh oranges is used to make a simple custard-based ice cream, or a refreshing sorbet, often flavored with orange-flower water as well.

Like rose water, orange-flower water is splashed into many fruit compotes, creamy desserts, and confections for its perfumed flavor, and it is often added to sugar syrups to pour over the traditional sweet pastries. Mix it with lemon juice to make a fragrant salad dressing. A drop is sometimes added to Turkish coffee, and a teaspoon of orange-flower water stirred into a coffee cup of boiling water, with or without sugar, makes a healthy, soothing tisane called "white coffee" in Lebanon. Dried bitter-orange peel from Iran can also be used to make a digestive tisane, but it is mostly used in stews and aromatic rice such as *morasa' polow* (p 77).

So many dishes in the Middle East are claimed by Arabs and Turks, Jews, and Kurds, but I have only ever had the following dish in an Armenian household. Like the Persians, the Armenians have long enjoyed the combination of fruit and meat.

ERİK KURUSU DOLMASI

(STUFFED PRUNES WITH ORANGES)

Serves 4–6
Preparation time 25–30 minutes
Cooking time 30 minutes

1 cup ground lamb or beef
1 small onion, grated
2–3 tablespoons pine nuts
1 teaspoon dried mint
1 teaspoon ground cinnamon
2–3 fresh oranges, sliced
2⅔ cups moist, pitted prunes
⅓ cup fresh orange juice
1 tablespoon olive oil
1 tablespoon sugar
A small bunch fresh mint and cilantro, finely chopped
Salt and freshly ground black pepper

Preheat the oven to 350°F.

Put the ground meat in a bowl with the onion and knead it with your hands. Add the pine nuts, dried mint, cinnamon, and seasoning, and knead until it resembles a paste.

Line a baking dish with half the orange slices. Then, using your finger, enlarge the opening of each prune, stuff with some of the meat mixture, and arrange them on top of the oranges.

Mix together the orange juice, olive oil, and sugar, and pour over the stuffed prunes. Cover them with a lid or some foil and pop them in the oven for about 30 minutes, until the prunes are tender and slightly caramelized.

Lift the prunes onto a serving dish, leaving the orange slices behind. Sprinkle the prunes with mint and cilantro, and then garnish with the orange slices.

This exquisite-looking preserve is a Persian specialty, often spooned over creamy rice or milk puddings. It is made with the native bitter oranges, for which the Seville variety can be substituted. A little time is required for preparation, but it is well worth the effort.

Orange-seller, Syria

MORABBÂ-YE KHALÂL-E NÂRANJ
(ORANGE-PEEL PRESERVE)

Makes 3–4 jars
Preparation time approximately 13 hours
Cooking time 25 minutes

8 bitter oranges, well washed and dried
1½ cups sugar
1 tablespoon whole cardamom pods

Peel each orange in a thin, wide, continuous strip. Cut each strip into four equal pieces and roll them into the shape of a tight rosebud. Pack the rosebuds into a deep bowl or container so that they don't unravel and cover with cold water. Leave them to soak for approximately 12 hours.

Squeeze the peeled oranges and reserve the juice.

Drain the orange rosebuds and put them in a heavy-based pan. Cover with water and bring to a boil. Reduce the heat and simmer gently for 1 hour. Drain and refresh them under running cold water.

Put the sugar into a heavy-based pan with roughly 5 cups of water and bring to a boil, stirring all the time. Boil gently for about 5 minutes, then stir in the cardamom pods, orange-peel rosebuds, and orange juice. Reduce the heat and simmer gently until the rosebuds are transparent and tender and the syrup is thick. Remove from the heat and pack the orange-peel rosebuds into sterilized jars. Pour in the syrup, through a strainer to catch the cardamom pods, and seal the jars immediately.

Salads of oranges and onions, often with herbs and olives, are popular in the orange-growing regions of Turkey, Syria, and Lebanon. This recipe is from Syria, where lemons are also added to the salad.

SALATA NARANJ
(ORANGE AND ONION SALAD)

Serves 4

Preparation time 15–20 minutes

3 sweet, juicy oranges, peeled (with pith removed), seeded, and sliced
1 juicy lemon, peeled (with pith removed), seeded, and sliced
1 red or white onion, finely sliced
Roughly 12 black olives
½ teaspoon cumin seeds, crushed
A small bunch fresh mint leaves, chopped, or a teaspoon fresh or dried thyme, or oregano

2 tablespoons olive oil
Salt

Arrange the orange and lemon slices on a dish. Place the onion slices and black olives on top.

Sprinkle with the cumin seeds, herbs, and salt, and drizzle with the oil. You can toss it lightly and serve at once, or leave it for a while to allow the flavors to mingle.

Salata naranj

MELON

(SHAMAMA) *Cucumis melo*

Fresh melon

Some people say that the best melons come from Afghanistan and Iran. This may be true, as wild ancestors of the modern melon were thought to have grown naturally in the area stretching from Egypt to Iran and northwest India, but it wasn't until after the fall of the Roman Empire that the melon was first cultivated. Watermelon, *Citrullus lanatus*, on the other hand, is not from the same genus as the melon and has a longer history of cultivation. It was grown and eaten in Egypt before 2000 BC. Although quite distinct from one another, I have joined melon and watermelon here, as they are often sold side by side and consumed in much the same way, as a *mezze* or dessert fruit. The seeds of both are also eaten, roasted and salted as a snack, or blanched.

Fresh watermelon

HOW IT GROWS

Melons are one of the world's agricultural wonders. Like weeds, they sprawl over the soil and grow at great speed. If allowed to, they would take over. Harvested in the hot summer months, they are much appreciated to quench the thirst. And those harvested in the winter provide a burst of honey-sweet, fruity delight. As mentioned earlier, the best are reputed to be grown in Iran, but all the regions of the Middle East grow a range of delicious specimens.

A netted melon ready to harvest

APPEARANCE AND TASTE

Nothing beats a ripe, golden-fleshed melon with a taste of pure honey. Most of the melons in the Middle East are like a cross between a cantaloupe and a honeydew, often with a green skin and orange or yellow flesh, or they are of the netted variety. All have juicy flesh that is so sweet it's like nectar. Winter melons, such as the Turkish Casaba melon, are more oval-shaped, like a football, and they have a rough green or green and yellow skin with a pale yellow flesh. In Iran, some of the melons are white-fleshed and taste like cotton candy. Watermelons are large and round, like basketballs, and a deep green, sometimes striped with light green or tinged with yellow. They are incredibly refreshing and dribble with juice as you tuck into the mild, pink flesh.

BUYING AND STORING

The best way to tell if a melon is ripe or not is by pressing the end opposite the stem to see if it yields or not. With some melons, such as galia and other cantaloupe varieties, you can tell if it's sweet or not by smelling the same end. Watermelons should have a rich, hollow sound when tapped. Both keep for weeks in a cool, dry place.

Melon sellers, Istanbul, Turkey

CULINARY USES

Ripe melons and watermelons are generally eaten fresh as *mezze* or dessert. A popular Turkish *meze* consists of cubes of sweet melon with cubes of white, feta-style cheese. Sweet melons are also served stuffed with other summer fruits and scented with rose water, or crushed and made into a chilled dessert or drink. The pale flesh of unripe watermelons, or the white flesh near the rind of a ripening fruit is often pickled or used for making a syrupy jam. Even the watermelon rind is preserved in a cardamom-flavored syrup in Iran.

In the heat of summer in Iran, the following recipe is often served as a chilled dessert or, diluted with ice, as a refreshing drink. Sprinkle crushed, scented rose petals over the dessert for an air of sophistication.

PÂLOODEH GARMAK
(ICED MELON WITH ROSE WATER)

Serves 2–4
Preparation time 10–15 minutes
Cooking time –

1 sweet, ripe melon (e.g. galia, honeydew, or cantaloupe)
2 tablespoons rose water
1–2 teaspoons sugar
2 pinches of rose petals

Halve and seed the melon, and cut out the flesh. On a plate to catch the juice, chop the flesh and crush it lightly with the back of a fork. Tip the crushed melon and juice into a bowl, then stir in the rose water and sugar. Put it into the refrigerator to chill and serve ice-cold with sprinkled with crushed rose petals.

Fruit often forms part of the *mezze* table in the summer and autumn months, and melon is very popular. Sweet and juicy, it complements white cheese beautifully, and it acts as a refreshing palate cleanser between dishes or courses. As a variation on the theme, modern recipes like this one crop up in the more cosmopolitan cities of the Middle East. It is not traditional, but very characteristic. The firm, crumbly regional cheeses can be replaced by feta and although the ingredients for the salad can be prepared ahead of time, they should be mixed together only just before eating, as the melon tends to weep.

KAVUN SALATASI
(MELON SALAD)

Serves 3–4
Preparation time 10–15 minutes
Cooking time –

1 ripe, juicy melon
1½ cups white cheese (feta)
A small bunch fresh purple basil and mint, chopped
2–3 tablespoons olive oil
A squeeze of lemon juice
2–3 tablespoons black olives

Halve and seed the melon, and cut out the flesh. Chop it into bite-size cubes and cut the cheese into similar-size cubes.

Watermelon jam

Put the melon and the cheese into a bowl with the herbs. Dress with the oil and a squeeze of lemon, and garnish with the black olives.

Kavun salatası

QUINCE

(SAFARJAL) *Cydonia oblonga*

Fresh quince

In the Song of Solomon, the "apples" mentioned are likely to be quinces, as this ancient, scented fruit was cultivated in the Levant before the apple. It is also believed that the "golden apple" given by Paris to Aphrodite, which led to the fall of Troy, was a quince. The name *Cydonia* comes from Kydonia in Crete, where a superior variety of quince was cultivated. The Romans called the quince *melimelum*, derived from the Greek for "honey apple," because the sour fruit was always preserved in honey. Other fruit and vegetables had been preserved in honey or vinegar by this time, but the quince was the first to be cooked before being preserved, which led to the discovery of pectin. Quince preserves with honey—the first jam—appeared in the medieval Arab world and are still enjoyed today throughout the Middle East.

Quince jam

HOW IT GROWS

The quince, which is related to the apple and the pear, originally came from the Caucuasus, where the wild, twisted trees still grow. It is cultivated throughout the Levant, Turkey, and Iran.

APPEARANCE AND TASTE

The quince is usually matt yellow or golden and looks like a large, bulging pear. The flesh is firm and simultaneously sour and scented, with lots of seeds. The raw fruit has a distinctive texture that can make your tongue feel as if it is sticking to the roof of your mouth, but when cooked with sugar, it turns a pretty shade of pink and emits a lovely, floral fragrance that wafts enticingly through the house.

BUYING AND STORING

The fresh fruit keeps quite well in a cool place. It is available in Middle Eastern stores and some well-stocked fruit stores from October to February. Most quince preserves keep for months and are intended to last the year.

CULINARY USES

In Turkey, the fresh fruit is cut into thin slices, with a little lemon juice squeezed over them so they don't discolor, to eat as *meze* or as a refreshing nibble with a drink. Throughout the Middle East, quinces are preserved in a sugar syrup, flavored with the juice of lemons or limes, or they are cubed or shredded and made into a syrupy jam, sometimes flavored with cloves or cardamom seeds. They are poached with sugar to make a fragrant, pink dessert, served with clotted cream, and cooked quinces are pureed to make a fruity paste that is eaten as a sweetmeat, decorated with blanched almonds. The Armenians combine quince with other vegetables in soups and stews, and they often sauté them with sugar and cinnamon to serve as an accompaniment to poultry or lamb. In Iran and Turkey, quinces are often cooked with meat or poultry in stews, or they are cooked whole and filled with a ground meat stuffing.

When the Arabs spread Islam throughout the Middle East, they also spread restrictions on all consumption of wine and spirits. The transition was slow, and for those who had enjoyed wine for so long, something had to be found to replace it. And so the sherbet, *sharab* ("drink" in Arabic), came about. Based on a fruit syrup, diluted with water, and served chilled with ice, sherbets are varied and refreshing.

One of the earliest, and most unusual, sherbets was made from a mint and vinegar syrup, just one step away from the forbidden wine, but the more common syrups are made from lemons, sour cherries, pomegranates, mulberries, and rose water. This delightful syrup is from Iran.

SHARBAT-E BEH-LIMOO
(QUINCE AND LIME SYRUP)

Makes roughly 3¾ cups
Preparation time 10 minutes
Cooking time approximately 40 minutes

¼ cup sugar
1 cup water
1 large quince, peeled, cored, and chopped into small cubes (keep in cold water with a splash of lime juice to prevent it from turning brown)
½ cup fresh lime juice

Put the sugar and water into a pan and bring it to a boil, stirring all the time. Drain the quince and add it to the pan.

Bring the liquid back to a boil, then reduce the heat and simmer for about 15 minutes. Strain the syrup through cheesecloth, pressing the quince with the back of a wooden spoon to extract the flavor.

Return the strained syrup to the pan, stir in the lime juice, and boil it gently until the syrup is thick. Leave it to cool in the pan, then pour into a sterilized bottle.

To serve, drop some ice cubes into a tall glass and put it in the freezer to frost. Pour 1–2 tablespoons of the syrup over the ice and dilute with it cold water.

This is a classic autumn dessert, enjoyed particularly in Turkey. It is quite magical, as the pale yellow fruit transforms into a pretty shade of pink, and the natural pectin in the fruit and seeds turns the syrup into a gelatin. If for no other reason, it is worth making this dessert for the heavenly perfume it emits in your kitchen.

AYVA TATLISI
(QUINCE DESSERT)

Serves 6
Preparation time 15 minutes
Cooking time approximately 1 hour

1 cup sugar
2 cups water
Juice of ½ lemon
6–8 cloves
2¼ pounds fresh quinces, peeled, halved from head to stalk, and cored (keep them in water with a splash of lemon juice until you're ready to use them)—retain the seeds

Put the sugar and water into a heavy-based pan and bring it to a boil, stirring all the time. Add the lemon juice, cloves, and quince seeds.

Slip in the quince halves, then reduce the heat and poach gently for about 50 minutes, until the fruit is tender and has turned pink.

Pick out the quince seeds and leave the quinces to cool in the syrup, which will become like a gelatin.

Serve chilled or at room temperature with clotted cream.

Ayva tatlısı

Fresh figs

FIG

(TEEN) *Ficus carica*

Muhammad is reputed to have said that if any fruit came from Paradise, it was the fig. In the West, figs are something of a luxury and are often disappointing, as they haven't matured on the tree, but in their natural habitat they are juicy and sweet and grow in abundance. The cultivation of figs first began somewhere between 4000 and 2700 BC in Egypt or Arabia. By 800 BC, figs were growing in mainland Greece and acquired the species name *carica*, as the Greeks thought they had originally come from Caria in Asia Minor. Figs are often referred to in the Bible.

Dried figs

HOW IT GROWS

The fig tree is descended from a wild tree, the caprifig, which spread from western Asia to the Mediterranean region in prehistoric times. Its evolution involved one of nature's little wonders. If a fig tree was to bear formed, edible fruit, the flower had to be visited by a tiny fig wasp. Amazingly, Aristotle was aware of this fact in the fourth century BC. This is still true of the caprifig and Smyrna figs, but in the long period since the Roman Empire new types of fig have appeared that don't require a wasp. With the caprifig though, the wasp inhabits the immature syconium, the vase-shaped outer shell, which contains both male and female flowers that are unable to fertilize one another. When she is impregnated, the female wasp crawls around inside the syconium, getting covered in pollen from the male flowers, and finds a way out through a little hole opposite the stem. She then flies to another syconium, crawls through the hole and lays her eggs down the style of a female flower, managing to pollenate the other female flowers as she passes them, so that they form seeds.

Botanically, the fig fruit is regarded as a series of fruits but as you eat it it looks more like a pocket full of seeds.

APPEARANCE AND TASTE

Smyrna figs still grow in their natural habitat in Turkey and closely resemble their ancient ancestors from Asia Minor all those years ago. Bigger than the ones we are used to and amber in color, they have a nutty flavor. In Turkey, Greece, North Africa, and California, where they now grow, they are eaten fresh, but for export they are dried. Also common in Turkey are Bardajic figs, which, are reddish-brown with a pinkish flesh, and Franciscan figs, which, have a purple-black skin and red, sweet flesh, and are the ones most of us are familiar with. Dried figs taste quite different from the fresh one. In parts of the Middle East figs are picked when they are very small and then dried, so that you can just pop them in your mouth like chewy, honey-flavored candy.

BUYING AND STORING

When buying fresh, ripe figs make sure they are soft to the touch so that the juice will ooze out of them. If they are firm, they will usually be tasteless and a bit dry. Really ripe figs need to be eaten immediately. Dried figs, on the other hand, keep for quite a long time if stored in an airtight container in a dry, cool place. The semi-dried figs are still moist and can just be popped into the mouth.

Crates of figs, Egypt

Yeşil incir reçeli

Some of the Middle Eastern jams are exquisite. There is the scent of antiquity in the delicate rose-petal jam, a striking novelty to the magnificent eggplant jam, and a delectable honeycomb flavor to this glorious conserve of tender, baby green figs floating in syrup. To stabilize the color, shape, and texture, the freshly picked, immature fruits are soaked in lime water (slaked lime powder diluted with water) before being poached in syrup. This, of course, may not be possible in your home, in which case the figs in the resulting jam will lose shape and become soft. The jam will still taste delicious.

YEŞİL İNCİR REÇELİ
(GREEN FIG JAM)

Makes roughly 5 cups of jam
Preparation time 5–10 minutes
Cooking time roughly 30 minutes

1 pound small, immature green
  figs, washed and patted dry
2 cups sugar
1¼ cups water
Juice of ½ lemon

If the figs are perfect with unblemished skins, there is no need to peel them; if not, remove the skins and trim the stalks.

Put the sugar and water into a heavy-based pan and bring to a boil, stirring all the time. Stir in the lemon juice and figs, and boil rapidly for about 5 minutes.

Reduce the heat and simmer for about 20 minutes, until the syrup thickens and the figs are beautifully tender.

Leave the figs to cool in the syrup, then spoon them into scalded jars. Leave them to stand for a few days before eating them.

CULINARY USES

Fresh, ripe figs are generally eaten as they are, with the juice dribbling down one's chin. Dried figs are added to fruit compotes, are used in stuffings and stews, poached into jam, and are occasionally used to make *rakı*, Turkey's national alcoholic drink. Dried figs are also stuffed and baked with honey and milk or cream. Immature figs are picked when they are small and green and are poached with sugar to make a delectable, honey-tasting, syrupy jam, which is more akin to a conserve.

Both fresh and dried figs are delicious baked with honey. Dried figs are also popular baked in a scented syrup, as in this homely winter dish, which is moist and sticky with a hint of roses.

İNCİR TATLISI
(STUFFED FIGS BAKED IN ROSE SYRUP)

Serves 4
Preparation time 15–20 minutes
  (+ soaking overnight)
Cooking time 20–25 minutes

2 cups dried figs, soaked
  overnight, or boiled for 5
  minutes, until soft and plump
¾ cup chopped blanched almonds
¾ cup chopped walnuts
1 cup sugar
⅔ cup water
2 tablespoons rose water

Preheat the oven to 350°F.

Drain the figs and cut off the stalks. Push a teaspoon of chopped nuts inside each fig, and place them all upright in a shallow ovenproof dish. In a pan, bring the sugar and water to a boil, stirring all the time. Reduce the heat, stir in the rose water, and simmer for 10–15 minutes, until the syrup coats the back of a spoon. Pour the syrup over the figs and place them in the oven for about 20 minutes, until they are tender and sticky. Serve hot or cold with clotted cream.

DATE

(TAMR) *Phoenix dactylifera*

Fresh dates on a stick

Dates are a staple food in the desert regions of the Middle East and North Africa. They were so important in the diet of the nomads and oasis-dwellers of Arabia that the date palm can be seen in early Egyptian and Mesopotamian carvings. In classical times, the Romans acquired a taste for the sweet, succulent fruit and imported dates from Jericho in Palestine to use as a sweetener or to stuff as a sweetmeat.

Finding dates in the desert must have been like stumbling across gold. Delicious fresh or dried, they could be carried by travelers and nomadic herdsmen, such as the disappearing Bedouin. They have a high sugar content and are fairly nutritional, so some desert Arabs thrive for long periods of time on a diet of dates and fermented milk. The Arabs say that the Bedouin can't get to sleep under the palms with the fruit hanging over their heads, such is their love of dates and all things sweet.

As the date is integral to the lives of both the nomadic and settled Arabs, it is one of the most extensively cultivated crops in the Middle East. Such is the appreciation of the date in Iraq and the Gulf, there are reputed to be over 350 varieties in Basra alone. Generally, the dates fall into three main types: soft, juicy dates, which are grown for eating fresh, although some of the crop is dried and compressed into blocks; hard, dry, fibrous dates—also known as "bread" or "camel" dates, which used to be the staple date of Arab nomads and which are dried further for their intense, sweet flavor or ground to a powder; and semi-dry dates, which are less sweet but moist and popular in Iran. Believed to increase prosperity and enhance life, dates play such an important role in the culinary cultures of the Middle East that the biggest producers, worldwide, are Egypt, Iraq, Iran, and Saudi Arabia. Even the degree of ripeness is internationally classified in Arabic.

Dried dates

HOW IT GROWS

Dates are the fruit of a palm tree that grows in irrigated environments as well as in extreme desert conditions, for its deep rooting system can reach water other crops can't. Like all palms, they flower and fruit at the top and, if left, they can grow to 107 feet in height. Obviously, this makes them difficult to harvest, so commercial growers tend to cut the trees at about 54 feet. Harvested in late summer, the fruits grow in large bunches that may contain as many as a thousand dates. A single tree can produce anything from 110 to 330 pounds of fruit.

APPEARANCE AND TASTE

Generally speaking, a fresh date fruit is roughly 2 inches long and yellow. However, its color, taste, quality, and uses vary according to the variety being grown. In Iraq, there is the Asharasi date, which is dry with a nutty taste; the soft, richly flavored Khadrawi from the south; the Khustawi, which is so sweet and delicious it is generally eaten as a dessert date; and the Zahidi, which is Iraq's main commercial date, sold in different stages of maturity from soft to dry. In Arabia there are the Bahri and the Khalas, both of which are rich in flavor, fresh and dried; and the Hilali, which has a lovely flavor but is eaten only fresh, as it doesn't dry well. Egypt has the large maroon-colored Khidri date, which is chewy with a mild flavor, and the Gulf region has the small, sweet Mactoum, which originally came from Iraq. In Oman and the United Arab Emirates, there is the reddish-brown Fardh, which is a staple date, and the Naghal, which ripens early and is eaten fresh.

BUYING AND STORING

Some fresh dates have better keeping qualities than others. For example, the Fardh and Khustawi keep well. Dried dates, on the other hand, keep for a long time, if stored in a cool, dry place. Most often, dried dates are packed in bags or boxes and dry out on keeping, but look for the moist, dark dates of Iran (available in Iranian and Middle Eastern stores), which are packed semi-dried in boxes or cans: they keep well in the refrigerator.

MANUFACTURING

In the Middle East, the principal manufactured products from date palms are sugar and molasses. As the Zahidi palm is prolific, producing fruit with a high sugar content, it is used as an industrial source of sugar. And a thick, sticky molasses (pekmez in Turkey, dibs in the Arab world) is extracted from the pressed fruit of a variety of date palms. It is sold in jars and used as a sweetener, or it is spooned onto bread like honey. Date syrup mixed with tahini makes a nourishing spread or dip.

*Dibs (pekmez):
date syrup*

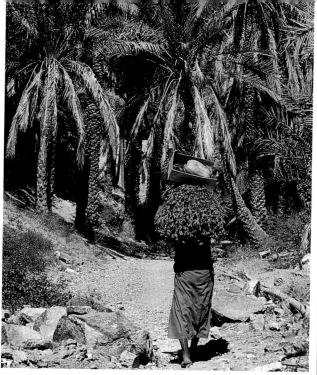

Carrying freshly picked dates and melons, Bahla, Oman

CULINARY USES

Fresh and dried dates have been combined with poultry and lamb since ancient times in the Arab world. The medieval recipe *rutabiya* consists of meatballs stuffed with almonds, flavored with spices, and garnished with dates. Throughout the Middle East, dried dates are often stuffed with blanched almonds, rose-scented almond paste, or crushed pistachios, and served as a sweetmeat. Pounded with cinnamon and a little rose water or orange-flower water, dried dates are often used as a filling for *ma' amoul* (p143), the special melt-in-the-mouth cookies baked by Christians at Easter and Muslims at *Ramadam*. Soft dates are used in Iraq to make little date-filled pies called *babee bi tamr*. In Iran, a delicious fudge-like candy, *ranginak*, is made with dates and walnuts, a combination that works well and is used in the popular sweetmeat *halwa tamr*, which is simply made of pressed dates and crushed walnuts rolled into balls. The Jewish communities make a date and raisin paste, *harosset*, to celebrate Passover, and dates are often married with raisins again in fruit compotes. Fresh and dried dates are quite often added to rice with nuts, or cooked with vegetables such as spinach and pumpkin. Fresh, sour dates are poached and preserved in syrup; the thick date syrup can be used as a sweetener in the preserves of other fruit and vegetables, such as turnips.

The Bedouin and the Marsh Arabs of southern Iraq pound semi-dried dates to a pulp and spread it on fish before roasting it over charcoal. Dates are also pulped and pureed and spread out thinly to dry in the sun to make the ubiquitous leathers (pp 96–8), which are chewed as a snack or added to winter stews for flavor. In some of the desert villages, the sap of date palms is used as a crude sweetener and a fermented drink is made from the fruit. And in parts of the Gulf and the United Arab Emirates, the flowers of the date palms are sold in the markets to be used as a dip for bread, made by pounding the flowers with a small dried fish.

The fat, moist, dark dates of Iran are the best I have ever tasted. They are sweet and fruity, and simply melt in the mouth.

Semi-dried harvested dates

Throughout the Middle East, a common way to eat dried dates as a sweetmeat is to remove the pit and replace it with a blanched almond, a walnut half, or rose-flavored almond paste. However, the Iranians go one step further and set the stuffed dates in a fudge-like mixture, which is garnished with ground pistachios and almonds for color, hence its name, *ranginak*, which means "colorful." In the following recipe, if the dates are really moist and sweet, you can omit the sugar.

RANGINAK
(STUFFED DATE FUDGE CAKE)

Makes 12–16 (depending on the size of slices)
Preparation time 25–30 minutes
Cooking time –

¾ cup halved walnuts
2⅔ cups moist, pitted dried dates
1 cup butter
2 tablespoons sugar
2 cups all-purpose flour
1 tablespoon ground almonds
1 tablespoon ground pistachios

Place half a walnut inside each date and close it up again. Lightly grease a shallow dish or baking pan and place the stuffed dates in it, packing them in together.

Melt the butter with the sugar and stir in the flour. Cook it gently until it turns golden, then pour it slowly over the dates, filling all the gaps.

Leave the mixture to set, then sprinkle with the ground nuts and cut the fudge cake into squares to serve as a sweetmeat with tea or coffee.

In Turkey, this dish of grains with nuts is sometimes called "Arab pilaf," because of the dates (which the Turks love but don't grow). Believed to be of Bedouin origin, it is a fairly versatile dish, as it can be made with rice or bulgur, sometimes colored with saffron and, occasionally, pepped up with chilies. My favorite way is with bulgur and lots of dates for their sweet, fruity flavor. With its use of two principal staples, wheat and dates, this simple dish captures the essence of the Middle East.

ARAP PİLAVI
(BULGUR WITH NUTS AND DATES)

Serves 4
Preparation time 5 minutes
(+ soaking of dates if necessary)
Cooking time 35 minutes

3 cups bulgur, rinsed and drained
2 tablespoons clarified butter (ghee)
2 tablespoons pine nuts
2 tablespoons pistachios
3 tablespoons blanched almonds, kept whole or halved
⅔ cup roughly chopped soft dried dates (soak them in water if hard)
Salt

Bring a pan of water to a boil, stir in some salt, and toss in the bulgur. Cook it vigorously for about 10 minutes, then drain.

Meanwhile, in a wide, heavy-based pan, melt the clarified butter and stir in the nuts. When they begin to brown, add the dates and cook for 1–2 minutes.

Splash in a about 2 tablespoons water to keep the dates moist. When it has bubbled up and been absorbed, tip in the bulgur, quickly tossing it about so that it is well mixed and doesn't stick to the bottom. Season if necessary and turn off the heat.

Cover with a clean dishtowel and a lid, and leave to steam for about 20 minutes. If you like, melt a little extra clarified butter and pour it over the bulgur, then toss with a fork. Serve hot with yogurt or kabobs.

A popular sweet in the Middle East: dates stuffed with almonds

Arap pilavı

APRICOT

(MISHMISH) *Prunus armeniaca*

Dried fruit, Turkey

Fresh apicots

It is believed that the apricot originated in China and traveled westward with the silk merchants, reaching Iran in the second or first century BC. Its botanical name is misleading, indicating the fruit is of Armenian origin, which is what the Greeks believed. At the end of the apricot season, villages in Anatolia are transformed into a feast of color as the bright orange fruits are laid out on the flat roofs to dry in the sun. Dried apricots are so appreciated in the Middle East that, when they are stuffed with blanched almonds or almond paste, some Muslims regard them as a gift from Allah.

HOW IT GROWS

The apricot, which belongs to the rose family and is related to the plum, cherry, peach, and almond, grows in warm temperate climates. In the Middle East, the trees grow mainly in central Anatolia in Turkey, in Isfahan in Iran, and on the oasis of al-Ghuta in Syria. Apricots come in a variety of colors, from white, orange, and pink to gray and black, and in differing sizes, some as small as a berry, others as large as a peach.

Treated dried apricots

APPEARANCE AND TASTE

A ripe, fresh, orange-yellow apricot is rather special. The taut skin, often tinged with rosy-red and dappled, is slightly furry and soft, like high-quality velvet or moleskin, and the juicy, golden flesh is delicate and sweet, like a fragrant honey. In Iran, they are known as *zardaloo*,

which means yellow plum. The white apricots, like white peaches, are often tinged with pink, and both their fragrance and their taste is delicately perfumed. Most commercial apricots end up dried and, if they have been dried in the sun, are full of that unmistakable apricot flavor, with an almost caramelized taste, and they look burned. The ubiquitous orange dried apricots have been treated with sulfur dioxide to retain the bright, appealing color.

MANUFACTURING

Throughout the Middle East, long thin strips of pressed, dried apricot, called "apricot leathers," are sold in the markets. These leathers come mainly from Turkey and Syria, where the washed and pitted fruit is pureed, spread very thinly on trays, and left in the sun to dry. Leathers, which are made of all kinds of fruit,

such as mulberries, plums, apples, and grapes, are popular as a chewy snack, or melted down and used to flavor stews and sauces, or diluted and made into a chilled drink. Apricot leathers are regarded as a luxury by the Bedouin, who are reputed to have a sweet tooth.

BUYING AND STORING

Sadly, many commercial fresh apricots are disappointing, as they are picked before they have fully ripened and the flesh can be sponge-like and tasteless, leaving you to wonder why on earth people rave about them. If you are lucky and do find ripe, juicy ones, eat them immediately and enjoy them, as they don't keep. Sun-dried apricots keep for about six months, stored in an airtight container in a cool, dry place.

Unsulphered dried apricots

CULINARY USES

Fresh apricots are usually eaten as they are. Occasionally, they are cooked in meat stews, and in Iran and Turkey they are made into a syrupy jam. Dried apricots are stuffed with almonds or almond paste as a sweetmeat, and they are used in a number of desserts and compotes, and in rice dishes and stews. In Turkey, they are poached in a scented syrup and filled with clotted buffalo cream in the delicious dessert *kaymaklı kayısı*. In Syria, dried apricots are poached and pureed, then mixed with chopped nuts and rose water, and served as a special dish for Ramadan.

This is a delicious fruity, aromatic dish of Arabic origin. Traditionally, the dried apricots were soaked and pureed before being added to the stew, but more modern versions found in Turkey, Iran, and North Africa use whole apricots. Try to find the sharp-tasting, naturally sun-dried apricots for the right flavor.

MISHMISHIYA
(LAMB AND APRICOT STEW)

Serves 6
Preparation time 40 minutes
Cooking time 1½ hours

2¼ pounds lean shoulder of lamb, cubed
2 teaspoons ground cinnamon
1 teaspoon ground coriander
1 teaspoon ground cumin
½ teaspoon chili powder
1⅓ cups dried apricots
A knob fresh ginger (about 1 inch)
3–4 cloves garlic
2 tablespoons olive oil with a little butter
2 onions, chopped
2 pinches saffron threads or about 2 teaspoons powdered saffron
About ½ tablespoon all-purpose flour
Salt and freshly ground black pepper

Toss the meat in the ground spices and leave to sit for about 30 minutes.

Pour boiling water over the apricots and leave them to soak for 30 minutes, then drain. Reserve the soaking water, top it up with ordinary water to make

Apricots ripening on tree

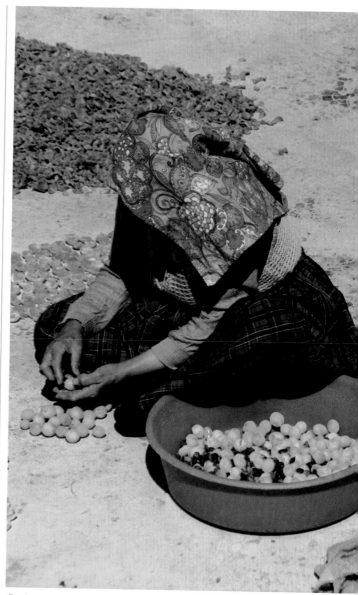

Drying apricots in the sun on a roof top, Cappedocia, Turkey

roughly 2½ cups, and puree a third of the apricots in about half of this water.

Using a mortar and pestle, grind the ginger and garlic to a paste.

In a heavy-based pan, heat the oil with the butter and fry the onions until soft. Stir in the saffron threads and add the spiced meat. Turn the pieces of meat over quickly so that the spices don't burn, and stir in the ginger and garlic paste.

Sprinkle with the flour and cover with the remaining water and pureed apricots. Stir well and bring to a boil, then turn the heat down and simmer gently, with the lid on, for about 1 hour, turning the meat from time to time.

Add the apricots and continue to cook for about 30 minutes, until both the apricots and meat are tender. Season well with salt and pepper.

THE MIDDLE EASTERN KITCHEN

Dried apricots are often cooked in syrup and preserved in jars but in this delicious Turkish recipe they are filled with a clotted cream made from buffalo milk (*kaymak* in Turkish, *eishta* in Arabic) and served chilled as a delightful winter or spring treat.

KAYMAKLI KAYISI
(APRICOTS FILLED WITH CLOTTED CREAM)

Serves 6
Preparation time 5 minutes +
6–8 hours' soaking of apricots
Cooking time 15–20 minutes

1⅓ cups dried apricots, soaked for
at least 6 hours or overnight
¾ cup sugar
1 tablespoon orange-flower water
¾ cup kaymak, clotted cream, or
heavy cream whipped until stiff
A few fresh mint leaves

Drain the apricots and reserve 1 cup plus 2 tablespoons of the soaking water. Put the water into a heavy-based pan with the sugar and bring the liquid to a boil, stirring all the time.

Boil the liquid for a few minutes, then stir in the orange-flower water and the apricots. Return the liquid to a boil, reduce the heat, and poach the apricots gently for 10–15 minutes. Turn off the heat and leave the apricots to cool in the syrup.

Lift the apricots out of the syrup, slit each one open with a knife, and fill with a teaspoon of *kaymak* or clotted cream. Place them on a plate, spoon some of the syrup around them, and put them in the refrigerator to chill.

Serve chilled, decorated with the fresh mint leaves.

The thin sheets of compressed dried apricot are extremely popular in Turkey and Syria. Traditionally, the peasant woman would crush the apricots with their feet, remove the kernels, then spread the apricot pulp out to dry in the sun. More modern methods employ machines to do the pureeing, but with a spell of hot summer weather apricot leather, *amardine*, can be made at home and kept in the refrigerator or freezer. Intensely fruity, the leather is dissolved in water and sweetened to make a refreshing drink, or added to stews. The dissolved, sweetened mixture can also be gently cooked to form a thick cream, which is chilled and spooned over yogurt or served as a dessert with blanched almonds and clotted cream.

AMARDINE
(APRICOT LEATHER)

Makes 2 leathers
Preparation time 1–2 days
Cooking time –

Roughly 2 pounds fresh apricots,
peeled and pitted
½ cup sugar

Prepare two large, rimmed baking trays with a sheet of plastic wrap pulled tight over the edges (you may need to secure it with tape).

Whiz the apricots in a food processor to form a puree. Add the sugar and blend until the mixture is very smooth. Now empty the puree onto the baking trays, spreading it thinly and evenly.

Apricot leather

Cover the trays with cheesecloth, pulled tight and fastened with tape to prevent it from touching the puree, and place them outside in the sunlight until the puree is dry and pliable enough to peel off the plastic underneath. Depending on the heat of the sun, this might take two days—be careful not to let the fruit dry out and become hard.

Roll up the leather in the plastic wrap and twist the ends to seal. Store it in a cool, dry place, in the refrigerator or freezer.

Kaymaklı kayısı

CHERRY

(KARAZ) *Prunus avium*

The word "cherry" is derived from the ancient Greek name *kerasos*, which probably came from the Black Sea port Kerasanda (modern-day Giresun in Turkey), meaning "place of plentiful cherries," as it was surrounded by cherry forests. The wealthy Roman general Lucullus is thought to have brought cherries, or cherry trees, back to Rome from this port, which was then known as Kerasunt, after defeating the Pontic king Mithridates around 70 BC. Cherries were then spread across Europe by the Roman legions, and even today their variety names—for instance, Black Tartarian, Circassian, and Turkey Heart—reflect their origins. Both the sweet cherry, *Prunus avium*, and the sour cherry, *Prunus cerasus*, are native to the eastern Mediterranean region, particularly to Turkey, Syria, and Iran.

Fresh sweet cherries

HOW IT GROWS

There are a number of species of cherry that belong to the *Prunus* genus, which includes apricots, plums, and almonds, all of which are native to western Asia. The white blossom of the cherry tree appears in April or May and the fruit usually matures in June. As the fruit grows at the top of the trees, which can reach 65 feet in height, tall ladders made out of chestnut wood are used for harvesting. The fruit has to be picked quickly, so groups of women and children climb up and fill the wicker baskets that have been strapped to the ladders until the cherry orchards have been cleared.

Wild cherries, best left to ripen on the tree

APPEARANCE AND TASTE

As one would expect, sweet cherries are sweet and juicy, and sour cherries generally need sweetening. Most of the sweet cherries in the Middle East are small and round, and a deep red or black when ripe. Sour cherries are slightly smaller, firmer, and light red. In Syria, you also get sour cherries that are black, and in Turkey there are sweet cherries that are white. Dried sour cherries are considerably smaller than fresh ones, and their flavor and color are intensified.

BUYING AND STORING

Ripe sweet cherries don't last long and are best eaten fresh. Sour cherries are delicious fresh too, but they are usually preserved in syrup to be used throughout the year until the next cherry season. Dried sour cherries keep for about a year in an airtight container.

MEDICINAL AND OTHER USES

"If the mulberry didn't follow me, I would turn people into my stalk," the sweet cherry says in Turkish lore, as sweet cherries are packed with vitamins and help stimulate the metabolism, so are regarded as "thinning." The dried cherry stalks, believed to contain diuretic properties, are used to make an herbal tisane to lower high blood pressure. The resin of cherry trees, cherry gum, is diluted with vinegar to soothe skin rashes and to treat coughs and colds. Bees use it to seal their hives and, at one time, it was used as a stiffener by textile manufacturers. The strong, deep red wood of the cherry tree was once used to make fine furniture and musical intruments.

Cherries and cucumbers in a market

Ground *mahlab (malep)*

CULINARY USES

Generally, ripe sweet cherries are eaten fresh as a snack or dessert, but sour cherries are often poached with sugar or cooked with meat or poultry to give a tart, fruity flavor. Both sweet and sour cherries are made into jams and desserts, such as the popular summer syrupy bread pudding that can be made with cherries, mulberries, peaches, or apricots. Sour cherries are boiled with sugar and strained to make a fruity syrup that is used as the basis of a cool, refreshing drink. Sour cherries are also preserved whole in syrup or poached, pureed and dried into "leathers." They are dried whole and used to flavor stews and rice dishes in Syria, Turkey, and Iran. The kernels of the *mahlab* (*malep* in Turkish) cherries are ground to a powder and used to flavor breads and crackers.

The following medieval Arab dish is made with sour cherries, which lend a lovely fruity flavor to the meatballs. Traditionally, the meatballs are served on pieces of flat bread and the cherry sauce is spooned over them.

LAHMA BIL KARAZ
(MEATBALLS WITH CINNAMON AND CHERRIES)

Serves 6
Preparation time 25–30 minutes
Cooking time 25 minutes

1 pound lean lamb or veal, passed through a meat grinder 2–3 times
1 teaspoon ground cinnamon
½ teaspoon ground cumin

Black cherry kernels

½ teaspoon ground cloves
Sunflower oil for frying
1 tablespoon clarified or ordinary butter
½ cups fresh sour cherries, pitted, or dried cherries soaked overnight
1–2 tablespoons sugar
1 teaspoon ground cinnamon
Salt and freshly ground black pepper

Put the ground meat into a bowl and squash it with your knuckles, then knead it vigorously, slapping it into the bowl, until it becomes smooth and pasty. Add the spices and seasoning and knead again.

Take walnut-size pieces out of the bowl and roll them into balls. Heat enough sunflower oil to cover the base of a pan and fry the meatballs in it until they are brown all over, then remove and drain on paper towels.

Melt the butter in a heavy-based pan and add the cherries. Cook for a minute, then add a little water to stew them. Stir in the sugar and cinnamon, bring to a boil, then pop in the meatballs and simmer for about 20 minutes or until they are cooked and the cherries are soft.

Crush most of the cherries and bubble up the sauce to caramelize it, adding a little more water if necessary. Serve the meatballs on flat breads or with rice.

Lahma bil karaz

Throughout the Middle East, dried fruit and nuts are often employed in the stuffing of meat and poultry. Sometimes they are combined with rice or bulgur, and sometimes they are bound with a tart fruit molasses or tomato paste, as in this Iranian recipe, which is also ideal for turkey.

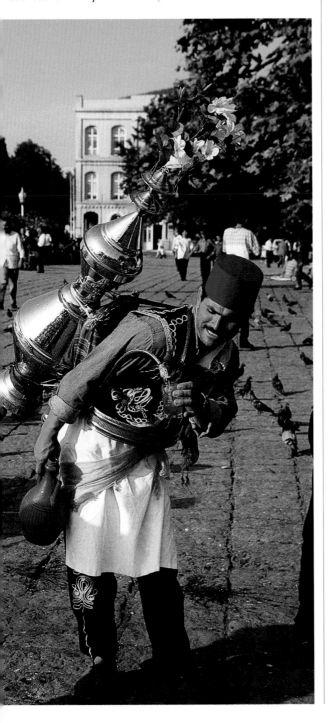

MORGH TU-POR
(CHICKEN WITH DRIED FRUIT STUFFING)

Serves 6
Preparation time 40 minutes
Cooking time approximately
  1 hour 30 minutes

I free-range, organic chicken,
  approximately 4½ pounds
½ onion
2 pinches saffron threads
1 teaspoon sugar
⅓ cup butter
Juice of 1 lemon
Salt

For the stuffing:
2 onions, chopped
2 tablespoons olive oil
½ cup chopped walnuts
½ cup chopped pistachios,
1 cup dried barberries
½ cup dried cherries
⅔ cup chopped dried prunes
⅔ cup chopped dried apricots
3–4 tablespoons tomato paste
Salt

Preheat the oven to 350°F.

First prepare the stuffing. Fry the onions in the olive oil until they begin to turn golden, then stir in the walnuts and pistachios. Fry for 1 minute, then add the dried fruit. Season with a little salt and stir in the tomato paste. Bind it together well, then leave to cool.

Rub the chicken lightly with salt, inside and out, and fill it with the stuffing. Block the cavity with the ½ onion and hold it closed with a skewer, or sew it up with a poultry needle and string. Lay a large sheet of foil, big enough to form a package over the chicken, in a baking dish and place the stuffed chicken on it.

Using a mortar and pestle, grind the saffron threads with the sugar and add a little boiling water to extract the color. Melt the butter in a pan, stir in the lemon juice and the liquid saffron, and pour it over the chicken.

Fold the foil tightly over the chicken and place the dish in the

oven for about 1 hour. Open the foil, baste the chicken with the juices, and roast uncovered for an addirional 30 minutes, until the chicken is cooked and golden.

A tall glass of ice-cold, deep-red cherry juice is a refreshing drink in Turkey and Iran. Every bar, café, teahouse, and caravanserai has bottles of ready-made cherry juice to serve with ice. But if you have the pleasure of tasting the homemade syrup poured over ice and diluted with a little water, it will transport you through centuries of delightful hospitality.

SHARBAT-E ÂLBÂLOO
(CHERRY SYRUP)

Makes 1 bottle
Preparation time 3 hours
Cooking time 35 minutes

3 cups sour cherries, washed and
  pitted
4 cups sugar
1 cup water

Place the cherries in a deep, heavy-based pan, cover with the sugar, and leave to stand for 2–3 hours to draw out the juice.

Add the water and bring the mixture to a boil, stirring until the sugar has dissolved. Reduce the heat and simmer for 10–15 minutes. Strain the mixture through cheesecloth, press all the juice out of the fruit, and return the strained liquid to the pan. Boil gently for a further 10 minutes, until the syrup is thick, then leave it to cool in the pan.

Cherry-juice seller in traditional Ottoman costume, Istanbul, Turkey

POMEGRANATE

(ROMAN) *Punica granatum*

With its leathery skin and jewel-like seeds, the pomegranate has the appearance of a fruit that has an ancient history—the dinosaur of the fruit kingdom. Like the fig and the grape, it has been so intricately woven into the tapestry of the Middle East that it appears in myth and legend. The goddess Aphrodite is said to have planted a pomegranate tree in her birthplace in Cyprus, the fruit is depicted in Egyptian tomb murals that date back to 1547 BC, and it is mentioned in the Old Testament.

The Romans called the pomegranate, *Malum punicum*, apple of Carthage, or *Malum granatum*, apple with grains, and it featured in a Latin proverb: "*Omni malo punico inest granum putre*"—"In every pomegranate is a rotten seed." The fruit was consumed in vast quantities by the Romans. The juice was fermented and made into wine, Nero's favorite digestive drink was made from pomegranates and quinces, and the fruit was dipped in the salty sea and dried in the sun to preserve it for winter.

Later, in medieval times, Islamic mystics believed that pomegranates could "raise" the soul and purge it of rage, hatred, and envy. During the period of the Ottoman Empire there were sweet and sour pomegranates as well as white pomegranates, which had white skins and pink, sweet grains, and "black" pomegranates from Baghdad, which had a purple skin and large, sour grains. Once used as a souring agent before the arrival of lemons, sour pomegranates are still grown for their juice, which is used to make a refreshing drink.

Fresh sweet pomegranates

HOW IT GROWS

The pomegranate is the fruit of a small bush-like tree that grows wild in its native habitat in the forests in northern Iran, to the south of the Caspian Sea and in Azerbaijan. It thrives in hot, arid regions and is cultivated in Iran, Turkey, Iraq, and in the eastern Mediterranean. The small leaves have a scarlet edging, and when the tree flowers, it bursts into color with tiny vermilion blooms. The fruit starts off pale green, like small bobbles, then gradually swells and the skin becomes leathery and coral red. The fruit matures in the late autumn.

APPEARANCE AND TASTE

In the Middle East, there are several varieties of pomegranate, both sweet and sour. Generally, they are round, the size of a tennis ball or bigger, with pink, leathery skin that conceals the treasure of translucent ruby seeds inside. The seeds of a ripe, sweet pomegranate, the "eating" variety, are fruity and juicy but the pith surrounding the clusters of seeds is very bitter. The seeds and juice of sour pomegranates are sour, or sweet–sour, to taste.

Pomegranates, not yet fully ripened

BUYING AND STORING

In the Middle East, fresh pomegranates come into season in the autumn and last for a few months. Both sweet and sour varieties are sold in some Middle Eastern stores but most of the pomegranates available in the supermarkets are sweet and come from elsewhere, such as Spain. They don't have the same intensity of color and taste. The dark pomegranate syrup or molasses (*pekmez* in Turkish, *dibs* in Arabic, *robb* in Farsi) is sold in jars in Middle Eastern and whole-food stores and keeps for months. If you want to make an authentic *fesenjân*, you will need to look for the tart, black *robb-e anâr* from Iran. The dried seeds can be found in some Middle Eastern stores.

MEDICINAL AND OTHER USES

The Prophet Muhammad commanded: "Eat the pomegranate, for it purges the system of envy and hatred." Certainly, the pomegranate is believed to cool and cleanse the system and aid digestion. Hippocrates recommended drinking pomegranate juice to reduce fever, and, some time later, the dried skin and flowers were used as astringents. A Turkish pharmacist who died in 1417 recommended crushing sweet and sour pomegranate grains with sugar to reduce anxiety. At the beginning of the twentieth century, the bark and root of the pomegranate tree were ground to a powder and sold as a remedy against tapeworm. But the most ancient use of the pomegranate was as a natural dye, found in the leathery skin and bark, used to tan leather and to color cotton and wool a reddish brown.

CULINARY USES

Fresh, ripe sweet pomegranates are generally eaten as a dessert fruit or squeezed for their refreshing juice to quench thirst in the middle of the day. The fresh seeds are used in a few salads and are often added to fruit compotes and sprinkled over desserts for color and texture. The seeds taste so sweet and are so delightful to look at, they are sometimes sprinkled with rose water, decorated with blanched almonds, and served chilled as a dessert. The juice of sour pomegranates was used liberally before lemons took over, but it is still used to add to marinades and soups, to make salad dressings and a tangy

Pomegranate leather

sorbet, and to make a tart, fruity sugar syrup that is the basis of a refreshing sherbet drink. The juice of both sweet and sour pomegranates is reduced to a thick, dark syrup or molasses, which is used in sweet and savory dishes, such as soups and stews, and in *muhammara* (p136), a red pepper and walnut dip. Like all the other fruit molasses, it is also mixed with tahini to make a thick, sweet paste to eat with bread or to use as a dip. Sour pomegranate molasses is particularly important in the *fesanjân* dishes of Iran, as the syrupy sharpness combines with the ground walnuts to produce a magnificent sauce. Dried wild pomegranate seeds, with their tart flavors, are scattered over some tahini dishes and hummus.

The *fesenjân* dishes of Iran are unique with their rich, dark, textured sauces made of ground walnuts and tart pomegranate syrup. For an authentic taste, you really need to use the Iranian pomegranate syrup, *robb-e anâr*. The most common *fesenjân*

dishes are made with dark meat, such as wild duck and other game birds, but there are also *fesenjân* dishes made with meatballs, fish, and eggplant.

KHORESHT-E FESENJÂN
(DUCK WITH WALNUTS AND POMEGRANATE SYRUP)

Serves 2–3
Preparation time 25 minutes (+ 1–2 hours' simmering of stock)
Cooking time approximately 1 hour 20 minutes

1 wild duck, cut into 6 pieces (keep the carcass for stock)

For the stock:
1 onion
A few celery leaves
A few peppercorns
Salt and freshly ground black pepper

1½ cups ground or finely chopped walnuts
2–3 tablespoons olive oil
1 onion, chopped
3 tablespoons pomegranate syrup
2 tablespoons sugar or honey

Put the duck carcass and the onion, celery leaves, and peppercorns into a pot. Cover with water and simmer for 1–2 hours to make a light stock. Then season with salt and strain.

In a heavy-based pan, fry the walnuts in a little of the olive oil, until they begin to darken and give off a lovely, nutty aroma, then put them aside.

Fry the chopped onion in the rest of the olive oil, until it begins to color, then add the duck to the pan. Brown the meat on all sides, then turn off the heat and remove the skin.

Pour in enough of the stock (about 2¼ cups) to just cover the duck, bring it to a boil, then cover the pan, reduce the heat, and simmer for about 20 minutes.

Stir in the ground walnuts and continue to cook gently for a further 20 minutes.

Add the pomegranate syrup with the sugar, and cook for another 15–20 minutes, until the duck is tender. Season and serve with plain rice.

In Turkey and Iran, pomegranate seeds are often added to salads and fruit compotes for a light, refreshing bite. The following salad is from Iran, but variations of it, particularly with grated fresh coconut, are served with grilled meat or as a *meze* dish in Turkey.

KHIYAR-O ANÂR
(POMEGRANATE AND CUCUMBER SALAD)

Serves 4
Preparation time 20–25 minutes
Cooking time –

3–4 pomegranates
1 long cucumber
1 red or white onion
Juice of 1 lemon
A small bunch of fresh mint, chopped, or 1 teaspoon dried mint
Salt and freshly ground black pepper

Split open the pomegranates and take out all the seeds. Remove any of the bitter membrane.

Peel the cucumber, quarter it lengthwise, then hold it together and slice it finely.

Quarter the onion and slice it finely, so the pieces are much the same size as the cucumber.

Put the pomegranate seeds, cucumber, and onion into a bowl, dress with the lemon juice, and toss in the mint. Leave to sit for about 30 minutes, and season before serving.

Left: Pomegranate seeds
Right: *Khiyar-o anâr*

Currants

Dried green grapes

GRAPE

(EINAB) *Vitis vinifera*

The vine and its fruit have been celebrated in food and wine since ancient times. There are paintings of different vines on the walls of early Egyptian tombs; the Bible mentions cultivated vineyards from the time of Noah, who was reputed to have planted vines in the foothills of Mount Ararat when the Great Flood subsided; and the seafaring Phoenicians brought the vine to Greece. As the frontiers of the Roman Empire advanced, the cultivation of the vine spread; it also moved in the opposite direction to parts of India and China where the winters were cool. The Greeks, Romans, and ancient Persians cultivated vines for the fresh fruit, for making wine, and for a variety of grape products, all of which are still in production in the Middle East today.

There are thousands of grape varieties but only a few of these are commercially important, mainly for wine, though some are grown specifically for dried currants, raisins, and sultanas (golden raisins). Turkey still ranks as one of the leading table-grape producers in the world. Dried currants, raisins, and golden raisins are all dried grapes, most of which originally came from the Mediterranean, the Middle East (mainly Turkey), and western Asia (Afghanistan); the leading producer today is California. The leaves of the vine, poached and stuffed, are popular throughout the Middle East.

HOW IT GROWS

The original grapevine, *Vitis vinifera*, was indigenous from the southeast region of the Black Sea coast and the southern region of the Caspian Sea to Afghanistan, where it still grows. This vine, and its many cultivated successors, is a climbing plant that needs support and a cool winter, but, like the olive and the almond, it can grow in conditions with poor soil and low rainfall. The vines that grow around Damascus are particularly famous.

APPEARANCE AND TASTE

The ripe, fresh eating grapes of the Middle East are usually round or oblong, and vary in depth of color from black through purple, pink, red, and white to green and yellow. Whether they are as small as a berry or as large as a plum, fat

Sultanas

or thin, they are nearly all fleshy, juicy, and sweet. The exception is the Iranian sour grape, which is really an immature green grape, valued for its tart flavor in summer stews. Fresh vine leaves picked in the early summer are quite tender but the later leaves can be large and tough, so they need to be blanched in boiling water before being used. Generally, they have a pleasing, almost malty taste. Raisins range in color from pale or golden to dark brown, almost black; some are sweet, others sour. The most popular raisins in the Middle East are seedless and well flavored, dried from the yellow Thompson seedless grapes (also known as Oval Kishmish or Sultanina) and from the Smyrna Sultana, which is a pale yellow, seedless grape with a good flavor. Golden raisins are usually larger than raisins, while the dried currants are so tiny they are called *kuş üzümü*, "bird grape," in Turkish. Dried from the small, black Zante grape, currants are often quite hard when sold but plump up when soaked or cooked.

BUYING AND STORING

Fresh grapes of all kinds should be bought ripe, on the bunch, and eaten fairly quickly. The Iranian sour grapes are sold fresh and dried in some Iranian or Middle Eastern stores in the early summer. Outside the vine-growing regions, the leaves are

Large raisins

usually preserved in brine and sold in packages, cans, or jars, which are available in a variety of Mediterranean and Middle Eastern stores, whole-food stores, and supermarkets. They will need to be rinsed well before use. Raisins, golden raisins and dried currants, on the other hand, keep for a long time. If they have been semi-dried, they will still be quite moist, perfect for snacking on, but they are sold mainly for cooking and need to be poached or reconstituted in water to soften and plump them up. All of them keep well in an airtight container in a cool, dry place.

MANUFACTURING

A grape syrup or molasses (*dibs* in Arabic, *pekmez* in Turkish) is made by boiling the juice extracted from the fresh fruit. It is sold in its refined form in jars throughout the Middle East and can be found in a crude, almost fermented form in villages. It is used as a sweetener for sweet and savory dishes, or mixed with tahini to spread on bread. Like apricots, carob, and mulberries, fresh grapes are also pressed, pureed, and dried into leathers to chew or use in cooking. Verjuice, the juice of unripe grapes, is bottled and used as a

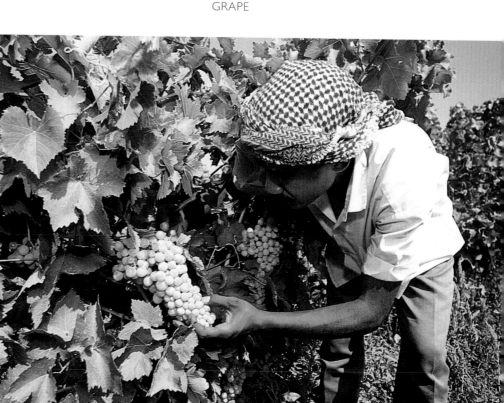

Harvesting of grapes by Egyptian worker, Jordan Valley

souring agent in cooking and dressings, just like vinegar. In some parts of the Middle East, grapes are grown for making a variety of red, white, and rosé wines, most of which remains in the country of origin. Some fairly refined vinegars are made from fermented wine. Fresh grapes, raisins, and dried currants are also employed in the making of Turkish *rakı*, which is a distilled alcoholic drink flavored with aniseed that turns cloudy when water is added.

Preserved vine leaves

CULINARY USES

Generally, bunches of fresh, ripe, sweet grapes are sold to be eaten as fruit. They are so sweet and delicious, there is little else you would want to do with them. In Iran, though, they are used to make the wonderful pickled delicacy *torshi-ye angoor*, which consists of huge, sweet, fleshy green and black grapes, symbolizing night and day, preserved in a syrupy vinegar to be consumed on Shab-e Yaldâ, the festival of the longest night. Also in Iran, the sour grapes, thinned from the crop of green grapes, are added to summer dishes, such as *khoresht-e-bâdenjân*, a delicious stew made with eggplant and lamb. Fresh vine leaves are often served with tabbouleh (p180), an Arab salad of bulgur and mint, or with a similar Turkish salad, *kısır*. The fresh or preserved leaves are usually stuffed with an aromatic rice mixture and served cold, or stuffed with a mixture of rice

and lamb and served hot. The tiny black dried currants are often added to stuffings, rice dishes, and *köfte*, Turkish meat- or fish balls. Raisins, golden raisins, and currants are used quite liberally to give a burst of fruity sweetness to a number of meat, poultry, vegetable, and rice dishes, as well as to numerous desserts. They are all included in the remarkable grain, pulse, and dried-fruit dessert, *aşure*, otherwise known as "Noah's dessert."

Raisins

According to legend, when the Flood subsided, Noah gathered up all the stores of grains and dried fruit on the Ark and made this dessert. Traditionally, it is made in large quantities, offered to friends and neighbors, and eaten on the tenth day of Muharram, which is the first day of the Muslim calendar, to mark the martyrdom of the Prophet's grandson. It can be made with wheat or barley, and requires a lot of advance preparation.

AŞURE
(NOAH'S DESSERT)

Serves 12 or more
Preparation time 24 hours
Cooking time approximately
 1 hour

1 cup whole barley, with husks
 removed, soaked for 24 hours in
 plenty of water
⅓ cup haricot beans, soaked for
 8 hours, or overnight, and
 cooked until tender
⅓ cup skinned fava beans, soaked
 for 8 hours, or overnight, and
 cooked until tender
¼ cup chickpeas, soaked for 8
 hours, or overnight, and cooked
 until tender
⅓ cup short-grain rice, washed
 and drained
⅔ cup halved dried apricots
⅓ cup golden raisins
⅓ cup raisins
⅓ cup dried currants
2 cups sugar
2 tablespoons cornstarch, mixed
 to a loose paste with a little
 water
½ cup rose water

To decorate:
A handful sliced dried figs
A handful sliced dried apricots
A handful golden raisins, soaked
 in water
A handful pine nuts
Fresh seeds of ½ pomegranate

In a large, deep pot, cook the barley in its soaking water, topping it up if necessary, until it is tender (about 45 minutes). Add the cooked beans, chickpeas, and the rice. Bring the liquid to a boil, then reduce the heat and simmer for 10–15 minutes.

Meanwhile, soak the dried fruit in boiling water for 5–10 minutes, drain, and then add to the pot. Simmer the dried fruit with the barley and pulses for about 10 minutes, then gradually add the sugar, stirring all the time, until the mixture thickens.

Spoon a little of the hot liquid into the cornstarch paste and tip it into the pot. Bring the liquid to a boil again, stir in the rose water, then reduce the heat and simmer for a further 10–15 minutes.

Tip the mixture into a large serving bowl, or spoon it into individual bowls, and leave to cool. Sprinkle with the ingredients for decorating and serve at room temperature.

Stuffed vine leaves are a classic delicacy. They are popular everywhere in the Middle East and, with the spread of the Ottoman Empire, they became widely known in the Balkans and in parts of North Africa. In Turkey cold vine leaves stuffed with aromatic rice are called *yalancı yaprak dolması*, meaning "false" or "lying," as they contain no meat. With their delicate spicy aroma, pierced by the sharp taste of lemon, these cold, stuffed vine leaves are particularly exquisite. They can be made with fresh or preserved vine leaves and in Iraq they are often made with chard or spinach leaves.

WARA EINAB
(VINE LEAVES STUFFED WITH AROMATIC RICE AND HERBS)

Serves 6
Preparation time roughly 40
 minutes (+ 20 minutes' soaking
 of leaves)
Cooking time approximately
 1 hour

Roughly 30 fresh or preserved vine
 leaves (and a few extra to line
 the pan)
2 tablespoons olive oil
2 onions, finely chopped
2 cloves garlic, finely chopped
2–3 tablespoons pine nuts
1 teaspoon sugar
½ teaspoon ground cinnamon
½ teaspoon ground allspice
1 tablespoon dried mint
1¼ cups short-grain rice, well
 rinsed and drained
Salt and freshly ground black
 pepper
A small bunch fresh mint, dill, and
 parsley, finely chopped

For the cooking liquid:
⅔ cup olive oil
⅔ cup water
Juice of 1 lemon
1 teaspoon sugar

If using fresh vine leaves, plunge them into boiling water to soften, then drain and refresh with cold water. If using preserved vine leaves, put them in a bowl and pour boiling water over them. Soak them for about 15 minutes, making sure the water gets in between the layers. Drain the leaves, then soak them in cold water, and drain again. This gets rid of the salt.

Heat the oil in a heavy-based pan and stir in the onions. When they have softened, add the garlic, pine nuts, and sugar. Fry for 1–2 minutes, until

they begin to color, then stir in the spices and mint, followed by the rice and seasoning.

Pour in enough water to just cover the rice and bring to a boil. Reduce the heat and simmer for about 10 minutes, until the water has been absorbed—the rice should be soft on the outside but firm in the middle. Using a fork, carefully toss in the fresh herbs and leave to cool a little.

Place a vine leaf, vein side up, on a plate or board. Put 1 heaping teaspoon of the rice at the bottom of the leaf, near where the stem would have been, in the center. Fold the stem edge over the filling to seal it in, then fold both of the side edges in toward the middle and roll up the leaf like a small fat cigar. Squeeze it lightly in the palm of your hand to fix the shape, then repeat the process with the other leaves.

Line the bottom of a shallow pan with the extra vine leaves, then pack the stuffed leaves, side by side, on top. Mix together the ingredients for the cooking liquid and pour it over the stuffed leaves.

Place a plate on top of the leaves to prevent them from unraveling, then put the lid on and simmer gently for 1 hour, topping up the liquid if you need to. Leave the stuffed leaves to cool in the pan. Serve cold with wedges of lemon to squeeze over them.

Aşure

PULSES, CEREALS, & GRAINS

Chickpeas

CHICKPEAS

(HUMMUS) *Cicer arietinum*

Like lentils and beans, chickpeas are a staple of the Middle East, constantly referred to as "the food of the poor." They were first grown in the Levant and ancient Egypt, from where they spread throughout the Middle East and North Africa to India. Wherever the Arabs traveled, they took chickpeas with them, so they later became incorporated into the cuisine of places such as Sicily and Spain. The botanical name *arietinum* comes from the seeds, which are curled at the sides and look like a ram's (*aries* in Latin) skull. The Arabic word for chickpea is *hummus*, which is also the name given to the famous Middle Eastern dish of cooked chickpeas crushed with olive oil, tahini, lemon juice, and garlic.

HOW THEY GROW

Chickpeas are cultivated all over the Middle East, particularly in Egypt, where they are a staple crop. The plants are small and bushy, bearing pods that contain two or three seeds. The harvested pods are dried and threshed to release the chickpeas, which are further dried in the sun to rid them of any moisture.

APPEARANCE AND TASTE

Dried chickpeas are small and hard, about the size of a pea, pale tan in color, and wrinkled from drying in the sun. They have thick, fibrous skins, which become apparent with soaking and cooking, and are removed in cold water before the chickpeas are added to dishes. When cooked, chickpeas have a slightly earthy taste with a meaty texture that is ideal for absorbing strong flavors. Roast chickpeas look like hazelnuts and are eaten salted as a nibble, or they are coated in sugar and eaten like candy. Fresh chickpeas, which have a lemony taste, are brilliant green and eaten raw or cooked at the beginning of the season in late spring.

BUYING AND STORING

Dried chickpeas are available in Middle Eastern and Asian stores, whole-food stores, and most big supermarkets. If stored in an airtight container, they will keep for a year or more. Cooked chickpeas, preserved in brine, are available in cans in the same places, but even after a lot of rinsing they have a slightly salty, metallic taste and, as they have been cooked until they are soft, they don't really absorb the flavors of a dish.

CULINARY USES

Before being used, dried chickpeas must be soaked in plenty of water for at least eight hours, during which time they will almost double in size. For all dishes, apart from falafel, they must be cooked in water for about one hour, until they are *al dente*. For purees, such as hummus, they need to be cooked a little longer, until they are soft. Once cooked and drained, they are put into a bowl of cold water so that the loose skins float to the top; the remaining skins have to be rubbed off by hand. Chickpeas are used extensively in soups, rice dishes, and stews, such as *dfeena*, an Egyptian specialty consisting of beef, a calf's foot, eggs in their shells, and haricot beans, as well as chickpeas. It is also a popular Sabbath meal in Jewish households. Chickpeas are tossed into hearty gypsy salads with onions, peppers, tomatoes, and cheese. They are crushed and bound into hummus-style garlicky dips with olive oil and lemon—variations include tahini, yogurt, crushed nuts, tomato paste, the pounded smoked eggplant, and red pepper paste. Pureed chickpeas are sometimes bound with mashed potato to make the Armenian dish *topik*, which is stuffed with dried currants, nuts, and spices. You can roast your own cooked chickpeas by drying them on paper towels for about one hour, tossing them in a hot, oiled, heavy-based pan until they are brown and crisp, then sprinkling them with salt.

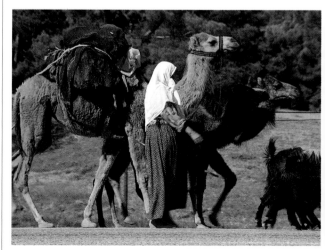

Camels are still sometimes used to transport household goods and dried ingredients, including spices and pulses

Sicak humus

FALAFEL
(SPICY CHICKPEA BALLS)

Serves 8–10 people
Preparation time 25 minutes +
soaking time
Cooking time 5–10 minutes

1 heaping cup dried chickpeas,
soaked for 24 hours
1⅓ cups dried white fava beans,
soaked for 24 hours
1 teaspoon baking soda
1 teaspoon ground coriander
2 teaspoons ground cumin
2 teaspoons ground or flaked
Middle Eastern red pepper
(p152)
1 large red onion, very finely
chopped
5–6 cloves garlic, crushed
A bunch fresh flat-leaf parsley,
finely chopped
A bunch cilantro, finely chopped
Salt and freshly ground black
pepper
Sunflower oil for deep-frying

Rinse and drain the chickpeas and beans. Pat them dry with a clean dishtowel, then grind them in a food processor until they form a fine paste. Season with salt and pepper, then add the baking soda, coriander, cumin, and the Middle Eastern red pepper. Grind the paste once more. Tip into a big bowl, add the rest of the ingredients, and knead thoroughly.

Take small lumps of the mixture in your hands, shape them into flat rounds about 2 inches in diameter and ¾ inch thick, and place them on a plate. In a wide pan, heat enough oil for deep-frying, then fry the *falafel* in batches until they are crisp and brown all over. Drain them on paper towels and serve hot, as above, or with lemon wedges to squeeze over them and a cucumber and tomato salad.

This recipe is a specialty from the east of Turkey, particularly popular with the people who live in the mountains, where the air is cold. It is served by itself or as part of a hot *meze* spread, with plenty of fresh bread to scoop it up.

SICAK HUMUS
(HOT CHICKPEA PUREE)

Serves 4–6
Preparation time 10 minutes (if
using an electric mixer)
+ 8 hours' soaking of the
chickpeas and 1½ hours'
cooking
Cooking time 25 minutes

2¼ cups dried chickpeas, soaked,
cooked, and drained with skins
removed
Roughly ½ cup olive oil
Juice of 2 lemons
2–3 cloves garlic, crushed
1–2 teaspoons cumin seeds

2 tablespoons light or dark tahini
Roughly 2 cups thick, strained
yogurt
Salt and freshly ground black
pepper

For the top:
2 tablespoons pine nuts
Roughly 3 tablespoons butter
1 teaspoon Middle Eastern red
pepper (p152)

Preheat the oven to 400°F.

Pounding the chickpeas by hand is laborious, so if you have a liquidizer or food processor, whiz all the hummus ingredients together. Season well and spoon into an ovenproof dish.

In a flat heavy-based pan, roast the pine nuts until they are brown. Quickly add the butter and allow it to melt before stirring in the red pepper. Spoon the melted butter over the top

of the hummus and bake it in the oven for about 25 minutes, until it has risen slightly and most of the butter has been absorbed. Serve hot with lots of crusty or flat bread.

Also known as *ta'amia*, these spicy vegetable balls can be made with dried white fava beans or chickpeas, or both. In Egypt, where they are claimed as a national dish, they are usually made with fava beans, but in Syria, Lebanon, and Jordan, falafel are commonly made with chickpeas. They are eaten for breakfast, lunch or as a snack, tucked into the pocket of pita bread with pickles, tahini, yogurt, hummus, or *baba ghanoush* (p82).

FAVA BEANS

(FUL) *Vicia faba*

Fava beans are among the oldest food plants. They are legumes of such antiquity that there is an Arab saying, "Beans have even satisfied the pharaohs." However, they were treated with suspicion in ancient times, associated with the dead and eaten at funeral feasts. Although fava beans have long been a part of the diet of the Middle East, they are by no means the only bean in culinary use. The black-eyed peas (*Vigna unguiculata*) and members of the haricot bean family (*Phaseolus vulgaris*), such as the fresh long green beans and the pinky-beige, speckled cranberry beans, are also prized. Like chickpeas and lentils, beans have traditionally been regarded as a staple food of the poor, but they are so versatile and tasty, the rich have never been able to resist them, hence the Egyptian proverb, "The man of good breeding eats beans and returns to his breeding."

Fresh fava beans

Egyptian brown beans need a long soaking and long, slow simmering. Beans should be seasoned with salt only after they are cooked, otherwise they don't soften. They should be tender, not soft and squidgy, almost meaty in texture, each with its own distinctive character. And, no matter how you cook them, there is no escaping the fact that beans do cause a bit of flatulence.

BUYING AND STORING

The season of fresh fava beans is short—just a few months in the summer. They are best eaten fresh, for if they are stored for a few days, the sugars turn to carbohydrate, which alters the taste and texture. Fresh cranberry beans and other haricot beans are also best eaten soon after picking. Dried beans, on the other hand, store for a long time. In the markets of the Middle East, the dried beans have been picked from the year's crop, which means they look appetizing, require less soaking, and taste fresh when cooked. In the supermarkets, whole-food stores, and Middle Eastern stores, all of which sell a wide range of dried beans, they might be as much as two or three years old, so they will need longer soaking and, when cooked, may be tough or taste a little woody. It's worth checking the expiration dates on the packages. Most beans are available in cans, but, as with chickpeas, they are often too soft, even mushy, and taste of the can.

HOW THEY GROW

The primitive fava bean was small, similar to the horse bean, which is grown only as a fodder crop. Nowadays, a range of fava beans are grown, varying in size, shape, and color. They thrive in most climates and are harvested in the summer.

Dried fava beans

APPEARANCE AND TASTE

There are two types of fava bean in the Middle East: the large, fresh green bean, called *ful akhdar* in Arabic, which can be eaten fresh or dried (*ful nabed*), and the small brown bean, *ful baladi*, which is eaten only dried. The very young fresh fava beans are green and tender, and can be eaten raw or cooked lightly with or without their pods. The more mature beans are shelled before they are cooked or dried. Dried fava beans are brown unless they have been skinned and split, in which case they are pale green,

cream, or white. The small variety of fava bean, the Egyptian brown bean, is round and dusty brown in color. Fresh beans are favored in season, but the dried beans, which have greater nutritional qualities, can be enjoyed all year. All dried haricot beans and the white and brown fava beans require lengthy soaking. This can be reduced by first blanching the beans in boiling water for two minutes, then soaking them for two hours. They need to be covered with a lot of water, as they swell and almost double in size. Cooking times differ from bean to bean—haricot beans may take one to two hours, black-eyed peas only thirty minutes, and the

Fresh cranberry beans

Sacks of black-eyed peas

CULINARY USES

Like lentils and chickpeas, all beans are used extensively in traditional peasant soups and stews. Fresh green beans and young fava beans in their pods are generally cooked lightly in olive oil or added to summer vegetable stews, but dried beans are employed in a variety of exciting ways. There is a magnificent, nourishing soup called *âb ghooshte fasl*, which comes from the Persian *âbgoosht*, a name given to lamb-based soups. It calls for beans and lentils, vegetables and dried fruit, spices and herbs, all cooked slowly in a large cauldron, enriched with the sheep's head and feet. Another Persian invention is *âsh-e nazri*, a huge, bean-filled soup served at prayer meetings. It is provided for, and made by, a community wishing for the recovery of a sick child or the safe return of a loved one who has gone on a long journey.

Fava beans marry deliciously with olive oil, either on their own or with other ingredients like artichoke hearts and dill, and they are popular mashed or pureed, known as *besara* in Egypt (*fava* in Turkey), and served with olive oil as a *mezze* dish. They are often added to rice dishes and feature in *fistuqia*, a medieval dish in which the beans are cooked with rice and yogurt. Popular in Jewish communities is an unusual dish of ancient origin called *mefarka*, a combination of fava beans, ground beef, spices and thyme, all bound together by eggs gently stirred into the dish, which is then turned out onto a plate and served cold.

Perhaps the best known of all fava bean dishes is *ful medames*.

Made with small brown beans, the dish is traditionally cooked in a pear-shaped, earthenware pot called a *damassa*, which is buried in the ashes of a fire or set over glowing coals and left to cook overnight. In Iraq, large brown beans are used in a dish called *badkila*, which is similar to *ful medames* and is often served in the street for breakfast

This is a great winter soup. In Iran it is served with bunches of fresh herbs, radishes, and pickles to pass around. Traditionally, it is a soup served in the bazaars

Egyptian brown beans

late at night or early in the morning, complete with every Westerner's nightmare: sheep's head, feet, and bobbing eyes.

ÂB GHOOSHTE FASL
(IRANIAN BEAN SOUP)

Serves 4–6
Preparation time 20 minutes (+ 6 hours' soaking of the beans)
Cooking time approximately 2 hours

½ cup dried, skinned fava beans, soaked for 6 hours
⅓ cup dried white haricot beans, soaked for 6 hours
⅓ cup dried black-eyed beans, soaked for 2 hours
½ cup yellow split peas
1 pound lamb, cut into small pieces
1 onion, coarsely chopped
⅓ cup pitted dried prunes
4 tomatoes, peeled and chopped
3–4 potatoes, peeled and cut into large dice
1–2 teaspoons ground cinnamon
1 teaspoon ground coriander
1 teaspoon ground turmeric
Salt and freshly ground black pepper
A bunch of fresh parsley, chopped

Put the beans, split peas, lamb, and onion into a deep saucepan and cover with about 8 cups of water. Bring the water to a boil, remove the foam, then cover and simmer for about 1 hour, until the beans are tender.

Add the prunes, tomatoes, spices, and potatoes. Cook for 1 hour more, until everything is tender, then add the parsley and season to taste.

Although basically a peasant dish, this simple salad of brown beans has become an Egyptian national dish, claimed by the Christian Copts, who regard themselves as representatives of the ancient pharaohs. Also popular in Syria, Lebanon, and Jordan, it is eaten in the street and in the fields, in primitive homes and in luxurious mansions, in rural villages and in expensive restaurants. It is often sold in the street for breakfast, sometimes tucked into Arab flat bread with a tahini dressing and sliced

Ful medames

tomato and onion. Some cooks add red lentils, carrots, or tomatoes for color; *bastirma* (p198) is occasionally added for flavor; and the dish is commonly served with hard-boiled eggs, olives, pickles, and lemon to squeeze over it, or lime in the Arabian Gulf. Traditionally, the plain, cooked beans are spooned into bowls and everyone helps themselves to olive oil, lemon, parsley, cumin, and seasoning, whatever they feel like. For the purposes of this book, though, I have prepared them as a salad.

FUL MEDAMES
(EGYPTIAN FAVA BEAN SALAD)

Serves 4
Preparation time 8 hours' soaking of the beans
Cooking time 1½–2 hours

1⅓ cups Egyptian brown beans, soaked for at least 8 hours, or overnight
2–3 tablespoons olive oil
Roughly 1 teaspoon cumin seeds
2 cloves garlic, crushed
Juice of 1 lemon
Salt and ground black pepper
A bunch fresh parsley, chopped

In a heavy-based pan, gently simmer the brown beans in plenty of water for about 1½ hours, or until they are tender but not too soft.

Drain them and, while they are still warm, toss them in the olive oil, cumin seeds, and garlic. Add the lemon juice and season to taste.

Toss in the parsley, serve warm or cold, and pass around pickles, olives, and hard-boiled eggs.

LENTILS

(ADAS) *Lens culinaris*

Red lentils

First cultivated in Egypt, lentils are legumes of antiquity, their name derived from the Latin, *lentus*, meaning slow. Lentils have stirred up mixed emotions. The Egyptians believed they could enlighten the minds of children and make them cheerful. The Persians classified them as a "cold" food, implying that they slowed the metabolism and had a calming effect. And the Romans maintained that lentils encouraged a mildness of character. One Roman general blamed his Persian defeat on lentils. His troops had been uncharacteristically slow-witted and sluggish because they had run out of their wheat supplies and had been forced to eat lentils. Along with beans and chickpeas, they have long been regarded as a food of the poor but they have also always been enjoyed by people of all classes.

HOW THEY GROW

The *Lens culinaris* is an annual plant that grows to about 16 inches in height, with short, broad seed pods, each containing two seeds. Ranging in size from tiny to small, the husked and unhusked seeds vary in color. Generally, they are dried before use.

APPEARANCE AND TASTE

The best-known lentils of the Middle East are the tiny red variety, sometimes known as Egyptian lentils. When the husks are removed, the lentils are pinkish. Also popular are the small pale yellow lentils, the bright orange ones, the brown ones, and the larger, matt-green ones. A little soaking in water helps to tenderize the lentils and shorten the cooking time, but the yellow, orange, and red lentils rarely need this. All lentils need to be cooked in lots of fresh water, but their cooking time and texture vary according to the soil they have been grown in and how much time has passed since they have been dried. When cooked, lentils should have an earthy texture, a sprout-like taste, and a nice bite to them, unless they have been specifically cooked to a pulp. They are filling and nourishing, for, apart from soybeans, they contain more protein than any other vegetable or pulse.

Lentils, nuts, and seeds displayed at a market stall

BUYING AND STORING

A number of Middle Eastern or Asian lentils are available in most supermarkets nowadays. Otherwise, they can be found in whole-food, Middle Eastern, and Asian stores, where they are often sold in large quantities and need to be picked over for tiny stones and grit.

CULINARY USES

Popular and important for their nutritional value, lentils can be married with a variety of spices and ingredients to make filling, tasty dishes. They are cheap and frequently used in stews and soups, such as *shourba bilsen*, a thick lentil and coriander soup from Yemen, and in rice dishes such as the Iranian *addas polow*, made with green lentils, rice, golden raisins, dates, and crispy fried onions, and served at *nazr* (thanksgiving ceremonies). Also in Iran, cooked lentils, lamb, and fried eggplant are pounded together to make a kind of porridge called *haleem bâdenjân*, which is blended with *kashk* (p125) and garnished with chopped walnuts and crispy fried onions.

Shula kalambar, a medieval Persian recipe used to heal the sick, calls for brown lentils to be cooked with spinach and spices, ingredients readily available in the street . An unusual Arab dish, *majroush*, is made with rice, spices, and yellow or brown lentils, which are pounded

Green lentils

together to make a paste or dip for bread. A medieval Arab dish of the poor, called *mujaddara* (*mujadarra*), is popular today in every household. It consists of brown lentils and rice cooked together, sometimes flavored with cumin, coriander, or mint, topped with browned and caramelized onions, and served with yogurt. Similarly, the Lebanese make a simple green (sometimes brown) lentil and bulgur dish, called *imjadra*, which is topped with fried onions and melted butter and is served with yogurt.

In Turkey, the green lentils are cooked with carrots in one of the sumptuous olive oil dishes, *zeytinyağlı havuç*. The Egyptians also cook red lentils with onion and spices in a dish called *masafi*, which looks like an Indian dhal. This lentil dish, which is cooked until all the water has been absorbed and the lentils appear pulped, is used as a bed for meat and vegetable stews. Sautéed simply in clarified butter and spices, lentils are often served with *rishta* (p125) or meat dishes, which can be made more substantial by frying peppers, eggplants, zucchini, carrots, or slices of *sujuk* (p166) or *basterma* (p198) with the lentils. And simple salads of lentils tossed in olive oil and lemon juice, often flavored with garlic, cumin, parsley, mint, or dill, teamed with chopped onions or tomatoes, and garnished with black olives, are served as *mezze*, or with meat dishes, such as kabobs.

This medieval dish is reputed to be a descendant of the "mess of pottage" with which Jacob bought Esau's birthright. Among Christian communities, it has traditionally been served during Lent. The name *mujaddara* comes from the Arabic word for smallpox, as the dots of lentils in the rice resemble pockmarks on a face. Aside from its less-than-appetizing name, it is a popular dish throughout the Arab world. In Egypt it is called *megadarra* and, in Lebanon, it is known as *mudardara*.

MUJADDARA
(LENTILS WITH RICE)

Serves 4–6
Preparation time 15 minutes
Cooking time 25–30 minutes

1 cup brown lentils
Roughly 3–4 tablespoons olive oil
2 onions, finely chopped
1 teaspoon ground cumin
1 teaspoon ground coriander
1¼ cups long-grain rice, well rinsed
2 onions, halved and sliced
Salt and freshly ground black pepper
A knob of butter

Put the lentils into a large pan. Cover with just enough water and boil them for about 15 minutes, until they are just tender, then drain and refresh them.

In the same pan, heat the olive oil and fry the chopped onions with the cumin and coriander until brown. Stir in the lentils and the rice, add the seasoning, and cover with just enough water.

Brown lentils

Bring the water to a boil and simmer gently for about 15 minutes, until the rice has cooked and almost all the water has been absorbed.

Turn off the heat, cover the pan with a clean dishtowel and then a lid, and leave the rice and lentils to steam for a further 15 minutes.

Meanwhile, heat a little extra olive oil with a knob of butter in another pan and fry the sliced onions until they are well browned and almost caramelized.

Tip the rice and lentils onto a serving dish and spoon the onions and oil over the top. Serve immediately with thick, creamy yogurt.

The mild *zeytinyağlı* vegetable dishes favored by the Ottomans were designed to be cooked in lots of olive oil and served cold, so that the vegetables were beautifully tender and the flavored oil could be fully appreciated. However, this dish defies the rule, as it crops up in different parts of Turkey, Syria, and Lebanon served both hot and cold, sometimes spicy and accompanied by yogurt.

ZEYTINYAĞLI HAVUÇ
(CARROTS AND GREEN LENTILS IN OLIVE OIL)

Serves 4
Preparation time 15 minutes (+ 1 hour's soaking)
Cooking time approximately 45 minutes

½ cup large green lentils, soaked for 1 hour
4–5 tablespoons olive oil
1 onion, halved and sliced
2–3 cloves garlic, chopped
1 teaspoon coriander seeds
3–4 carrots, peeled and sliced
1 tablespoon tomato paste
1 teaspoon sugar
Roughly 1 cup water
Salt and freshly ground black pepper
A bunch fresh dill and mint, chopped
Wedges of lemon to serve

Drain the lentils and put them in a pan, covered with plenty of water. Boil them for about 15 minutes, until they are tender but not soft, then drain and refresh them.

In a wide pan, heat the oil and stir in the onion. When the onion begins to color, stir in the garlic, coriander seeds, and the carrots. Cook for a few minutes, then add the lentils.

Stir in the tomato paste and sugar, followed by the water. Mix well and bring the liquid to a boil, then cover the pan and simmer gently for about 35 minutes, until the carrots are tender. Remove the lid, season to taste, and continue to simmer for a further 10 minutes, until most of the liquid has gone.

Toss in most of the herbs and serve immediately with yogurt, or leave it to cool in the pan and garnish with the rest of the herbs. Serve with lemon to squeeze over it.

Yellow lentils

Zeytinyağlı havuç

Long-grain rice

RICE

(ROZ) Oryza sativa

HOW IT GROWS

Descended from a wild grass that probably originated in the Himalayas, cultivated rice gives higher and better yields than wheat or barley. In the Middle East, the rice is grown mainly in shallow water, fed by rain or by drainage systems. Old methods of sowing the rice in nursery beds, transplanting plants by hand, and reaping with a sickle are still in use. In the rice-growing communities, the irrigated rice can be grown on the same land year after year, sometimes yielding two harvests annually. It grows mainly along the Caspian littoral in the north of Iran, in parts of Anatolia and Syria, in the southern marshlands of Iraq, and in Egypt.

Rice was already established in northern India, China and Southeast Asia by about 2000 BC, but it didn't make an impact in the Middle East until much later. The ancient Greeks and Romans imported rice, but it was expensive and used mainly for medicinal purposes. The Turkic tribes probably brought rice to Persia some two thousand years ago, but it wasn't grown in Egypt until the sixth or seventh century AD. During the Ottoman times, there was such a demand for rice, it had to be imported. The long-grain variety came overland from India and, after the Ottoman conquest of Egypt in 1517, the short-grain was bought by sea from the Nile delta, making rice a luxury like sugar, which was also imported from Egypt. Rice was thus used sparingly, reserved mainly for extravagant feasts and wedding ceremonies.

In the Middle East today, rice is part of everyday fare in the cities but in most rural areas, apart from the rice-growing regions of southern Iraq, it is still used sparingly, bread and wheat being the cheaper staples. Light, nourishing, often elaborate, and cooked with pride, rice continues in its role as the food of feasts and hospitality. Cooked simply in clarified butter, it is reputed to have been a favorite dish of the Prophet Muhammad. The traditional method of cooking rice in the Middle East is called *pilaf* (or *pilau*), which originates from the medieval Persian word *pulaw* (*polow* in modern Iran). Descriptions of this technique first appeared in the Arabic books *Kitab al-Tabikh al-Baghdadi, Kitab al-Tabikh al-Warraq* and *Kitab al-Wulsa Ila'L-Habib*, written in Baghdad and Syria in the thirteenth century. The Persians were particularly imaginative with their elegant and artistic pilafs bursting with colorful fruits such as sour cherries, barberries, mulberries, and pomegranates, recipes that still exist in modern Iran. When the Arabs conquered Persia, they adopted these creative pilafs and spread them throughout the region, so that variations crop up all over the Middle East, each with a national stamp.

APPEARANCE AND TASTE

Generally, white rice is grown and used in the Middle East. Some grains are long and scented, others are short, stubby, and starchy. The long, fragrant grains, used for pilafs, have a good flavor and texture when cooked, absorbing the flavors of the other ingredients. There are many different types, some requiring longer cooking, but all absorb the cooking liquid and expand greatly. The Arabic name for plainly cooked rice is *ruzz mufalfal*, meaning "peppered rice," which doesn't imply that the rice is flavored with pepper but that the cooked, plump grains should be separate like individual peppercorns. The short grains, used mainly for stuffings and desserts, have less flavor and are more

Short-grain rice

Harvesting rice, northern Iran

glutinous, but still retain a bite when cooked. Rice is also ground into a fine, white flour, which is used particularly for the traditional milk and rice puddings of the Middle East.

BUYING AND STORING

The harvested grain contains little moisture, which is further reduced by drying, so as long as it is stored in a cool, dry, dark place, rice can keep for anything between three and ten years. For savory dishes, it is important to use a fragrant long-grain rice but, apart from the small quantities found in Middle Eastern stores, the rice from Iran, Turkey, Egypt, and other countries is not exported. However, American long-grain and Basmati rice make excellent substitutes in most dishes. Sweet-rice dishes require a stubby, short-grain rice, for which a standard pudding rice can be substituted. Rice flour (not ground rice) is sold in Middle Eastern stores and whole-food stores.

CULINARY USES

In the Middle East, rice is not the main staple crop (wheat is) but it is the everyday food of the cities. It is the key element in a wide variety of dishes based on the traditional *pilaf* (*pilau*)—a method of cooking rice, often with other ingredients, with each grain remaining separate. Spices, nuts, dried fruit, meat, and vegetables may be cooked or steamed with the rice, but plain rice (*ruzz mufalfal* in Arabic, *sade pilav* in Turkish, and *chelow* or *katteh* in Farsi) can also be cooked this way. Rice can be tinted gold with saffron, tinged pink with tomatoes, or scented with sweet fruit and spices. It is often served in a mound as a meal in itself or as an accompaniment to a dish. Some recipes call for it to be tipped out of the pan, upside down, in a layered mold, like in the Palestinian specialty *makloub* (p131). A medieval specialty, called *seleq*, still popular in Saudi Arabia today, consists of rice cooked in milk until it resembles

a soft cream; this is served as a bed for a whole roast lamb or kid. Typical *pilafs* include lentils, fava beans, black-eyed beans, pine nuts, almonds, herbs and spices, chicken, noodles, eggplant, spinach, chickpeas, and lamb.

A classic Persian specialty is the *khoresht*, a sour-tasting, thin vegetable or fruit stew, sometimes containing a little meat, which is served with, or spooned over, plain rice (*chelow*) as standard fare in every Iranian household. The Iranians also make a traditonal baked rice dish, *tahcheen*, which can be layered with meat or vegetables, with a yogurt-enhanced crusty bottom. Regarded as rather

special, the *tahcheen* dishes are often served on festive occasions. Turkey is also known for its elaborate *pilafs*, such as *perdeli pilav*, which is often served at weddings and consists of chicken, carrots, almonds, and dried currants cooked with rice and encased in a pastry dome. The Turks also cook a wide variety of ingredients with the rice rather than adding them in afterwards, and they make a number of *pilafs* using fish, such as anchovies, and shellfish. In the Arabian Gulf, fish and shellfish are also added to the rice dishes called *birian,* which, with the use of turmeric, ginger, and curry powder, are similar to an Indian *biryani.* The Turks, the Syrians, the Kurds, and the Armenians all make *pilafs* with bulgur too, particularly in the countryside where wheat is the cheaper grain. And the Bedouin make a simple, tasty bulgur or rice dish combining dates and almonds.

Short-grain rice is often pounded with ground lamb or beef to make meatballs, and it is used in the famous *koofteh Tabrizi*, a mammoth stuffed meat dumpling from Tabriz and Azerbaijan. One of the principal uses of short-grain rice is in the stuffed dishes called *dolma* in Turkey, *dolmeh* in Iran, and *mahshi* in the Arab world, which are thought to have originated in Ottoman Turkey and are now popular throughout the Middle East. The rice is combined either

Using oxen to till a rice paddy, Turkey

with spices, herbs, dried currants, and pine nuts, known as a "false" filling, or with spices, ground meat, and, occasionally, yellow split peas, and then used to stuff a variety of fruit and vegetables, such as eggplant, quince, apples, peppers, vine leaves, cabbage leaves, zuchinni and their flowers, as well as whole lamb, kid, pigeons, or poultry.

Short-grain rice is also used to make the ever-popular sweet rice puddings, which at the time of the Romans were made only to settle upset stomachs. The rice puddings of the Middle East, such as the Iranian *shollehzard*, are thick and creamy, usually flavored with saffron, rose water, or spices, and served chilled. Rice flour is used to give thickness and substance to the equally popular milk puddings, such as the traditional *muhallabia* (p187); the famous chicken breast pudding, *tavuk göğsu* (p62), from Ottoman Turkey; and the Iranian *fereni*, a delicate, rose-flavored rice cream. In Syria and Lebanon the birth of a son is celebrated with *meghlie* (p185), a spicy dish made with rice flour flavored with ginger, aniseed, cinnamon, and fennel.

Methods of cooking rice

To make a perfect *pilaf*, the grains of rice are thoroughly washed, sometimes soaked, to remove the starch, then the rice is covered with just enough water (usually one cup of rice to two cups of water) and cooked in an open pot, until the grains are al dente and almost all the water has been absorbed. The pot is then covered with a clean dishtowel, followed by the lid, and the rice is left to steam for a further twenty minutes off the heat.

In Iran, the rice is cooked and drained first, then butter, or a mixture of yogurt and beaten egg, is added to the pot. The drained rice is tipped over this, together with any additional flavorings—such as meat, fruit, or vegetables—covered, and left to steam over a low heat for about twenty minutes. The melted butter or yogurt at the bottom of the pot forms a golden brown crust, called tahdeeg, meaning "bottom of the pot," which is a traditional feature of Persian rice and highly relished.

Rice flour

This rice dish from the Arabian Gulf can be made with mussels, scallops, or squid. In the style of an Indian *biryani*, it also has echoes of India in its use of spices: turmeric, ginger, fenugreek, and even curry powder. As the population of the Arabian Gulf is heavily expatriate, and the Gulf has a history of trade with India, the flavors of this dish are not surprising.

MAYGOO POLOW
(RICE WITH SHRIMP)

Serves 3–4
Preparation time 5–10 minutes
Cooking time approximately
* 30 minutes*

1¼ cups long-grain rice, well rinsed
1 tablespoon clarified butter
  (ghee)
1 onion, sliced
A knob of ginger, sliced into small,
  thin sticks
1 teaspoon turmeric
1 teaspoon ground fenugreek
1 teaspoon curry powder
8 ounces fresh shrimp, shelled
Salt
A small bunch of cilantro, chopped

Put the rice into a pan and cover with just enough water. Sprinkle in a little salt and bring the water to a boil. Cook the rice for about 10 minutes, until it is tender but not fully cooked, with a bite to it, and the water has been absorbed.

In another pan, heat the clarified butter and stir in the onion. When it begins to color, stir in the ginger, and cook for

1–2 minutes, before stirring in the spices.

Quickly toss the shrimp in the spices and tip the rice into the pan with a little extra salt. Reduce the heat to very low, cover the pan with a clean dishtowel and the lid, and leave to steam for 10–15 minutes.

Toss in some cilantro and tip the rice onto a serving dish.

Literally translated as "laid on the bottom." *tahcheen* is a classic Persian dish served on special occasions like weddings and festive days. Traditionally, the dish was made in a wide-bottomed pan that was placed in the hot coals of a baker's oven, where it would bake for many hours so that a thick, crusty layer formed on the bottom. Lamb or chicken can be used in this recipe.

TAHCHEEN
(IRANIAN BAKED RICE)

Serves 4–6
Preparation time approximately
* 30 minutes (+ 1 hour soaking*
* the rice and 1 hour marinating*
* the chicken)*
Cooking time 30–40 minutes

2 pinches saffron threads
A sprinkling of sugar
¾ cup yogurt
2 eggs
1 onion, grated
1 small roast chicken, the meat
  stripped off and cut into pieces
2½ cups long-grain rice, washed
  and soaked in salted water for
  about 1 hour
Roughly ½ cup olive oil
Roughly ¼ cup butter, cut into
  pieces
Salt and freshly ground black
  pepper

In a small bowl, grind the saffron with the sugar. Add a few drops of boiling water and mix well.

Sacks of grains, pulses, dried fruit and spices in a open-air market, Turkey

Tahcheen

Mix the yogurt and egg together, beat in the grated onion and season with salt and pepper. Stir the saffron mixture into the yogurt, and marinate the chicken pieces in it for 1–2 hours.

Meanwhile, fill a large saucepan with water and bring it to a boil with a little salt. Toss in the drained rice and cook for about 5 minutes, until the grains are soft on the outside but firm in the middle. Drain and rinse under lukewarm water.

Remove the chicken from the marinade, then mix half of the cooked rice with the remaining yogurt mixture. Heat the oil in the bottom of a heavy-based pan and spread the rice and yogurt mixture across the base and up the sides. Lay the chicken on top, followed by the rest of the rice, or arrange the rice and chicken in alternate layers. Dot the butter on top.

Poke a few holes through the rice, then cover the pan with a clean dishtowel and the lid. Keep it on a high heat for 1–2 minutes, then reduce to the lowest heat and leave the rice to steam for about 30 minutes. Alternatively, bake it in a low oven, about 325°F for 30–40 minutes.

Spoon the cooked rice onto a serving dish and arrange the chicken on it with thick wedges of crispy bottom. If you prefer, you can turn the pan upside down onto a serving dish to present the rice in a mound.

WHEAT

(QAMAH) *Triticum*

APPEARANCE AND TASTE

Once stripped of their bran coats, the dried wheat grains are tan-colored and look a bit like large, fat grains of brown rice with a slit down one side. Whole immature wheat grains that are still green can also be eaten. Known as *freek*, they are usually roasted and then cooked like mature grains of wheat; they have a delicious smoky flavor.

Just after harvesting, some of the wheat is parboiled, drained, dried and rubbed to remove the bran, then crushed into coarse, medium, or fine grains, called *burghul* (bulgur). The color of bulgur varies from light to dark brown to gray, and it resembles hard pellets. These have to be soaked in boiling water, or boiled, before eating. The resulting taste is distinctly nutty with a delightful springy texture.

The hard durum wheat is coarsely milled to produce the brittle grains of semolina, which, when cooked, have a pleasantly light and grainy texture. Semolina can be further ground to a fine flour, which is used for pasta, or it can be processed to make couscous, which is available in Lebanon, and is generally eaten in North Africa. The hard-wheat flours used for bread and pasta are usually white, with a superior taste and texture when they have been stone-ground.

The ancient civilizations of Mesopotamia, Syria, Palestine, and Asia Minor subsisted mainly on wheat and barley (*Hordeum vulgare*), the oldest cultivated cereals. First was barley, which up until classical times was the staple grain in the eastern Mediterranean region, including Egypt, where it was used to make a kind of porridge and bread, and was malted for beer. Gradually, wheat took over, probably because the natural gluten found in wheat produces a better, lighter bread, but barley and millet remained the cheap staples for slaves and the poor. The ancient Egyptians were the first sophisticated bread-makers, using different kinds of wheat, but the Romans were the first to distinguish between "hard" and "soft" wheat—the "hardness" indicating a higher proportion of gluten, which gives bread a superior texture. The most important types of wheat cultivated today belong to the species *Triticum aestivum*, which is used for bread, and *Triticum durum*, which in its coarsely ground form is known as semolina. Finely ground, it is used for pasta. Traditional grinding stones, also known as saddle stones, depicted in ancient Egyptian paintings and on Assyrian reliefs, are still used in some villages, but most of the wheat is ground into flour at mills or factories.

Dried whole wheat

HOW IT GROWS

Along with barley, wheat was probably cultivated around 6000 BC. Over the centuries, it has developed so that it can adapt to most soils and climates. Like many other grasses and cereals, the wheat ear is formed like a tower, with each story containing two to five flowers, some of which develop into grains covered with bearded or beardless husks. To separate the grain from the husk and the ear, the harvested wheat is threshed, which is still done by traditional methods using oxen in some poorer parts of the Middle East.

Harvesting wheat on the plains of Anatolia, Turkey

BUYING AND STORING

Whole-wheat, semolina, and good-quality, stone-ground hard-wheat flours are available in whole-food stores and some supermarkets. Kept in airtight containers in a cool, dry place, they store quite well. Bulgur is available in the same outlets, as well as in Middle Eastern stores. If well stored, it keeps for a long time. *Freek* is available only in Middle Eastern stores.

CULINARY USES

Wheat grains

Boiled wheat, or sometimes bulgur, is used in some festive sweet dishes in the Middle East, particularly among the Lebanese Maronites and the Sephardic Jews. The fragrant dish *belila*, made with wheat or barley, is often served to celebrate happy occasions in Jordan, Lebanon, and Syria, while the Sephardic Jews traditionally serve it to celebrate the cutting of a baby's first tooth. Another famous sweet wheat dish, also made with barley, is *aşure* (p109), which in Muslim communities is served to commemorate the martyrdom of the Prophet's grandson on the tenth day of Muharram, the first month of the Muslim calendar. It is also the dish that, according to legend, Noah prepared with all the provisons that were left on the ark when the flood subsided. Wheat or barley is traditionally used to make the ancient dish *harrisa* or *harriseh*, which is a porridge-like soup made with meat. It is particularly popular among the Kurds and Armenians, who eat it as a

Fine-grain bulgur

hearty winter breakfast; in Syria and Lebanon, it is made when a sheep is slaughtered for special occasions, such as Assumption Day among Christians. The same dish is known as *haleem* by the Iranians, who claim that it became the Prophet Muhammad's favorite dish when the Arabs conquered Persia.

Bulgur

Bulgur is usually served like rice with meat or vegetables in it. The Kurds often eat it cooked plain and served in a mound with thick yogurt spooned into the hollowed out center and melted clarified butter poured on top. Bulgur is also used in some meatballs, particularly the traditional *kibbeh* of Lebanon and Syria, known as *kubba* in Iraq, which sometimes contain potatoes or pulses pounded with the bulgur instead of meat. And it is the basis of two distinct herb salads, the *tabbouleh* (p181) of the Arab world and North Africa, and *kısır* from southern Turkey. Generally, the coarse grade of bulgur is used for rice dishes, soups, and stews; the medium grade is used in *kibbeh* and stuffings, as in the Egyptian dish of pigeons stuffed with bulgur and raisins; and the fine grade is used for salads.

Kishk

In the wheat-growing areas of Lebanon, Syria, Turkey, and Armenia, a preserved food is made of yogurt and bulgur, which is mixed together and spread out on a wide tray to dry for several days in the sun. As the bulgur soaks up the moisture, the mixture is

rubbed between the palms daily to break it up until it resembles tiny grains, which are then spread out on clean cloths to dry in the sun. Commonly known as *kishk* (*tarhana* in Turkish), these fermented, dried grains are used to flavor and thicken stews and soups, and to make a sort of porridge for breakfast. The word *kishk* originally comes from the Persian word *kashk*, which referred to cracked wheat or barley, but in modern Iran it refers to dried buttermilk that is formed into balls or crushed into a powder and used in much the same way as *kishk*. Two medieval culinary manuals, the Arab *Wulsa* and the Egyptian *Kanz*, refer to recipes using *kishk*.

Semolina

Semolina is used in the popular Syrian dish *ma'mounia*, which is like a sweet, cinnamon-flavored porridge. It is also used in a variety of breads and cakes to give them a light texture, such as in the Turkish dessert *Revani*, a semolina cake soaked in syrup. And it is used in some traditional *halwa* or *helva* dishes, in which the semolina is cooked with butter and sugar and ingredients such as pine nuts, until the grains turn golden.

Flour

Wheat flour is the main flour used for risen loaves and flat breads, but a few bread doughs are made with barley or corn. Similarly, wheat is used in all flat bread or pastry doughs

Coarse bulgur

employed in *sanbusak* (p141) or *börek*, and in the numerous sweet pastries. Wheat flour is also used to make the Middle Eastern pasta which has been in existence since ancient times. Medieval culinary manuals refer to fresh noodles as *lakhsha*, a Persian word, and to dry noodles as *itriyya*. By the thirteenth century the word *lakhsha* was replaced by *rishta* (*reshteh* in Farsi), also a Persian word, which is what the noodles

Semolina

are called today. Although cheap and simple to make, *rishta* is not considered a dish of the poor but, instead, is regarded as rather grand.

Also popular in parts of the Middle East is the Turkish pasta dish *mantı*, which is thought to have originated from the Chinese noodle dough, *mantu*, and traveled across Central Asia to Anatolia with the Turkic-speaking peoples. *Mantı* dough can be filled with meat, nuts, or chickpeas, shaped like ravioli, and boiled, or it can be filled, shaped into little open dumplings, and baked in stock in the oven. However it is cooked, *mantı* is always served with garlic-flavored yogurt, often topped with melted butter, thyme, and Middle Eastern red pepper (p152). Different types of pasta, such as the small teardrops used in some soups and rice dishes, are manufactured in Turkey and among the Jewish people, who are proud of their *calsones*, which are rather like cheese-filled ravioli.

Rishta noodles

The Lebanese and the Syrians both claim *kibbeh* as their national dish. Basically, *kibbeh* are meatballs or patties and, once again, each country in the Middle East has its own version. The following Lebanese recipe for bulgur and lamb *kibbeh* would take a long time to prepare if we used the traditional method of grinding everything by hand but with an electric mixer it doesn't very take long at all.

KIBBEH
(BULGUR AND LAMB PATTIES)

Serves 6
Preparation time 20–25 minutes
   + 20 minutes' soaking of
   bulgur
Cooking time 3–5 minutes

Muslim farmers, Yemen

1⅓ cups bulgur
1 pound lean lamb, cut into small
   chunks
1 big onion, grated
1 teaspoon ground allspice
1 teaspoon Middle Eastern
   pepper (p152) or ground
   paprika
1–2 teaspoons salt
Sunflower oil for frying
A small bunch fresh flat-leaf
   parsley
Lemon wedges

Rinse the bulgur, put it into a bowl and cover with just enough boiling water. Leave it to soak for 20 minutes, then squeeze out any excess moisture and put it into a food processor. Blend it to a pasty mixture and pop it into a bowl.

Put the lamb into the food processor, blend it to a paste, and add it to the bulgur. Add the onion, spices, and salt to the lamb and bulgur, and, using your hands, knead them all together.

Divide the mixture into batches and blend each batch in the food processor. Knead it all together one more time, then shape the mixture into little balls (dip your hands in cold water from time to time, as the mixture is sticky), and flatten each ball in the palm of your hand.

Heat some sunflower oil in a heavy-based skillet and fry the *kibbeh* over a moderate heat until brown. Drain on paper towels and serve hot with fresh parsley and lemon to squeeze over them.

Sweet dishes often play a significant role in the Middle East. They are not just delights for those with a sweet tooth, but are served to celebrate a birth or a marriage, to commemorate the death of a religious figure, or to mark a religious event. In Syria and Lebanon *belila*, also known as *qamhiyya*, is traditionally made with young green wheat or barley, and is served at happy events such as the New Year. Often the cooked grains are bathed in syrup and served in individual bowls, allowing each person to sprinkle the nuts and cinnamon on top. This fragrant dish is offered to nursing mothers, as it is believed to enrich their milk. In Sephardic communities, it is served to celebrate the cutting of a baby's first tooth.

BELILA
(WHOLE-WHEAT IN A FRAGRANT SYRUP WITH NUTS)

Serves 10–12
Preparation time 20 minutes
   (+ soaking overnight)
Cooking time approximately
   1 hour

2⅔ cups whole-grain wheat,
   soaked overnight, drained and
   rinsed, with bits of husk removed
2 cups sugar
Juice of ½ lemon
3 tablespoons rose water
⅔ cup raisins, soaked in water for
   20 minutes
2 teaspoons ground cinnamon
1 cup coarsely chopped pistachios
1 cup coarsely chopped blanched
   almonds

Put the wheat into a heavy-based pot with plenty of water. Bring to a boil, then reduce the heat and simmer for about 1 hour, or until the wheat grains become tender and burst open (add more water if necessary). Drain and tip the cooked grains into a serving bowl.

Put the sugar into a heavy-based pan with roughly 2½ cups of water. Bring to a boil, stirring all the time. Add the lemon juice and rose water, then reduce the heat and simmer for 10–15 minutes, until the syrup coats the back of the spoon. Stir in the raisins at the end.

Pour the hot syrup over the cooked wheat. Sprinkle the top with cinnamon and nuts, and serve hot or cold, spooned into individual bowls or cups.

Kibbeh

NUTS & SEEDS

CHESTNUT

(KASTANA') *Castanea sativa*

Whole chestnuts

The chestnut tree, often referred to as Spanish, is of west Asian origin. Around 300 BC, the Greek writer Xenophon described how Persian nobles gave their children chestnuts to eat to fatten them up. The best chestnuts are thought to have come from Sardis in Asia Minor, not far from modern-day Izmir in Turkey, and the Greeks took them from there to Europe. Wild chestnuts, which are slightly smaller than the cultivated variety, were often regarded as a staple for the poor. They contain more starch and less oil than other nuts and, therefore, provide nourishment during the winter, often used instead of potatoes. In the Mediterranean regions, where the chestnut trees grow, the shiny brown shells are split and the nuts are roasted over charcoal grills in the streets. The strong, flexible bark and branches of the chestnut tree are used to make orchard ladders and domestic tools.

Roast chestnut seller, Istanbul, Turkey

CULINARY USES

Chestnuts appear mainly in the cooking of Turkey, Syria, Lebanon, and the Palestinian territories. An old substitute for potatoes, chestnuts are sometimes cooked with lamb in a hearty stew. They figure in *makloub*, a stunning, molded rice dish thought to be Palestinian. And they figure in a number of dishes from Istanbul and Bursa in Turkey, particularly in stuffed cabbage leaves, *lahana dolması*.

This is a winter dish from Bursa, the first seat of the Ottoman dynasty, which lies at the foot of the ancient Mount Olympus. The chestnuts from the surrounding groves are roasted over braziers in the streets, poached in syrup, or wrapped in cabbage leaves. Boiled fresh or dried chestnuts can be used, but the flavor and texture of roast chestnuts are best. Occasionally, the stuffed leaves are served hot with an egg and lemon sauce, but usually they are eaten cold with a *tahini* dressing, or simply with lemon to squeeze over them.

HOW IT GROWS

Like almond trees, chestnut trees grow in a temperate climate and are happiest in the Mediterranean region. They are medium-sized, hardy trees and live for a long, long time. Their fruit is round, green, and spiky, with a leathery inner shell that preserves the vitamins in the kernel, which ripens in October and November. The best chestnuts grow around Bursa in Turkey.

APPEARANCE AND TASTE

Enclosed in hard, shiny brown shells, chestnuts are pale beige. They are meaty nuts that dry well and can be preserved in syrup. Roasting brings out the best flavor, which is mild and distinct, with a slightly floury texture.

Dried chestnuts

BUYING AND STORING

Fresh chestnuts are easily available in season. The shell should be hard and unbroken. In a cool, dry place, they keep for a few months. Dried chestnuts are available in some supermarkets and specialty stores and should be stored in an airtight container. The syrupy preserves, in the style of *marrons glacés*, are available in Middle Eastern and Mediterranean stores.

LAHANA DOLMASI
(STUFFED CABBAGE LEAVES WITH CHESTNUTS)

Serves 4–5
Preparation time approximately 1 hour
Cooking time 25 minutes

- 1 green cabbage to give roughly 16–20 leaves
- 2 tablespoons olive oil
- 1 onion, finely chopped
- 1 teaspoon ground allspice
- 1 teaspoon ground cinnamon
- ½ cup short-grain rice
- 8 ounces fresh chestnuts, roasted, shelled, and chopped
- A small bunch fresh dill and flat-leaf parsley, finely chopped
- Juice of ½ lemon mixed with 1 tablespoon olive oil
- Salt and freshly ground black pepper

Put the whole cabbage into a big pan of boiling water and cook until tender. Drain and refresh, then carefully tear off the leaves. Choose roughly 16 of the best inner leaves and cut out the base of the central vein.

Heat the oil in a pan and soften the onion. Stir in the spices and rice and pour in enough water to cover. Season with salt and pepper and bring the water to a boil. Reduce the heat and simmer until the liquid is absorbed. Gently toss in the chestnuts and herbs.

Place a cabbage leaf flat on a surface. Spoon some of the rice mixture just above the cut-away base, fold over the two sides to seal it in, then roll up the leaf from the base into a tight log shape. Repeat with the other leaves and pack them snugly into a shallow pan.

Add a little water to the lemon juice and olive oil and pour it over the stuffed leaves. Place a plate directly on top, then cover the pan and cook gently for about 25 minutes. Serve hot or cold with wedges of lemon.

In Arabic the word *makloub* (*maqlubi*) means "turned over," which is exactly what this Palestinian dish is. Popular in Syria, Lebanon, and Jordan, the rice is cooked on top of layers of vegetables and meat, and then turned upside down so that the meat or vegetables are on top. All kinds of vegetables are used, but an unusual version includes chestnuts.

MAKLOUB
(PALESTINIAN RICE WITH CHESTNUTS)

Serves 4–6
Preparation time approximately 50 minutes
Cooking time 40 minutes

- 8 ounces chestnuts
- 2 tablespoons clarified butter (ghee)
- 1 onion, chopped
- 8 ounces lamb, cut into small pieces
- 1 teaspoon baharat (p162)
- 2½ cups lamb or beef stock, or water
- A little oil
- 2½ cups long-grain rice, soaked in boiling water for 10 minutes and drained

Cut 1–2 gashes in the chestnut shells and put them in a pan of boiling water. Reduce the heat and simmer for 20 minutes. Then drain the chestnuts, remove the shells, and halve the nuts.

Meanwhile, in a heavy-based pan, melt the clarified butter and stir in the onion. When it begins to brown, add the meat and cook it until it begins to brown. Then stir in the spices, followed by the stock. Bring the liquid to a boil, reduce the heat, and simmer for about 40 minutes, until the meat is tender. Drain the meat and add water to the stock to make it back up to 2½ cups.

Brush a little oil on the base and sides of a heavy-based saucepan, preferably one with sloping sides. Arrange the meat on the bottom, followed by a layer of chestnuts.

Cover with the rice, spread evenly over the top, then carefully pour in the stock, taking care not to disturb the layers. Don't stir. Put the lid on and cook it gently for about 25 minutes, until the liquid has been absorbed. Turn off the heat, cover with a clean dishtowel, followed by the lid, and leave to steam for another 15 minutes.

To serve, loosen the edges with a sharp knife, then place an inverted, flat serving dish over the top of the pan. Using both hands to grasp the pan and the dish firmly together, turn them upside down. Carefully lift the pan off, leaving the rice mold with the meat on top.

Makloub

HAZELNUT

(BUNDUK) *Corylus colurna*

Wild hazel trees were probably first brought from Asia Minor and cultivated in Europe. Pliny mentions that hazelnuts came from the Black Sea coast, where most hazelnuts are still grown. In fact, Turkey is the largest producer of hazelnuts. Hazel wood is believed to contain magical and medicinal qualities and the nuts contain so much protein, they are often mixed with almonds, raisins, and cinnamon and given to children as a nutritious snack.

Whole hazelnuts

APPEARANCE AND TASTE

Ripe hazelnuts are round and beige, and encased in a hard, brown shell. Like almonds, they can be eaten when they are immature and juicy, and have a milky, sharp taste. Ripe hazelnuts are dried until they are firm and quite sweet. Roasting improves their flavor and texture.

BUYING AND STORING

Hazelnuts are sold in and out of their shells, chopped or ground. Shelled hazelnuts are often sold with their brown skins on; if you roast or blanch the nuts, these will rub off easily. Hazelnuts still in their shells keep fresh for longer, but the shelled nuts also keep surprisingly well.

Roast, shelled hazelnuts

CULINARY USES

Hazelnuts feature mainly in the dishes of Turkey and Egypt. Ground hazelnuts are used in cookies and sweetmeats, such as *helva* (or *halva*). Roast hazelnuts combine deliciously with chocolate and are used in a range of Turkish Delights. Hazelnuts are occasionally used in rice dishes, but are more commonly used in salads and sweet pastries. They are also used to make a Black Sea version of *tarator* (p209), a sauce made with nuts, garlic, bread, and lemon juice, and served to accompany fish and deep-fried shellfish in Turkey, Syria, Lebanon, and Egypt. As the taste and texture of hazelnuts complement fish so well, they are often fried with onions and dried currants and served with fish, or they are combined with pine nuts, onions, tomatoes, and parsley to make an Egyptian sauce served with fried fish, such as red mullet. Again in Egypt, hazelnuts are used in the sweet pastry *om Ali*. Hazelnuts are also used in *dukkah* (p163), an Egyptian spice and nut mixture that is served with olive oil as a dip for bread.

HOW IT GROWS

Indigenous to Anatolia, hazelnuts grow profusely along the Black Sea coast where 300,000 tons are harvested a year. The fruits, which ripen from late August to October, are picked and laid out to form long hazelnut carpets by the roadside, at the edges of gardens, or in any available flat space, so that the husks split and fall off and the nuts dry in the sun.

Jars of mixed hazelnuts and pistachios in honey

This syrupy bread-and-nut dessert is a homey dish in Egypt. Some families make it with thin pancakes, others with thin pastry, but the most common is with flat bread. Sheets of phyllo pastry toasted or fried work well in this dish, which is usually made in individual bowls.

OM ALI
(EGYPTIAN BREAD PUDDING WITH NUTS)

Serves 6
Preparation time approximately 25 minutes
Cooking time 25 minutes

Roughly 6 sheets of phyllo
2–3 tablespoons clarified or ordinary butter
1½ cups chopped hazelnuts, almonds, and pistachios
⅔ cup golden raisins
4½ cups milk
1¼ cups light cream
½ cup sugar
1–2 teaspoons ground cinnamon

Preheat the oven to 450°F.

If you prefer to toast the phyllo, pop the sheets in a low oven for about 15 minutes, until they are crisp and brown, then crumble them. Otherwise, melt the butter in a wide pan, tear the phyllo into pieces and fry them in the butter until they are crisp and brown.

Arrange the crispy phyllo, layered with the nuts and golden raisins, in individual ovenproof bowls, or in a big ovenproof dish.

In a heavy-based pan, bring the milk, cream, and sugar to a boil, stirring all the time. Keep boiling for a few minutes, then pour it over the layered phyllo. Pop the dishes, or dish, into the oven and bake for about 25 minutes, until the top is brown. Sprinkle the top with ground cinnamon, and serve hot.

Taratorlu kabak

Steamed or fried vegetables in a crushed nut-and-garlic sauce, *tarator*, are popular in most regions of the Middle East. I particularly like the following Turkish *meze* recipe, as the combination is light and fruity. The zucchini and apple can be deep-fried or steamed.

TARATORLU KABAK
(ZUCCHINI AND APPLE IN A HAZELNUT AND GARLIC SAUCE)

Serves 3–4
Preparation time 20 minutes
Cooking time –

2 zucchini, partially peeled and sliced
1 apple, quartered, cored, and sliced
Sunflower oil (optional)
½ cup hazelnuts
2 cloves garlic
2 tablespoons olive oil
Juice of 1 lemon
2 tablespoons creamy yogurt
A small bunch flat-leaf parsley
Salt and freshly ground black pepper
A handful roasted hazelnuts, roughly chopped

Steam the zucchini with the apple for about 5 minutes, until tender, and then refresh them under cold running water. Or deep-fry them in sunflower oil until golden.

Using a mortar and pestle, pound the hazelnuts with the garlic and bind with the olive oil and lemon juice. Beat in the yogurt and parsley, and season to taste.

Arrange the zucchini and apple mixture on a plate, spoon the sauce over the top, and garnish with the roasted hazelnuts.

Whole dried
sunflower seeds
in their husks

SUNFLOWER SEED

(BISRA ABBAD AL-SHAMS) *Helianthus annuus*

Husked
sunflower seeds

Native to North America, sunflowers probably came to Turkey via Spain in the sixteenth century, along with tomatoes, peppers, and corn, articles of trade with the New World. Apart from the ornamental uses of its spectacular head, it is the seeds of the sunflower that are in demand for culinary purposes. It is often thought that the flower got its name from its resemblance to the sun, but it could also have acquired the name from its ability to turn its handsome head toward the sun, so that it faces east at sunrise and west at sunset.

Sunflower seeds for sale, Iraq

HOW IT GROWS

Sunflowers grow in sunny temperate climates and can reach up to 12 feet in height. One flower head can contain hundreds, sometimes thousands, of seeds. Sunflowers grow wild in the Mediterranean regions of the Middle East, and they are cultivated in Turkey for the seeds and oil. At harvest time the edges of country roads are strewn with the drying heads.

APPEARANCE AND TASTE

The seeds are flat and gray, with a pleasant taste and a bite to them. The dried pods, which are long and black, are edible, but they are quite fibrous and chewy. As with most nuts and seeds, flavor improves with roasting.

BUYING AND STORING

The dried seeds are sold both in their pods and out, plain or roasted. They keep well in an airtight container.

MANUFACTURING

In Turkey the seeds are pressed to make a light, general-purpose cooking oil, high in polyunsaturates and without cholesterol. Tasteless, it is used mainly for frying and for salad dressings in areas where olive oil is unavailable or too expensive.

CULINARY USES

Roasted and salted, sunflower seeds are often sold to nibble on. Children love them and buy bags of them on their way home from school. They are often added to a mixture of nuts and spices or served with a glass of *rakı* (p184). They are also added to salads, sprinkled on breads, and used in some rice dishes. But the main role of sunflower seeds is in the light oil.

The following Turkish recipe is popular in the summer months, when fish is usually cooked on the outdoor grill. Surplus catch or leftover cooked fish will be deftly turned into aromatic or spicy balls and served with a fresh seasonal salad and rice.

BALIK KÖFTESI
(FISH BALLS WITH DRIED CURRANTS AND SUNFLOWER SEEDS)

Serves 4–6
Preparation time approximately 30 minutes
Cooking time 10 minutes

1 pound trimmed fresh fish filets
2 slices day-old bread, soaked in a little water and squeezed out
1 red onion, finely chopped
2 cloves garlic, crushed or finely chopped
2 tablespoons sunflower seeds
2 tablespoons dried currants, soaked in water for 15 minutes and drained
2 teaspoons tomato paste
1–2 teaspoons ground cinnamon
A bunch fresh parsley and dill, finely chopped
1 egg
Salt and freshly ground black pepper
A little all-purpose flour for coating
Sunflower oil for frying
A lemon, cut into wedges

In a bowl, break up the fish with a fork, removing any remaining bones. Add all the other ingredients and knead well with your hands. Form the mixture into balls, flatten them a little, and lightly coat them in flour.

Heat some sunflower oil in a skillet and fry the fish balls over a gentle heat until they are cooked through and golden brown all over. Drain on paper towels and serve hot with lemon to squeeze over them.

In the Middle East, dishes that are referred to as salads often form part of the *mezze* spread. However, increasingly in the big cosmopolitan cities like Istanbul and Damascus, salads like this one are served as a side dish or as the main dish for wealthy, lunching ladies. Similar salads are made with carrots, cabbage, leeks, and onions.

Roast the sunflower seeds in a heavy-based pan, until they brown and give off a nutty aroma.

TAHİNLİ KARNABAHAR SALATASI
(CAULIFLOWER WITH SUNFLOWER SEEDS IN A SESAME DRESSING)

Serves 3–4
Preparation time roughly 20 minutes
Cooking time –

I small cauliflower, washed and broken into small florets
I apple, peeled and diced
A bunch of fresh parsley, mint, and cilantro, chopped
2–3 tablespoons roasted sunflower seeds
I–2 tablespoons light tahini
Juice of ½ lemon
I–2 cloves garlic, crushed
Salt and freshly ground black pepper

Put the cauliflower, apple, fresh herbs, and roasted sunflower seeds into a bowl.

In a small bowl, mix together the tahini, lemon juice, and garlic with a little water, until it is the consistency of heavy cream. Season the dressing and pour over the salad.

Toss well and garnish with some extra roasted sunflower seeds.

Tahinli karnabahar salatası

Whole walnuts

BUYING AND STORING

Ripe walnuts are sometimes sold in their shells but usually they are sold shelled, in half-kernels or broken pieces. As with all nuts, walnuts in their shells store well for several months.

MANUFACTURING

Walnuts are pressed for their pungent, topaz-colored oil. Walnut juice is used as a dark brown dye.

CULINARY USES

Walnuts are used in a variety of syrupy desserts and pastries, such as *kalburabastı*, a Turkish dish of walnut spongecake soaked in syrup, and the much-loved baklava. It is the nut used in the Persian *fesenjân* (p104) dishes that combine crushed walnuts with tart pomegranate syrup in a sauce for duck, fish, and eggplant. It is the principal flavoring and texture in *çerkez tavuğu* (p62), the delightful Circassian dish of walnuts and chicken. Walnuts are also used in savory pastries, such as the spinach pies *fatayer bi sabanikh*, and they are pounded with red peppers in the delicious *mezze* dish *muhammara*. Crushed with garlic, bread, and olive oil, walnuts are used to make a strong-tasting version of the popular sauce *tarator* (p209), which is served with fish and shellfish such as *midye tavası*. In Istanbul, the traditional *tarator* is always made with walnuts. Chopped walnuts are stuffed into figs and baked in honey, or

Shelled walnuts

they are stuffed into tiny eggplants and pickled, and they are used in numerous spicy fruit and nut fillings for poultry and fish, particularly in the famous Turkish mackerel dish *uskumru dolması*. Green walnuts are preserved in syrup.

This vividly flavored and textured *mezze* dip is particularly popular in Aleppo in Syria and in Gaziantep in Turkey, the two places famous for their hot red peppers. Some variations of *muhammara* include tahini or white cheese.

MUHAMMARA
(RED PEPPER AND WALNUT DIP)

Serves 4
Preparation time 25–30 minutes
Cooking time –

2 red bell peppers, grilled over charcoal or roasted in the oven
1 cup coarsely ground walnuts
2–3 cloves garlic, crushed
1 teaspoon flaked Middle Eastern red pepper (p152), or 1 chili, finely chopped
Juice of ½ a lemon
2 tablespoons olive oil
½ cup yogurt cheese (yogurt strained overnight)
Salt and freshly ground black pepper

Peel and seed the bell peppers and chop to a pulp. Using a big mortar and pestle, pound the peppers, walnuts, and garlic together to make a textured paste. Beat in the Middle Eastern red pepper, olive oil, and lemon juice. Then beat in the yogurt

WALNUT

(JAWZ) *Juglans regia*

Walnut trees have grown wild across Asia since prehistoric times, and walnuts have long been regarded as the king of nuts. Their Latin name means "Jupiter's acorn," in accordance with the ancient myth that the gods ate walnuts while men lived on acorns. The walnut tree was so highly regarded by the ancient Persians that the nuts were reserved solely for the king. And when the king of Greece was sent some walnut trees by the Persian king, he, too, made sure that he was the only one to enjoy them.

HOW IT GROWS

Walnut trees generally grow in temperate climates. The most important species is the Persian walnut, which grows wild across Asia but is also cultivated for its superior nuts. These trees bear green fruit with flesh surrounding a hard-shelled pit that holds the edible kernel. When it is immature and green, the entire fruit can be eaten or pickled, but as the fruit ripens, the fleshy part becomes leathery.

APPEARANCE AND TASTE

Walnut shells appear like two half-shells seamed together. When they are opened, each half contains a half-kernel that looks a bit like a diagram of a brain. In fact, in Afghanistan walnuts are called *charmarghz*, which means "four brains." The green, unripe fruit are very sour but the half-ripe nuts can be preserved in syrup. Ripe walnuts are quite oily, with a strong, slightly bitter, woody taste.

cheese until thoroughly blended, and season it to taste.

Spoon the mixture into a serving bowl and drizzle a little olive oil over the top to keep it moist. Garnish with a few extra walnuts, fresh mint, or black olives. Serve with flat breads to scoop it up.

A legacy of the Ottoman Empire, baklava is arguably the grandest of the Middle Eastern syrupy pastries. Certainly, it is the best known and the most misunderstood. The magnificent creation of the pastry chefs in the Topkapı Palace, the classic baklava was made with eight layers of a special pastry dough, clarified butter, and seven layers of nuts.

In the Middle East, baklava is generally associated with celebrations, such as births, weddings, festivals, the Jewish bar mitzvah and the Muslim Ramadan. As vast quantities are consumed, most people buy their baklava from the specialty pastry stores, where they will be enticed by other syrupy pastries too. However, if you use sheets of phyllo pastry, a straightforward baklava is easy to prepare at home. Once again, pistachios are often regarded as the most prestigious filling, but walnuts are traditional.

BAKLAVA
(LAYERED PASTRY WITH WALNUTS AND SYRUP)

Serves 8–12
Preparation time 30 minutes
Cooking time approximately 1 hour

¾ cup clarified or ordinary butter
½ cup sunflower oil
1 pound phyllo pastry
4 cups finely chopped walnuts
1 teaspoon ground cinnamon

For the syrup:
2 cups sugar
1 cup + 2 tablespoons water
Juice of ½ lemon, or 2 tablespoons rose water

Preheat the oven to 325°F.

Melt the butter with the oil in a pan and brush a little of it on the base and sides of a 12-inch baking pan. Place a sheet of phyllo pastry in the bottom and brush with the melted butter and oil. Do the same with half the quantity of phyllo pastry sheets, easing them into the corners and trimming the edges if they flop over the rim.

Baklava

Spread the chopped walnuts over the top sheet and, if you like, sprinkle with cinnamon. Continue with the phyllo pastry sheets, brushing each layer with the melted butter and oil. Brush the top and, using a sharp-pointed knife, cut parallel lines right through all the layers to the bottom, making small diamond shapes. Then pop it in the oven for about 1 hour. If the top is not golden brown at the end of the hour, turn the oven up to 400°F for a few minutes.

Meanwhile, make the syrup. Put the sugar and water into a pan and bring to a boil, stirring all the time. Stir in the lemon juice,

reduce the heat and simmer for 10–15 minutes—if using rose water, add it at this stage. Leave the syrup to cool.

Take the golden baklava out of the oven and pour the cold syrup over the hot pastry. You can zap it back into the oven for 5 minutes if you like, to help the pastry absorb the syrup, or just let it cool. When they have cooled, lift the diamond-shaped pieces out of the pan and arrange on a serving dish.

POPPY SEED

(KASHAKISH) *Papaver somniferum*

The poppy was valued by the ancient Egyptians and the ancient Greeks, who grew it for opium to use as a painkiller and sleeping potion, hence its botanical name, meaning "sleep-bearing." Opium is derived from the alkaloids in the sap of the unripe seed pods, which also produce the medicinal derivatives morphine and codeine. With such addictive properties, the poppy was much in demand, and cultivation spread to parts of Arabia and Persia, India and China. Opium-smoking, which first became fashionable in the nineteenth century, has led to bans on poppy cultivation without a permit in most countries. The east of Turkey is famed for its dark, almost black, honey made from pollen of the opium poppy. Fiery, with hallucinatory properties, it is aptly called *deli bal*, meaning "crazy honey."

An Arab resting in the desert, title-page from *The Valley of the Nile*

Poppy seeds

HOW IT GROWS

Related to the wild poppies that grow all over the eastern Mediterranean, the opium poppy is cultivated in Turkey and Iran. It is an annual plant with quite thick, hairy stems, large, frilly leaves, and splendid pink, white, or lilac flowers. When the flowers die, they leave behind oval seed pods, which are dried and then split to release the tiny seeds.

APPEARANCE AND TASTE

The tiny seeds, which are not narcotic when ripe, are usually slate-blue or camel-brown; there is also a beige variety from India. They have a crunchy texture and a mild, nutty flavor, which is enhanced when they are roasted.

BUYING AND STORING

The seeds are always sold whole. Like other spices, they can be ground at home. They store well in airtight containers kept in a cool, dry place.

CULINARY USES

The seeds and leaves of the opium poppy are edible. In the Middle East, the seeds are occasionally pressed to extract a pleasantly flavored oil, or are ground with the oil and used as a paste in some dishes. Usually, though, they are used whole, sprinkled liberally over breads and crackers, and added to pickles, salads, or egg dishes for a delightful crunch. In Jewish communities poppy seeds are sprinkled over the braided egg dough *Hallah*, the Sabbath and holiday bread, as the seeds represent the manna that fell from heaven. Also in Jewish communities, poppy seeds are added to the cakes and cookie doughs made for the festival of Purim. In Egypt and other parts of North Africa, the sweet couscous dishes, which the Jews serve at Hanukkah, sometimes contain poppy seeds. Believed to give strength, poppy seeds are occasionally added to honey doughs and syrups in Egypt and Yemen, and the roasted seeds are ground into some spice mixtures, particularly in Armenian communities.

Poppy seedheads

Poppy seed cakes, cookies, and pastries are specialties of the Jewish festival Purim, a day of jubilation commemorating Queen Esther, a Jewess who was married to a Persian king, and her outwitting of the Persian vizier Haman, who had decreed all Jews should be sentenced to death. As Queen Esther was said to have broken her three-day fast by eating poppy seeds after praying for the decree to be repealed, they have become symbolic. These little semolina cakes, which are popular in Egypt, Lebanon, and Jordan, and not just among the Jewish communities, can be made with almonds, coconut, and poppy seeds.

BASBOUSA
(SEMOLINA CAKES WITH POPPY SEEDS)

Serves 6–8
Preparation time approximately 30 minutes
Cooking time 35 minutes

½ cup clarified or ordinary butter
¾ cup sugar
2 tablespoons poppy seeds
1 teaspoon vanilla essence
2 eggs
2⅓ cups fine semolina
1 teaspoon baking powder
½ teaspoon baking soda
¾ cup strained yogurt
12 almonds, blanched and halved

For the syrup:
1 cup water
2 cups sugar
Juice of ½ lemon

Preheat the oven to 375°F.

First make the syrup. Bring the water and sugar to a boil, stirring all the time. Add the lemon juice and continue to boil for a few minutes, then reduce the heat and simmer for about 10 minutes, until the syrup coats the back of the spoon. Leave the syrup to cool.

In a bowl, cream the butter with the sugar until light and fluffy. Beat in the poppy seeds and vanilla essence, then beat in the eggs, one at a time. Sift the semolina with the baking powder and baking soda onto a plate, then fold it into the creamed butter with the yogurt. Tip the batter into a greased rectangular baking pan, roughly 8 × 12 inches, and spread it evenly. Arrange the almond halves in lines over the top, so that a nut will be in the center of each piece when the cake is cut.

Bake it in the oven for 30 minutes, or until a skewer inserted into the cake comes out clean. Quickly pour the cold syrup over the hot cake, cut it into lozenge shapes and return it to the oven for 4–5 minutes. Serve warm or at room temperature with eishta, the thick cream made from buffalo milk, or clotted cream.

The pickled foods of Iran are both exotic and exciting, full of fruits, spices, and seeds. These persimmon pickles are particularly delicious, reflecting some of the key flavors and textures of the Middle East.

TORSHI KHRAMLU
(PERSIMMON PICKLES)

Makes 2 big jars
Preparation time 30 minutes
Cooking time –

2 dried limes
3 teaspoons white mustard seeds
3 teaspoons roasted coriander seeds
3 teaspoons roasted poppy seeds
2 teaspoons black peppercorns
1 teaspoon cardamom seeds
4–6 cloves
1 teaspoon ground cinnamon
2 pounds ripe persimmons, cored and cut into wedges
8–10 cloves garlic, peeled
12 fresh or dried dates, pitted and halved
3¾ cups white wine vinegar
2 teaspoons salt
¼ cup sugar

Break the dried limes into pieces. Mix the spices together with the ground cinnamon.

Place some of the persimmon pieces in a sterilized jar with some of the lime, spices, garlic, and dates. Repeat in layers.

Put the vinegar, salt, and sugar in a pan and bring to a boil, stirring until the sugar is dissolved. Pour the hot vinegar over the persimmons, leave to cool, and then seal the jars. Store for a couple of weeks before eating.

Basbousa

PINE NUT

(SNUBAR) *Pinus pinea*

The use of pine nuts in the Middle East goes back to ancient times, when they were included in the cornucopias of fruit placed on statues that had been erected to symbolize the wealth of a city. The medieval Arabs used them liberally in savory dishes and confectionery, and the Ottomans acquired a taste for them in many of their lavish dishes. Today they are one of the most widely used nuts in Middle Eastern cooking, found concealed in almost every stuffing and scattered over numerous dishes.

HOW IT GROWS

The pine nut comes from the woody cones of the umbrella-shaped stone pine, *Pinus pinea*, which grows at low altitudes and in relatively poor soil around the Mediterranean coastline. Some cones open at maturity, others remain closed for several seasons. Just as the heat of a forest fire will open the cones like an exploding grenade, heat is used to prise them open commercially.

Roast pine nuts

APPEARANCE AND TASTE

Pine nuts are the small, edible seeds of a range of pine trees. Most of them are ivory in color and shaped like long teardrops. They are creamy in texture and have a sweet, pleasant taste of pine resin.

BUYING AND STORING

Good pine nuts are the second most expensive nut after macadamias. They are sold shelled and keep well in an airtight container for a month or two. If they are stored for too long, they go soft and rancid, owing to their high oil content.

CULINARY USES

In the Middle East, pine nuts are used in desserts, fruit compotes, jams, and sweetmeats such as the Turkish *un helvası*, prepared for births and weddings. They are frequently used in rice dishes, and there is practically no aromatic rice filling or ground lamb stuffing for poultry, vegetables, and pastries such as *sanbusak* that doesn't include pine nuts. They are also added to some meat, fish, and vegetable balls. Lightly roasted, they are a popular finish to many dishes, particularly sprinkled over syrupy pastries and cakes. Ground pine nuts are used in a very smooth, sumptuous version of the popular *tarator* (p 209) sauce served with fish and shellfish, particularly in Turkey, Lebanon, Syria, and Egypt.

Helva or *halva* made at home is quite different from the hard, manufactured blocks made with sesame seeds. It should be quite light and soft, able to be eaten with a fork. This recipe is for a popular Turkish *helva*, served at happy events such as a wedding or the birth of a child.

UN HELVASI
(FESTIVE HELVA WITH PINE NUTS)

Serves 8
Preparation time –
Cooking time approximately 50 minutes

¾ cup butter
1½ cups all-purpose flour, sifted
1 tablespoon sunflower oil
⅓ cup pine nuts
2½ cups milk
1 cup sugar
⅔ cup) water
Confectioners' sugar for sprinkling

Melt the butter in a large, heavy-based pan. Stir in the flour to form a thick roux and cook it for a few minutes, until it begins to change color.

Stir in the sunflower oil and continue to cook until the roux turns camel-brown and comes away from the sides of the pan. Then add the pine nuts and cool until they turn golden.

At the same time, keeping an eye on the roux, heat the milk and sugar in another saucepan and bring to a boil, stirring all the time. Then reduce the heat and simmer for about 10 minutes, until the syrup coats the back of the spoon.

For the next stage, which requires some fast work, use oven gloves to protect your hands against the steam. Quickly pour the water into the roux and stir madly, then pour in the hot milk syrup and stir equally madly, pressing the doughy balls against the side of the pan until the mixture binds together in a thick, gooey paste. Punch the paste with the wooden spoon and flip it against the sides of the pan, cooking it until the pine nuts begin to drop out of the mixture, which should have become soft and spongy.

Reduce the heat to very, very low and cover the pan with a clean dishtowel, followed by the lid. Make sure you lift the hanging flaps of dishtowel up over the lid to prevent them from catching fire. Leave the mixture to steam for about 20 minutes, then turn off the heat and leave the mixture to cool.

Serve the *helva* at room temperature, scooping it out in thin layers and sprinkling it with confectioners' sugar.

Extolled in poems recited at the courts of Abassid caliphs in tenth-century Baghdad, these savory pastries are particularly popular in Egypt, Lebanon, Jordan, and Syria. The Turks make a variety of similar pastries, called *börek*, and the Jews make little filled pies, called *pasteles*, with the same dough. Generally, the fillings are much the same—the traditional ground lamb or beef filling, called *tatbila*, with cinnamon and pine nuts, or white cheese with mint and dill, spinach with cheese or nuts, and a Jewish eggplant and tomato filling called *khandrajo*. Traditional *sanbusak* are shaped like half-moons and sprinkled with sesame seeds.

SANBUSAK
(SAVORY PASTRIES FILLED WITH GROUND MEAT AND PINE NUTS)

Serves 6 (makes roughly
   30 pastries)
Preparation time roughly
   45 minutes
Cooking time 40 minutes

For the filling:
1 onion, finely chopped
1 tablespoon clarified or ordinary
   butter, or olive oil
2 cups finely ground lamb or beef
2–3 tablespoons pine nuts
1 teaspoon ground cinnamon
½ teaspoon ground allspice
Salt and freshly ground black
   pepper

For the dough:
½ cup sunflower oil
½ cup melted clarified or ordinary
   butter
½ cup warm water
1 teaspoon salt
4 cups all-purpose flour

For the top:
1–2 eggs, beaten
2–3 tablespoons sesame seeds

Preheat the oven to 350°F.

To make the filling, soften the onion in the butter and stir in the meat. Cook for a few minutes, until the meat changes color, then stir in the pine nuts. Cook for another 1–2 minutes, until the nuts begin to color, then stir in the spices and season. Sprinkle 4–5 tablespoons of water over the meat, cook it for a few minutes more, then put it aside.

Sanbusak

Now make the dough. In a large bowl, mix the oil and melted butter with the warm water and salt. Sift the flour and add it gradually to the bowl, using a knife to mix it until it is stiff enough to use your hands. Form the dough into a soft, oily ball, adding a little extra flour if necessary. Take a walnut-size lump of dough, roll it into a ball, and flatten it between the palms of your hands. Place it on a floured surface and repeat with the rest of the dough.

Put a heaping teaspoonful of the filling in the middle of one half of each circle, then fold over the other half to make a half-moon shape. Pinch the edges together to seal them and place them on a greased baking sheet. Brush the surface with the beaten egg and sprinkle lightly with sesame seeds, then pop them into the oven for 35–40 minutes, until they are pale golden. The pastries can be served hot or cold, but they are best straight out of the oven.

PISTACHIO

(FUSTUK HALIBI) *Pistacia vera*

Whole roast pistachios

CULINARY USES

The small tree *Pistacia vera* is native to parts of western Asia and the Levant, particularly in the area between Turkey and Afghanistan, and in Lebanon and Syria, where the highly prized nut has been eaten since about 7000 BC. The name pistachio comes from *pesteh*, the Persian word for the nut. The genus *Pistacia* includes trees producing an edible resin (mastic).

The Romans introduced pistachio trees into Europe in the first century AD. Of all the culinary cultures in the Middle East, it is the Turkish and Iranian that make the most of pistachios. There are stores dedicated to displaying and selling them—in or out of their shells, packed in boxes, embedded in toffee or *lokum*, wrapped in cellophane, or tied up with ribbons. When they are freshly roasted and still warm, they are quite irresistible.

Slivered pistachios

As a snack, pistachios are roasted and salted. In Iran they are sometimes roasted in lemon juice to bring out their flavor. Ground pistachios are used to make a sweetmeat like marzipan and as the basis for a delectable creamy, green ice cream. They are also sprinkled over a variety of cookies and syrupy pastries for color. Chopped pistachios appear in a variety of sweet dishes, such as the grain-based *belila* (p126), given to nursing mothers and eaten to celebrate a baby's first tooth, and the wobbly, blancmange-style *balouza* and its syrupy version, *balta*. They are used in the Egyptian dessert *om Ali* (p133), in the Arab pancakes *ataif*, and in a number of rice dishes throughout the Middle East. Along with almonds and walnuts, they figure in the rice stuffing for *qouzi mahshi*, an impressive Saudi Arabian specialty of a whole roast kid served on a tray surrounded by mountains of rice.

During the Ottoman period, pistachios were incorporated into specific syrupy pastries such as *kadaif*, a shredded pastry bathed in syrup and filled with pistachio nuts; *şöbiyet*, the diamond-shaped pastries; and *bülbül yuvası*, meaning nightingale's nests; and they were packed into the paper-thin rolls called *dürüm*. In Turkey they are used in a highly prized *helva*, embedded in varieties of Turkish Delight, and concealed in *fistikli kabobi*, a ground meat kabob, rolled like a sausage and filled with whole pistachios. In Iran, they are pounded with fresh basil to make a paste for the noodles, *rishta*, and ground and added to an exotic version of the spice mixture advieh (p168).

HOW IT GROWS

Remarkably, the pistachio tree grows in arid areas where no other plants, apart from shrubs, survive. Generally, the tree produces a good crop in alternate years. The small, dry fruits of the tree look like olives and grow in clusters. Inside the pit of the fruit is the kernel, which is the nut that we eat. When the fruit is ripe, the shell of the kernel opens at one end, which the Iranians call *khandan* (laughing).

APPEARANCE AND TASTE

The skin of the fruit is soft and pinky-red, enveloping the hard, beige shell. Inside, the kernel is green all the way through and has a distinctive taste. Some are yellowy green with a hint of red, others are almost cream-colored, but the most highly prized are dark green. Plain pistachios are delicious, but when they have been roasted, their flavor is quite exquisite.

BUYING AND STORING

Pistachios, like pine nuts, are expensive. They are sold both in and out of their shells. Generally, if they are kept in an airtight container, the nuts in their shells will store well, but if they have already been shelled and stored badly, they tend to get soft and chewy. Ground pistachios don't keep well. They lose their flavor and begin to look dull.

Shelled roast pistachios

taif is a medieval dish of pancakes dipped in syrup, sprinkled with pistachios, and eaten with thick, clotted cream, *ishta*. In the tenth century a poem written about the dish was recited at a lavish banquet in honor of the Caliph Mustakfi of Baghdad, who was particularly fond of *ataif*. It is also a dish served at festivals and weddings, and to break the fast of Ramadan. Nowadays, people often buy ready-made pancakes from the baker's and fill them with nuts before dipping them in syrup. The following recipe is based on the medieval recipe.

ATAIF
(ARAB PANCAKES DIPPED IN SYRUP)

Serves 4–6 (roughly 16 pancakes)
Preparation time 1¼ hours
Cooking time 3–4 minutes for
  each pancake

1 cake compressed fresh yeast, or
  1 teaspoon active dry yeast
1 teaspoon sugar
1 cup + 2 tablespoons lukewarm
  water
2 cups all-purpose flour
Sunflower oil

For the syrup:
2 cups sugar
1¼ cups water
Juice of ½ lemon
1–2 tablespoons orange-flower
  water

To serve:
2–3 handfuls pistachios, chopped
Clotted cream

Dissolve the yeast with the sugar in a little of the lukewarm water and leave it to froth.

Sift the flour into a bowl and make a well in the middle. Pour the yeast into the well, along with the remaining water, and beat it all together to form a smooth batter. Cover the bowl

with a dishtowel and leave it in a warm place for about 1 hour, until the batter rises a little and becomes bubbly and elastic.

To make the syrup, bring the sugar and water to a boil in a pan, stirring all the time. Stir in the lemon juice, reduce the heat, and simmer for 10–15 minutes, until it coats the back of the spoon. Add the orange-flower water and simmer for a further 5 minutes. Leave the syrup to cool, then chill in the refrigerator.

When the batter is ready, heat a heavy-based skillet and, using a piece of paper towel, rub it lightly with a little sunflower oil. Pour ½ cup of batter into the hot pan, tilting it slightly to spread it a little—the pancake should be quite fat and roundish.

Reduce the heat a little and fry the pancake for 1–2 minutes, until it begins to bubble and lifts off the base of the pan, then flip it over and fry the other side.

Dip each hot pancake into the cold syrup, spread or serve with cream, and sprinkle with the chopped pistachios.

These delicious little stuffed cookies are called *ma'amoul* by the Arabs and *menena* by the Jews. Christians regard them as an Easter specialty and Muslims eat them during Ramadan. Usually they are filled with walnuts or pistachios, or with a paste made of softened dates. The pistachio-filled *ma'amoul* are considered the most desirable.

MA'AMOUL
(COOKIES STUFFED WITH PISTACHIOS)

Makes roughly 20 cookies
Preparation time 30–40 minutes
Cooking time 25 minutes

2 cups all-purpose flour
½ cup butter
1 tablespoon sugar
1 tablespoon orange flower or
  rose water
Roughly 1 tablespoon milk
Confectioners' sugar for dusting

For the filling:
1 cup finely chopped pistachios
2 tablespoons sugar
1 tablespoon orange-flower or
  rose water

Preheat the oven to 325°F.

Mix together the ingredients for the filling and put aside. Sift the flour into a bowl and rub in the butter until the mixture looks like fine bread crumbs. Stir in the sugar and the orange-flower or rose water, then bind with enough milk to form a soft, malleable dough.

Ataif

Take a walnut-size lump of dough in your fingers and shape it into a little pot with thin sides. Fill the pot with the chopped nuts to about three-quarters full, then pinch the top edge together to close the opening and form a ball. Flatten the ball slightly in the palm of your hand and place it on a baking sheet with the smooth side on top.

Repeat with the rest of the dough. Prick the tops with a fork to make a pattern and bake for about 25 minutes. They should come out of the oven soft and pale, not brown.

Leave them on the baking sheet to cool until firm, then transfer them to a wire rack or plate, and dust with confectioners' sugar before serving.

Whole blanched almonds

ALMOND

(LOZ) *Prunus amygdalus*

Almond trees have grown along the Mediterranean and in Central Asia for thousands of years. The oldest mention of their cultivation is in the Bible (Numbers 17:8)—Aaron's miraculous rod is made of almond wood. The ancient Greeks cultivated almonds and the Romans regarded them as a Greek nut. They played an important role in early Arabic cooking, not least for the milk that was extracted from them and used in desserts and drinks. The fruit of the almond trees are eaten fresh and dried. Immature almonds are eaten along with their velvety green husks before the shells harden. Often sold by street peddlers as a snack, they are dipped in salt and then popped whole into the mouth. There are old recipes for meat stews using these green almonds, but nowadays the mature, dried almonds are used instead.

HOW IT GROWS

The almond tree fruits only in temperate climates. It doesn't like frost or tropical humidity, so it grows only in western Asia and around the Mediterranean. Although it belongs to the same genus as the apricot and cherry tree, its leathery fruit is quite different: It can be eaten immature and it has a large pit and kernel.

APPEARANCE AND TASTE

Knocked off the trees in their hard, pockmarked, beige shells, whole almonds are oval-shaped, slightly swollen and about 1 inch long. Their ridged, cinnamon-colored skins are very thin and can easily be removed by soaking the nuts in water. After blanching in this way, a pearly white nut with a delicate aroma, a creamy texture, and sweet taste remains. Blanched almonds can be flaked or ground to a coarse powder for different recipes. The immature green almonds, which are eaten whole, have a crunchy texture with a slightly astringent, watery nut inside. As you might imagine, they taste like young shoots, but the salt lifts and sweetens them.

BUYING AND STORING

Almonds are best bought in their shells or skins, as they keep fresh longer that way. You can then blanch them yourself, which gives you a softer, creamier nut—the blanched ones you buy have usually dried out and can be quite brittle. The same applies to the bought flaked and ground almonds, which have usually lost a lot of their delicate flavor and moisture from sitting. Almonds in their skins, flaked, chopped, and ground, are available in most supermarkets and whole-food stores, but ready-blanched almonds are more difficult to find. As with all nuts, almonds should be stored in an airtight container in a cool, dry place, where they will keep for about eight months.

CULINARY USES

Blanched almonds are often eaten plain or toasted as a nibble. To blanch, place the shelled almonds in a bowl and pour boiling water over them. Leave them to soak for about five minutes, until the skins loosen. Then drain and refresh them under running cold water and rub the skins off between your fingertips—some may be more stubborn than others. To toast, pat the blanched nuts dry, place them on a baking sheet and put them in a hot oven (400°F) for about ten minutes, until they are crisp and lightly browned, then toss them in salt and eat as a snack. Or roast them in a hot, heavy-based pan until they turn brown and glisten, giving off a lovely nutty aroma.

Blanched and flaked almonds are used in rice dishes; meat and poultry stews; vegetable and fruit stuffings; fruit compotes, such as *khoshaf*; cookies, such as the almond bracelets *kahk bi loz* (p163); and candy. Along with walnuts and pistachios, they are one of the nuts popular in the sweet, syrupy pastries, particularly in the Turkish specialty *sütlü nüriye*, a melt-in-the-mouth pastry filled with shaved almonds and

Assorted dried fruit and nuts

bathed in a milk syrup. Whole blanched almonds are also popular with roast chicken and duck, such as the classic Middle Eastern roast duck with honey and almonds. Blanched almonds are coated in sugar for festivals, births, circumcisions, and other feasts and ceremonies. Ground almonds are used in cookies , candies, and desserts, particularly *keşkul*, the famous almond milk pudding from the Ottoman palace kitchens. They are pounded and kneaded with sugar to form the paste we call marzipan, the basis of the delightful dusted almond balls, *orass bi loz*, which are colored yellow with saffron in Iraq. Freshly ground almonds are bound with olive oil, lemon juice, and garlic to make *tarator* (p209), a sauce for fish, seafood, and chicken. They are also tied up in cheesecloth and poached in water to extract their natural creamy milk, which is then used to make a delicate syrup that is diluted and served as a cool, refreshing drink.

Khoshaf

Syrupy fruit compotes are very popular in the Middle East. *Khoshaf* (*hoşaf* in Turkish) is the classic combination of dried fruit and nuts, served as a winter dessert and at ceremonial feasts.

KHOSHAF
(DRIED FRUIT AND NUT COMPOTE)

Serves 8
Preparation time 5 minutes + 48 hours' soaking time
Cooking time –

2⅔ cups dried apricots
1⅓ cups prunes
⅔ cup golden raisins
¾ cup blanched almonds
⅓ cup pine nuts
1 cup sugar (less if you prefer)
2 tablespoons rose water
1 tablespoon orange-flower water

Put the dried fruit and nuts into a large bowl and cover with water. Add the sugar, rose water, and orange-flower water, and gently stir it all together.

Cover the bowl and let the fruit and nuts soak for 48 hours. During that time the water and sugar will form a golden syrup with the juices of the fruit.

Serve chilled.

The name of this recipe probably originated in Persia, where the beggars, *fuqara*, who regarded themselves as the "paupers of God," went from house to house begging for food to be placed in the oval bowl, the *keshkul*, which was suspended on a chain from their shoulders. Hence, this delicately flavored dessert (*keshkul* in Arabic, *keşkul* in Turkish), which was a favorite of the Ottomans, is always served in individual bowls, sprinkled with ground nuts or grated coconut to symbolize the *keshkul* being filled.

KEŞKUL
(ALMOND CREAM)

Serves 4
Preparation time 10 minutes (+ 20 minutes blanching and peeling almonds)
Cooking time 35 minutes

¾ cup blanched almonds
2½ cups milk
5 teaspoons rice flour
½ cup sugar
1–2 tablespoons finely ground pistachios or coconut

With a mortar and pestle, pound the almonds to a smooth paste and blend with a little of the milk. In a small bowl, slake the rice flour with a little milk, then pour the rest of the milk into a saucepan. Add the sugar and bring the milk to a boil, stirring all the time.

Stir a little of the hot milk into the rice flour, then add the rice flour to the pan. Keep stirring the milk and add the almond paste.

Reduce the heat and let the mixture simmer for about 25 minutes, stirring from time to time, until it thickens. Pour the mixture into individual bowls and leave to cool.

Serve chilled with finely ground pistachios or coconut on top.

SESAME SEED

(SIMSIM) *Sesamum indicum*

Light tahini

Thought to have originated in India or China, sesame was one of the first oil-yielding plants to be cultivated in Egypt and the Near East. Often mentioned in the works of classical writers, the seeds have been crushed to a paste and used in confectionery and spice mixtures since medieval times. When sugar cane was introduced to the Arabs in the early Middle Ages, the Jews played a leading role in the ensuing sugar industry, acquiring recognition for their good cooking and confectionery, which often used sesame seeds and sesame oil. As Jews are restricted to vegetable oils in their cooking, they rely on olive oil and the pungent sesame oil for flavor. In nineteenth-century Egypt and Iraq, a Jewish house was said to be detectable from miles away, because of the strong-smelling sesame oil, *siraj*.

BUYING AND STORING

The seeds are best bought whole and then roasted when needed. They store well in an airtight container, away from direct sunlight. Tahini comes in light and dark varieties, smooth and coarse. The darker, coarser version is made from roast sesame seeds and the husks, and there are some excellent organic brands available. Sesame oil is available in Middle Eastern, Asian, and Chinese stores, as well as supermarkets and whole-food stores. It needs to be stored away from the light.

CULINARY USES

Roasted seeds are used in a variety of spice mixes and blends, such as *zaatar* (p198) and *dukkah* (p163). They are often sprinkled over rice and meat dishes for a bit of crunch and nutty flavor. Similarly, they are sprinkled liberally over savory pastries and breads such as *fatayer bi semsem*, sweet sesame rolls, and *semit*, the ubiquitous bread rings—sold on every street—which would be naked without their sesame seeds. They are used in confectionery, such as the popular *simsimiyya*, made with sesame seeds, almonds, honey, and cinnamon. In savory dishes, the seeds are never a principal ingredient or flavoring, but tahini often is. The light tahini, which is cream-colored and smooth in texture, is regarded as superior and is ideal for a number of *mezze* dishes, like *baba ghanoush* (p82) and hummus, whereas the coarser, darker variety, which includes the husks, is used for the delicious mixture *tahin*

HOW IT GROWS

Sesame is an upright annual herb with deeply veined, oval leaves and white or pink flowers, which form small sausage-shaped pods that contain the seeds. The seeds are harvested while they are still immature and green, as the ripened seeds have a tendency to burst out of the pods and scatter, which may be where the command, "Open, sesame" in *Ali Baba and the Forty Thieves* comes from.

APPEARANCE AND TASTE

The tiny seeds are almost flat and teardrop-shaped, varying from pearl-colored to brown and black. The black seeds hold more flavor, but the lighter-colored seeds are more common in the Middle East. They have a crunchy texture and a mild nutty flavor, which is enhanced when they are roasted. Although tiny, the seed is rich, containing 50 percent oil, which is extracted by crushing it.

MANUFACTURING

Sesame seeds are crushed to make a nutty cooking oil that is high in polyunsaturated fatty acids and keeps well. As a source of oil, the sesame plant has a low yield, even lower than the olive, so the oil is valued highly. The seeds are also ground into a thick oily paste called tahini or tahina (*tahin* in Turkish), from the Arabic word *tahana*, "to grind." To make tahini the seeds are soaked before they are crushed to loosen the bran from the kernels. They are then soaked again in salted water, which causes the bran to sink to the bottom and the kernels to float to the top. The kernels are then roasted and ground to extract the thick oily cream that we know as tahini.

Roast sesame seeds

Semit

bekmez, which is spread on bread. Tahini also features in the spicy pine-nut filling for the unusual Armenian dish *topik*, and it is used in some salad dressings and sauces. Both crushed sesame seeds and tahini are used to make blocks of *helva* (*halva*), which is made with sugar syrup and a variety of ingredients such as nuts, chocolate, and *bois de Panama*.

In Egypt, the Levant, and Turkey, these bread rings, liberally covered with toasted sesame seeds, are sold in the streets. The cry of *"semit, semit!"* (*simit* in Turkish) can be heard throughout the day as the street vendors walk around with baskets or shopping carts filled with the freshly baked rings, or carry long wooden poles onto which the rings are threaded. Standard breakfast or snack fare, these popular rings are easy to make at home.

SEMIT
(BREAD RINGS WITH SESAME SEEDS)

Makes 8 rings
Preparation time 40 minutes
   (+ approximately 2½ hours proving time)
Cooking time 25–30 minutes

1 cake compressed fresh yeast or
   1 teaspoon active dry yeast
½ teaspoon sugar
Roughly 1¼ cups lukewarm water
4 cups organic white bread flour
1 teaspoon salt
1 egg beaten with 2 tablespoons
   water
A shallow bowl full of sesame seeds

Preheat the oven to 400°F.

Cream the yeast with the sugar in a little of the lukewarm water, until it begins to froth. Sift the flour with the salt into a large bowl. Make a well in the center and pour in the yeast with the rest of the water and use your hands to draw in the flour from the sides.

Knead the mixture well until it forms a dough, then knead it on a lightly floured surface until it becomes smooth and elastic. Clean the bowl, add a drop of sunflower oil to the bottom, and roll the ball of dough in it. Cover the bowl with a damp dishtowel and leave the dough for 1–2 hours to prove and double in size.

Punch down the risen dough into an elastic ball. Divide the dough into 6–8 pieces (or more if you want smaller rings) and shape each piece into a ring, roughly 17 inches in diameter. Brush each ring with the beaten egg, dip it into the bowl of sesame seeds, then place it on an oiled baking sheet.

Cover again with a damp dishtowel and leave the rings in a warm place for about 30 minutes to double in size. Bake in the oven for 25–30 minutes, until the rings are golden-brown and sound hollow when tapped on the bottom.

Mixed with lemon juice, the sesame paste tahini makes a lovely dressing for salads and a tangy sauce for baked chicken or fish, as in this dish, found throughout the Middle East. Trout, sea bass, and red mullet work well, as do haddock filets.

Semit **seller**

TAJIN SAMAK BI TAHINA
(FISH BAKED IN TAHINI)

Serves 4–6
Preparation time 15 minutes
Cooking time approximately 30 minutes

1¼ cups light tahini
⅔ cup lemon juice
⅔ cup water
2 cloves garlic, crushed
1–2 tablespoons olive oil
2 onions, halved and sliced
1 teaspoon cumin seeds
1 whole fish, weighing roughly
   2¼ pounds, gutted and cleaned
Salt and freshly ground black
   pepper
A small bunch fresh flat-leaf
   parsley, finely chopped

Preheat oven to 325°F.

In a bowl, beat the tahini with the lemon juice and water to form a smooth, creamy sauce, then beat in the garlic and season to taste.

Heat the oil in a pan and fry the onions with the cumin seeds until they are golden brown.

Spread half of the onions in the base of a dish, add the fish, and cover with the remaining onions.

Pour the tahini sauce over the fish and bake in the oven for about 30 minutes, until the fish flakes easily. Serve hot, sprinkled with parsley.

FLAVORINGS

DILL

(SHIBIT) *Anethum graveolens*

The ancient Romans regarded dill as a symbol of vitality. The ancient Greeks used it as a cure for hiccups. And both the Romans and the Greeks are reputed to have drifted into peaceful slumber by wrapping fresh, aromatic dill leaves around their heads. The ancient Persians believed that "you are what you eat," which, similar to the yin and yang theory of ancient China, led to the consumption of "cold" foods to cool the blood and relieve fever, and "hot" foods to warm the blood and reduce melancholy or sickness. During the Ottoman period, this theory was also put into practice and dill, which was regarded as "warming," played an important role balancing the "cooling" vegetables such as marrows, zucchini, and fava beans.

Fresh dill

HOW IT GROWS

Indigenous to western Asia, dill belongs to the parsley family and is closely related to fennel. It is an annual herb that can grow up to 3 feet in height, with thin, feather-like leaves, crowned with clusters of tiny, yellow flowers and flat, oval fruits. When the fruits have ripened and turned yellow-brown, the seeds are extracted and dried.

APPEARANCE AND TASTE

Although the long, green, feathery fronds of fennel and dill look very similar, they taste quite different. Fennel has an anise flavor whereas dill is more akin to caraway. The flat, oval seeds are light brown with a warm aroma.

BUYING AND STORING

The fresh leaves should be bought on the stalk and kept in a plastic bag in the refrigerator or, like flowers, left to stand in a glass of water. They don't last long and if left in plastic, they begin to turn a bit like pond weed. Dried dill leaves are available but they smell and taste like dried cut grass. The seeds store quite well in an airtight container in a cool, dry place.

MEDICINAL USES

Dill has been cultivated for its medicinal qualities for a long time. It is believed to lower cholesterol and to stimulate the production of breast milk in nursing mothers. An infusion of the seeds in water is used to cure hiccups, flatulence, and stomach complaints, and is often given to infants to soothe colic and induce a restful sleep.

CULINARY USES

Fresh dill is particularly popular in Turkey and Iran, where it is often combined with mint to balance cooling vegetables. It is the favored herb in the splendid Ottoman olive oil dishes, such as *zeytinyağlı enginar* (p 221), artichoke hearts in olive oil. Dill is nearly always used in fava bean dishes such as *fava*, a puree of fava beans, and *bâghâli polow*, an Iranian rice dish with fava beans. Dill is also used to flavor yogurt dips, cucumber and yogurt salads, cheese pastries such as *sigarı böreği*, and rice dishes. It is often used with fish,

Dill plant with flowers

particularly in dishes that are served cold. In Iraq it is combined with yogurt to flavor an Assyrian soup made with rice and vegetables. Both the dill fronds and the seeds are used in preserves and pickles.

During his reign of the Ottoman Empire, Mehmet the Conqueror filled the kitchens of the Topkapı Palace in Istanbul with chefs who specialized in just one thing, such as the *börekçi*, the maker of savory pastries. Even to this day, there are specialist pastry-makers throughout the Middle East, and the Turks excel at it. The variety of *börek* is immense. Some are fried and others are baked or steamed; different types of pastry dough are used, but perhaps the most common are the ones made with paper-thin sheets of *yufka* (known as *fila* in the rest of the Middle East). Filled with ground meat, spinach, or cheese and herbs, these pastries are particularly popular when rolled into the shape of a cigar, *sigarı böreği*. If kept covered with a damp distowel in the refrigerator, they can be made in advance and fried at the last minute. For this recipe, I have used *fila* (sold as phyllo) rather than any other pastry, as it is more readily available outside the Middle East. For the cheese, I have used feta, which works well as a substitute for the Turkish white cheese—the latter is a great deal creamier and comes in different grades of texture and saltiness, depending on the region it is from.

SİGARA BÖREĞİ
(CHEESE-FILLED PASTRY ROLLS)

Makes approximately 30
Preparation time 25–30 minutes
Cooking time 15–20 minutes

3 cups feta cheese
4 eggs
A large bunch of fresh dill, mint,
    and parsley, chopped
Roughly 8 sheets of phyllo pastry
Sunflower oil for frying

Mash the cheese with the eggs in a bowl and beat in the herbs. Cut the phyllo into long strips, approximately 3 inches wide.

Take one strip and spoon a little of the cheese onto the end nearest to you. Fold the corners over the filling and roll it up tightl, until you are almost at the other end. Dip the far end into a cup of water, then seal the roll.

As you prepare the rolls, keep them under a damp dishtowel so they don't dry out.

Heat enough sunflower oil for deep-frying in a shallow pan. Fry the rolls in batches, until they are golden brown. Drain them on paper towels and serve while they are still warm

Sigara böreği

In Iran there are two superb rice dishes flavored with dill. One, *baghali polow*, consists of the classic combination of fava beans and dill. The other, *sheveed polow*, is simply a dish of plain rice flavored with dill, which is often served with preserved, salted fish from the Caspian Sea. The same combination is enjoyed along the Black Sea coast of Turkey, where the mackerel and anchovies are hung up to dry for dishes such as this.

SHEVEED POLOW
(RICE WITH DILL)

Serves 4–6
Preparation time approximately
    2 hours' soaking
Cooking time 50 minutes

2½ cups long-grain rice, well
    washed and drained
1–2 teaspoons salt
A big bunch of fresh dill, chopped
¼ cup butter, cut into pieces

Put the rice into a pan with the salt and enough water to just cover it, then leave it to soak for about 2 hours.

Bring the water to a boil and stir in the dill. Reduce the heat and simmer for about 10 minutes, until the water has been absorbed.

Scatter the pieces of butter over the rice, then wrap a clean dishtowel around the lid and place it over the pan.

Reduce the heat to very, very low and leave the rice to steam for about 40 minutes. Turn off the heat and let the rice stand for 5 minutes before opening the lid. Slide a knife down the sides of the rice to ease it away from the edges, then tip it upside down onto a serving plate. Serve immediately with preserved or fresh fish.

RED PEPPER

(FILFIL AHMAR HALABI) *Capsicum frutescens*

Oiled red pepper

Middle Eastern red pepper is difficult to define. Is it a chili or not? During the sixteenth century sweet and chili peppers came from the New World to Constantinople, from where they spread throughout the regions of the Ottoman Empire. Among them were long red peppers whose pungent flavors were instantly incorporated into the cooking of the empire, not least in Hungary, where the first peppers were called "Turkish peppers," the most likely ancestors of Hungarian paprika. Middle Eastern red peppers do come from the same family as the chili, and some would regard them as such, but in the Middle East the dried, ground spice is ranked in a class of its own, varying in strength from region to region, getting hotter the further south you go. It is such a popular spice that strings of dried red peppers hang from doorways and balconies, like bright decorations, and large sacks of red pepper flakes and powder are found in every market.

BUYING AND STORING

Whole dried red peppers and the flaked or ground spice are available in Middle Eastern stores, but make sure they are deep red. If they have begun to turn brown, they will taste stale. The whole peppers can hang in your kitchen for almost a year, but the flaked and ground spice must be stored in an airtight container and, even so, will begin to lose their intensity after six months.

HOW IT GROWS

Like all chilies, the red pepper is a perennial with sharp-tasting fruits. It can be cultivated in most regions of the Middle East but the bulk of it is grown in Gaziantep, Maraş and Urfa in southern Turkey, and in Aleppo in northern Syria, hence its other names: Antep (from Gaziantep) and Aleppo pepper.

Red peppers drying

APPEARANCE AND TASTE

The fresh peppers are long, thin, and horn-shaped, similar in appearance to the Guajillo chilies of Mexico. They are rarely eaten fresh, but are hung up on strings to dry before being crushed or ground and used as a spice. Hotter than paprika and milder than cayenne, the spice is surprisingly rich and fruity. The best-quality red pepper is deep red and flaked, and is rubbed with oil so that it keeps fresh and imparts its flavor. The flakes can also be roasted until dark, almost black, and oiled for a rich, nutty flavor that packs a punch.

CULINARY USES

Middle Eastern red pepper has many uses, but the one that sets it apart from other chilies is its liberal use as a condiment. In Syria and Turkey, bowls of it are often put on the table, alongside dried thyme, or oregano, and *sumac*, ready to be sprinkled over *mezze* dips, yogurt dishes, kabobs, grilled fish, and salads. It is added to rice dishes, soups, stews, and egg dishes, and it is often used to fire up meatballs and grilled meats such as *Adana kabobı*. In Turkey it is often combined with melted butter to drizzle over yogurt and meat dishes.

Ajvar

This is one of the most popular ways of cooking liver in the Middle East. The liver of goats, sheep, lambs, and chickens can all be cooked in the same way. The depth of fieriness and the addition of other spices may vary from region to region, but the red pepper remains a constant.

KIBDAH MAKLIYA
(LAMB'S LIVER SAUTÉED WITH RED PEPPER)

Serves 4
Preparation time 15 minutes
Cooking time 4–5 minutes

2–3 tablespoons olive oil
2 cloves garlic, chopped
1 teaspoon cumin seeds
2–3 tablespoons flour
1 pound lamb's liver, cut into thin strips, with cleaned and skinned
2 teaspoons Middle Eastern red pepper
Salt
1 lemon, cut into quarters

Heat the oil in a heavy-based skillet and stir in the garlic and cumin seeds.

Tip the flour onto a plate and quickly toss the liver in it so that it is lightly coated. Add it to the pan and sauté lightly, until just cooked.

Sprinkle with the red pepper and season with salt, then serve immediately with lemon to squeeze over it.

A dish of Arab origin, *ajvar* is popular in Syria and Iraq, and in southeastern Turkey (where it is called *acvar*). It is served warm with yogurt or lemon and lots of fresh bread.

AJVAR
(WARM GRILLED PEPPER AND EGGPLANT SALAD)

Serves 3–4
Preparation time 25–30 minutes
Cooking time 5 minutes

1 red bell pepper
1 fat eggplant
1 red onion, roughly chopped
2 cloves garlic, roughly chopped
A scant teaspoon sugar
2–3 tablespoons olive oil
1–2 teaspoons Middle Eastern red pepper
Juice of 1–2 lemons
1–2 teaspoons vinegar
1 bunch of fresh flat-leaf parsley, roughly chopped
Salt and freshly ground black pepper

Place the bell pepper and eggplant directly on a gas flame or over a charcoal grill and burn the skin all over. Pop them into a plastic bag to sweat for a few minutes and then hold them under running cold water while you remove the burned skin.

Put the pepper onto a board, cut it in half, discard the stalk, seeds, and pith, and chop it to a puree. Discard the stalk of the eggplant and chop the vegetable to a puree.

In a flat pan, sauté the onion and garlic with a little sugar in the olive oil until they just begin to color. Stir in the red pepper and add the pureed bell pepper and eggplant.

Beat in the lemon juice and vinegar, stir in most of the parsley, and season to taste. Serve warm with the rest of the parsley and fresh flat bread.

CHILI

(FILFIL HAR) *Capsicum frutescens*

Green chilies

Chilies are found in dishes all over the world, yet they are relatively new to most continents. First cultivated in Mexico as early as 7000 BC, chilies didn't reach Europe until Columbus took them back to Spain at the end of the fifteenth century. The Portuguese then took them to India, Asia, and Africa,. The Ottomans, who, with Spain, dominated the political stage in the sixteenth century, spread them around their vast empire. There are many different types of chili, and only the very hot varieties are covered in this section.

HOW IT GROWS

All chilies fall into the *Capsicum* genus, which belongs to the *Solanaceae* family that includes the tomato and eggplant. The two major species are *Capsicum annum*, which is an annual bush bearing larger, milder-tasting fruit, and *Capsicum frutescens*, which is a taller perennial with smaller, sharper, often fiery-tasting fruit. Generally, the unripe fruits are green and the mature fruits are red. The mature fruits are usually dried in the sun.

APPEARANCE AND TASTE

In the Middle East, the hot chilies can be either red or green, long or short, but they are always thin and fiery. They should not be confused with the milder, fruity flavored Middle Eastern red pepper (p152), which, although a member of the chili family, is often not regarded as such and is mainly used in its dried form. All chilies contain capsaicin their seeds, ribs, and skin, which makes them hot and mouth-tingling. Some are perfumed, sweet, and fiery, others burn like hell-fire.

Right: Hot green chilies, cucumbers, and tomatoes, Turkey

Left: Chili powder

BUYING AND STORING

When buying fresh chilies, look for firm, shiny ones. Dried chilies can be bought whole and store well in airtight containers. Crushed and ground dried chilies lose their flavor after a few months.

CULINARY USES

Generally, the young, green chilies are used fresh. They are chopped or sliced into stews and a few salads—such as *çingene pilavı*, a Turkish gypsy salad of onions, peppers, chilies, grated white cheese, and herbs—or fried and grilled whole in a variety of kabobs. The two Arab dishes *samak harra* and *battata harra* are well known for their chili content. The small, fiery green chilies are pickled in vinegar and salt. Red chilies are used fresh too, but more often they are dried and ground to intensify the flavor and then used in hot pastes, marinades, and winter stews. In Yemen, chilies are used to make *bisbas*, a fiery paste made with chilies, garlic, and salt, similar to harissa, which is used in North Africa, Jordan, and its neighboring countries. Both *bisbas* and harissa are used to flavor soups and stews, and as a dip for bread; only a small amount is needed. Chilies have the ability to cool the body in hot weather and warm it in the winter. If you find them insufferably hot, don't try gulping water; the only things that will soothe your throat and tongue are milk and yogurt.

Chilies and çarliston peppers in the market

The spices used in this popular Arab dish vary in Syria, Egypt, and Lebanon, but the chilies are always there. Serve it with a salad or one of the many yogurt dishes to put out the fire.

BATTATA HARRA
(HOT SPICY POTATOES)

Serves 4
Preparation time 20 minutes
Cooking time 20 minutes

4 tablespoons olive oil
2⅔ cups peeled and diced new potatoes
3 cloves garlic, crushed
2–3 hot chilies, chopped
1 teaspoon cumin seeds
Juice of ½ lemon
A small bunch of cilantro, chopped
Salt

Heat the olive oil in a heavy-based skillet and add the potatoes.

Fry until browned and crispy, then stir in the garlic, chilies, and cumin seeds.

Fry for 1–2 minutes longer, then season with salt, refresh with lemon juice, and sprinkle with the cilantro. Serve hot with grilled or roast meat, poultry, or fish.

Each region has its preferred chili paste or relish. In Turkey and Syria, the hot, dried red chili peppers are soaked and mashed to a paste, and sometimes they are roasted before being soaked to give them a rich flavor. In Yemen, the hot paste *bisbas* is made with fresh or dried chilies that are ground to a puree with garlic and salt. Similar pastes are *shatta*, used in other parts of the Middle East, and the North African relish harissa. Stored in the refrigerator, harissa keeps for a long time if it is always covered with a layer of oil. It is excellent added to stews, spread on bread, or stirred into yogurt to make a dip.

HARISSA
(CHILI RELISH)

Makes 1 medium-sized jar
Preparation time 10–15 minutes
   (+ 1 hour for soaking)
Cooking time —

8 ounces (16 cups) dried red chili peppers, soaked in water for 1 hour
1 whole head of garlic, peeled
1 tablespoon coriander seeds, ground
1 tablespoon dried mint
1 tablespoon salt
A small bunch of fresh cilantro leaves
A little olive oil

Drain the chili peppers, cut off the stalks, and remove the seeds.

Fresh chilies

Using a mortar and pestle, pound the chilies to a paste with all the other ingredients (or whiz them in a blender), adding enough olive oil to make a thick paste.

Spoon the relish into a jar and keep it in the refrigerator.

Battata harra

Hawayij

CARAWAY

(KARAWIYA) *Carum carvi*

Originally from the temperate areas of Asia, including the regions now known as Iran and Turkey, caraway has been used for culinary and medicinal purposes for over 5,000 years. Believing the aroma kept lovers from straying, the ancient Egyptians, Greeks, and Romans used caraway to make love potions. The name comes from the ancient Arabic *karawiya*, which is still the word used for it in the Arab world today.

HOW IT GROWS

The biennial plant is cultivated for its seeds, which are the split halves of the dried fruits. It grows up to 2 feet in height and has light-green feathery leaves, which have a mild caraway flavor.

APPEARANCE AND TASTE

The dried seeds are dark brown with light brown, almost green, ridges. They are hard, sometimes bow-shaped, with pointed ends and are no more than ¼ inch long. They have a warm, sweet aroma and a slightly spicy, pungent taste.

BUYING AND STORING

Dried seeds and ground caraway are available in most supermarkets and Asian stores, but, as with most spices, it is best to buy the seeds and grind them yourself. Both the dried seeds and the ground spice should be stored in airtight containers in a cool, dark place.

MEDICINAL USES

Apart from its role in ancient love potions, caraway is believed to "spring-clean" the body. Chewed or infused, it is reputed to freshen the breath, aid digestion, relieve flatulence and colic, activate the kidneys, and reduce nausea.

CULINARY USES

Caraway is used mainly to flavor breads, buns, and crackers. The seeds are sometimes used with vegetables such as carrots, leeks and cabbages, and in vegetable stews and dishes. Caraway is included in many versions of the Iranian spice mixture *advieh* (p168), and it is one of the main ingredients in *hawayij*, a peppery spice mixture from Yemen. To make a small quantity of *hawayij* to add to soups and stews, just grind to a powder 6 teaspoons black peppercorns, 3 teaspoons caraway seeds, and 1 teaspoon cardamom seeds, and blend them with 2 teaspoons ground turmeric.

In Yemen, the stews are often quite fiery, either from chilies or from one of the many hot spice mixtures prepared in every home. The use of *hawayij* gives this stew an enjoyable kick. Traditionally, it would be served with plain rice or flat bread.

AKUW'A
(YEMENI OXTAIL STEW)

Serves 5–6
Preparation time 25 minutes
Cooking time 3½–4 hours

2 oxtails, cut into pieces
4–5 tomatoes, peeled and chopped
6 small onions, peeled and left whole
4–5 cloves garlic, peeled and left whole
2 teaspoons hawayij
Salt

Wash the oxtail pieces and put them into a large pot. Cover with cold water and bring to a slow simmer. Skim the top, and add the tomatoes, onions, and garlic.

Stir in the *hawayij*, season with salt, then cover the pan and simmer gently for about 3 hours, until the meat is so tender it is practically falling off the bone and the liquid has reduced.

Serve hot with plain rice or flat bread to mop up the sauce.

In Turkey, cooked vegetables are mashed to a puree and then beaten, or served, with yogurt to make the delectable *ezme* dishes for the *meze* table, such as the following carrot dish.

HAVUÇ EZMESİ
(CARROT puree WITH CARAWAY SEEDS AND YOGURT)

Serves 4
Preparation time 15 minutes (+ 15 minutes' steaming)
Cooking time –

4 large carrots, peeled and steamed until soft
2 tablespoons olive oil
Juice of ½ lemon
1 teaspoon caraway seeds
Heaping ¼ cup thick yogurt
2–3 cloves garlic, crushed
Salt and freshly ground black pepper
A small bunch of fresh mint or dill

In a bowl, mash the carrots with a fork and blend with the olive oil, lemon juice, and caraway seeds (or whiz them all together in a blender). Season to taste, then spoon the mixture onto a serving dish, leaving a well in the middle. Beat the garlic into the yogurt, season to taste, and spoon into the well. Sprinkle with the mint or dill.

Caraway seeds

Havuç ezmesi

CAROB

(KHARRUB) *Ceratonia siliqua*

Gold Souk, Saudi Arabia

Often referred to as locust beans, these pods, which are rich in sugar, have been used as a source of food since ancient times. In the Bible, the reference to John the Baptist surviving in the desert on locusts and honey may, in fact, refer to these nutritious beans rather than the insect. In some parts of the Middle East, Africa, and Asia, carob pods are used primarily as animal fodder, but in the eastern Mediterranean region they have been cultivated for culinary purposes since the ancient Greeks first prized the pods as a sweetmeat and used the seeds as a weight for gold. The word "carat" derives from the Greek *keration*, which means "little horn," and is the name given to the carob seed.

Carob pods

HOW IT GROWS

The large, leathery pods are the fruit of an ancient evergreen tree, *Ceratonia siliqua*, which is cultivated and grows wild in the eastern Mediterranean region. When the pods ripen, they become full of a sweet gum. They are picked and pressed to extract the sticky juice, *dibs kharrub*, which is used for culinary purposes.

APPEARANCE AND TASTE

The ripened pods are long, brown and leathery, containing a sticky, dark gum that has a distinctive fruity smell and tastes like caramel. The thick molasses extracted from the pods is almost black, like molasses. Broken carob pods, called kibble, are roasted and ground to produce a brown powder that resembles powdered chocolate.

BUYING AND STORING

As carob powder has a fat content of only 0.7 percent, compared to the 25–50 percent of chocolate, it is often sold as a chocolate substitute in the "health-food" stores of the West. Otherwise carob pods and powder are available in Middle Eastern stores. Since there is not a huge demand for carob, it is best to use the pods fairly quickly, as they may not be at their freshest. Carob powder stores in an airtight container for about six months, and the molasses, which is sold in jars, keeps well in a cool, dark place.

Jar of thick, fruity carob molasses

CULINARY USES

Generally the pods are chewed as a snack, the powder is used in cookies, and the molasses is used like honey on bread or in sweet pastries. Like most of the fruit molasses made from grapes, mulberries, dates, and pomegranates, carob molasses is sometimes used to give a fruity sweetness to stews, sweetmeats, and a few *mezze* dishes, such as *nazuktan*, made with smoked eggplant puree and crushed almonds. And like the grape and date molasses, it is delectable when bound with tahini, in equal quantities, to form a paste that can be spooned onto bread and eaten as a snack or for breakfast. The same paste can be used as a filling in some flat-bread doughs, which are then baked in the oven, or it can be pepped up with lemon and mint to make a Turkish savory dip, *tahin tarama*.

Tahini mixed with a fruit molasses, in equal proportions, is a very popular combination in Turkey, Syria, Lebanon, and Jordan. It works particularly well with grape, date, and carob molasses. The Turks take this delicious combination one step further and present it as a *meze* dip, mixed with lemon juice and mint.

TAHİN TARAMA
(TAHINI DIP WITH CAROB AND MINT)

Serves 3–4
Preparation time 5–10 minutes
Cooking time —

Heaping ¼ cup smooth tahini
3–4 tablespoons carob molasses
Juice of 1 lemon
½ tablespoon dried mint

Carob pods in a basket

In a bowl, combine the tahini with the carob molasses.

Beat in the lemon juice, followed by the mint, and adjust the flavor according to your taste— a little more lemon, a little more mint—it is completely up to you. (If the tahini you use is particularly thick, you might need to add a tiny bit of water to thin it down.)

Serve with bread to scoop it up.

The following *mezze* is another one of those dishes that pops up in different parts of the Middle East under different guises. The Arabs and the Turks can make anything with a grilled or baked eggplant, and this dish, which is found in southern Turkey, Syria, and Jordan, is just one of the fine examples.

NAZUKTAN
(EGGPLANT PUREE WITH ALMONDS AND CAROB SYRUP)

Serves 4
Preparation time 25–30 minutes
Cooking time —

2 eggplants
Juice of ½ lemon
2 tablespoons carob molasses
2–3 cloves garlic, crushed

1 teaspoon Middle Eastern red pepper (p152) or 1 mild red chili, chopped
3 tablespoons almonds, roasted and chopped
A small bunch of fresh mint, chopped
3 tablespoons thick creamy yogurt
Salt

Grill the eggplants over charcoal, or directly over a gas flame until they are soft. Slit them open, scoop out the inside, and put it into a bowl.

Using a fork to break up the eggplant, mix it with the lemon juice, carob molasses, and garlic.

Add the red pepper, chopped almonds, and mint, and bind with the yogurt. Season to taste and garnish with a few whole roast almonds and mint.

Tahin tarama

CINNAMON

(QIRFA) *Cinnamomum verum*

Cinnamon has long been used as a spice and flavoring. Arab traders supplied the ancient Greeks and Romans but never revealed their source. Instead, they made up fantastic stories about the dangers of collecting cinnamon: They had to enter valleys infested with poisonous snakes and the bark burst into flames under the sun. However, the Arabic writers of the twelfth to fifteenth centuries put an end to the secrecy, revealing the true source as Ceylon. This led to the Portuguese occupying Ceylon for its wild cinnamon at the beginning of the sixteenth century, followed by the Dutch in 1636, who inherited the monopoly in cinnamon and began its cultivation.

Cinnamon sticks

Cinamon bark

HOW IT GROWS

Cinnamon is the dried bark of an evergreen tree of the laurel family. It is indigenous to Sri Lanka, which is the largest producer. The tree grows to a height of 33 feet, but some cinnamon cultivators grow straight shoots in a bush form and harvest them when they are 5–6 feet high. To get the cinnamon we cook with, the outer bark is stripped off the tree and dried in chunks, while the inner bark is prised off in sections, scraped clean, cut into equal sizes, rolled into scrolls by hand, and then dried in the sun.

APPEARANCE AND TASTE

Cinnamon is sold as loose chunks of crude bark or as brittle cinnamon sticks, which look like delicate, tan-colored scrolls. It is also sold as quillings, which are like offcuts of the inner bark, and in powder form. The bark should smell of cinnamon. The warm, sweet aroma is intensified when it is ground.

BUYING AND STORING

Cinnamon sticks are easy to grind so, as with most spices, it is best to store them in an airtight container and grind them when you need them. Ready-ground cinnamon doesn't retain its fresh, warm, spicy aroma for long.

MEDICINAL USES

An infusion of cinnamon in hot water is drunk to relieve nausea and for stimulating the digestion. A few drops of cinnamon bark oil in hot water make a pleasant, spicy inhalation for head colds.

Ground cinnamon

CULINARY USES

In the Middle East, cinnamon is used to flavor cookies, sweetmeats, desserts, savory rice and meat dishes. It is often sprinkled on top of milk puddings, such as the Turkish chicken breast pudding, *tavuk göğsu* (p62), and on top of milky drinks, such as *salep* (p178), made from ground orchid root. It is the favored spice to combine with nuts, so it's used in the fillings of a number of syrupy pastries, such as baklava (p137) and *konafa* (p47). The Iranian *khoresht* is often spiced with cinnamon, and in Lebanon, Syria, and Turkey, cinnamon is one of the only spices, along with allspice, used to flavor meat, particularly lamb. It is the principal flavoring in *ma'mounia*, a sweet semolina porridge served for breakfast, and it is often the main spice, along with allspice, to be used in the dried fruit and rice stuffings for meat and poultry, and in the meat and rice stuffings for vegetables and fruit, such as *dolmeh sib* (p182) or *dolmeh beh*, the stuffed apples and quinces of Iran. Cinnamon sticks are used to flavor soups, stews, and some pickles, such as the Turkish sweet-and-sour pears, *armut turşusu*. Cinnamon is one of the main spices in the ubiquitous Arab spice mix *baharat* (p162), which also includes ground cloves, cumin, coriander, and paprika. It is also always combined with cardamom seeds in the Iranian spice mixture, *advieh* (p168).

Spiced fruit and vegetables are popular as a snack or as part of a *mezze* spread. Unlike pickles, they are not usually made from immature fruit with the intention of preserving it, but with ripened fruit to be eaten that day or week. This recipe comes from Bursa, which lies beneath the snow-capped peaks of Mount Olympus, surrounded by lush fruit orchards.

ARMUT TURŞUSU
(SWEET-AND-SOUR PEARS)

Serves 6
Preparation time 10 minutes
Cooking time 30 minutes

1¼ cups white wine or cider vinegar
½ cup water
½ cup honey
2 cinnamon sticks
6–8 allspice berries
A pinch of saffron threads
3 large fresh pears, peeled, cored, and cut in half vertically with the stalks left on
A handful of walnuts, blanched and skinned
A small bunch of fresh mint leaves

Put the vinegar, water, honey, cinnamon, allspice, and saffron into a big, heavy-based pan and bring it to a boil, stirring all the time until the honey has dissolved.

Reduce the heat, put in the pears and poach them gently for about 25 minutes, until they are tender. Remove the pears with a slotted spoon and place them on a dish.

Add the walnuts to the vinegar syrup and let it bubble for about 5 minutes to reduce and thicken. Spoon it over the pears and leave to cool.

Serve the pears with plenty of fresh mint leaves.

Armut turşusu

Rice dishes with chicken or lamb are popular throughout the Middle East. Rice dishes made with the livers are particularly favored, especially on festive occasions when a hen or sheep is slaughtered and all the parts are consumed. The livers of both can be used for the following dish, an Istanbul specialty, which is eaten on its own with yogurt or served with a plain kabob.

İÇ PİLAVI
(AROMATIC RICE WITH CHICKEN LIVERS AND PINE NUTS)

Serves 4–6
Preparation time 15 minutes
Cooking time 40 minutes

1–2 tablespoons clarified butter (ghee) or olive oil
1 onion, chopped
2–3 tablespoons pine nuts
2 tablespoons dried currants, soaked in water for 15 minutes and drained
1 teaspoon ground allspice
½ teaspoon ground cinnamon
2 cups long-grain rice, soaked in water for 15 minutes and drained
Roughly 3 cups chicken stock or water
1½ cups chicken livers, trimmed and cut into small pieces
A small bunch of fresh parsley and dill, finely chopped
A handful of roasted pine nuts
Salt and freshly ground black pepper

Melt the clarified butter in a heavy-based saucepan and stir in the onion and pine nuts. When they begin to brown, add the dried currants, then stir in the spices and rice.

Pour in the stock or water, season with salt and pepper, and bring the liquid to a boil. Turn down the heat and simmer gently for about 15 minutes.

Meanwhile, sauté the chicken livers in a little extra clarified butter.

When all the liquid has been absorbed by the rice, toss the chicken livers and herbs through it, then cover the pan with a clean dishtowel, followed by the lid. Remove it from the heat and leave it to steam for a further 15–20 minutes.

Tip it out onto a serving dish, using a fork to make sure it is well mixed, and garnish with a few roast pine nuts.

Ground coriander

CORIANDER

(KUZBARA) *Coriandrum sativum*

Baharat mix

The coriander plant was cultivated in ancient Egypt for medicinal and culinary purposes and the seeds were found in the tombs of the pharaohs. Used as a spice since classical times, the seeds were likened to the color of manna in the Bible. The fresh leaves, known as cilantro, are used widely in the Middle East by the Iranians, the Circassian communities, and in the Arab regions, where they are sometimes called "Arab parsley." It is also one of the bitter herbs eaten at the Jewish Passover.

HOW IT GROWS

Coriander, which is related to parsley, is an ancient annual herb from the carrot family. Native to southern Europe and the Middle East, this pretty plant can grow up to 2 feet in height, with a long, thin stem and lots of wide, floppy, scalloped leaves two-thirds of the way up. The upper leaves are small and thin, resembling sparrows' claws, leading up to the delicate, pinkish-white flowers at the top. The seeds are picked when ripe and then dried for use.

APPEARANCE AND TASTE

The whole coriander plant has a distinctive spicy, citrus aroma. Although the large, bright green, scalloped leaves—cilantro—look a bit like flat-leaf parsley, they are quite different in aroma and taste. Cilantro leaves are soft and floppy, with a fresh smell and a bitter, fruity taste, with a hint of orange peel and ginger. The small, golden seeds have a warm, sweet aroma, which is intensified when roasted, and a slightly peppery, woody taste.

BUYING AND STORING

Unless you grow coriander yourself, the flowers and roots are rarely available, so it is the large green leaves and the seeds you will find. Sold in bunches, the stems can be floppy but check that the leaves are fresh-looking. Cilantro droops quickly and should be kept in water, like cut flowers. The seeds should be whole and gold in color, with a distinctive aroma. They keep well in an airtight container in a dry, cool place and can be dry-roasted for a more pungent, nutty flavor or ground to make your own powder. Ready-ground coriander loses its aroma and flavor quickly.

Cilantro

CULINARY USES

All parts of the coriander plant are used. The root can be used in spicy soups and stews, and the small, upper leaves and flowers are delicious in salads., but in the Middle East it is the lower leaves and the seeds that are the most commonly used. The leaves are used in salads, rice dishes, and stews in Iran and the Arab regions. The well-known Circassian dish Çerkez tavuğu (p 62), made with chicken, walnuts, and coriander, is traditionally made with fresh cilantro. Both the leaves and the seeds are used in pickled vegetables, such as the stuffed baby eggplant pickle of Iran and Turkey.

The aromatic seeds and the ground spice are used in vegetable stews, meatballs, and some cakes and breads, such as the medieval savory bracelets *kahk*. The seeds are roasted and crushed in the delicious Egyptian specialty *dukkah*, which is an appetizing dip made with nuts and spices. The seeds are often ground and used in an Arab condiment called *taqlia*, which is made of ground coriander mixed with fried, crushed garlic and salt, and is added to some meat and chicken dishes. The ground seeds are also used in the Iranian spice mixture *advieh* (p169), and in the ubiquitous Arab spice mixture *baharat*.

To make a basic *baharat* mixture, grind together 2 tablespoons black peppercorns, 1 tablespoon coriander seeds, 1 tablespoon broken cinnamon bark, 1 tablespoon cumin seeds, ½ tablespoon cloves, ½ tablespoon cardamom seeds, 1 whole nutmeg, and mix it all with 2 tablespoons ground paprika.

Coriander see

Dukkah

This loose, dry mixture of nuts and seeds is an old Egyptian favorite. Crushed to release the flavors, rather than ground, the mixture is used as a dip for bread that has first been dipped in olive oil. Served for breakfast, or as a snack or *mezze* dish, the recipe varies from family to family. It is served in a shallow bowl placed beside a bowl of olive oil to make the dipping swift and easy. A humble street version of *dukkah*, consisting of dried mint, salt, and pepper, is sold in paper cones, like *zaatar*, ready to be sprinkled on bread.

DUKKAH
(EGYPTIAN CORIANDER AND SESAME SEED DIP)

Makes roughly 2¾ cups
Preparation time 25–30 minutes
Cooking time –

A handful of , roast hazelnuts
2 cups roast sesame seeds
Heaping ½ cup roast coriander seeds
3 tablespoons cumin seeds, roasted and ground
Scant 1 teaspoon salt

Using a mortar and pestle, pound the roast seeds and nuts with the ground cumin and salt. The mixture should be finely crushed and dry, not worked into a paste.

Serve with bread and olive oil, or keep in an airtight container for a maximum of 1 month.

These traditional spice bracelets are mentioned in the medieval cooking manual, *Kittab al-Wulsa Ila'L-Habib*. Flavored mainly with coriander, they are sprinkled with sesame seeds and *mahlab* (p100), ground black cherry kernels, and are eaten for breakfast or as a snack during the day. In Yemen and Egypt, a little chili powder is also sometimes added to the dough.

KAHK
(SPICE BRACELETS)

Serves 6
Preparation time approximately 2½ hours
Cooking time 1 hour 20 minutes (+ 1–2 hours, cooling and drying out)

4 cups strong bread flour
1 tablespoon ground coriander
½ tablespoon ground cumin
½ tablespoon salt
2 cakes compressed fresh yeast, or 2 teaspoons active dry yeast
½ teaspoon sugar
½ cup clarified butter (ghee)
1 egg, lightly beaten
Roughly ¼ cup sesame seeds
1–2 tablespoons mahlab (p100)

Sift the flour with the spices and salt into a large mixing bowl.

Dissolve the yeast with the sugar in a little lukewarm water, until it begins to bubble. Melt the clarified butter and then leave to cool.

Make a well in the middle of the flour and pour in the yeast and clarified butter. Using your hand, draw the flour in from the sides and work the mixture into a dough, adding a little lukewarm water to help bind it. Knead the dough for about 10 minutes, until smooth and pliable. Take a walnut-size lump of the dough and roll it into a thin "cigarette," about 4 inches long, then bring the ends together, pressing them firmly, to make a bracelet. Repeat with the rest of the dough.

Brush the tops with the beaten egg, sprinkle with sesame seeds, and place the bracelets on an oiled baking sheet. Leave in a warm place for 1–2 hours, until they have risen. Meanwhile, heat the oven to 350°F.

Sprinkle the risen bracelets with *mahlab* and place them in the oven for 20 minutes. Reduce the heat to 300°F and bake them for 1 hour. Turn off the heat and leave the bracelets to cool and dry out in the oven. They should be firm and golden.

SAFFRON

Saffron

(ZAFFARAN) Crocus sativus

Safflower

The saffron crocus has been cultivated in western Asia and the Mediterranean region since ancient times. The wealthy and noble used saffron as a delicate scent in their banqueting halls and to color their food and dye their clothes. Cleopatra is said to have used saffron for her complexion and Nero is reputed to have ordered the streets of Rome to be sprinkled with saffron water before he entered it. Saffron traveled to India from Persia and then to Spain with the Arabs. It is not to be confused with safflower, a plant related to the thistle and sunflower, which is often called "poor man's saffron," as the deep orange-red flowers also yield yellow and red dyes. It is used as a cheap substitute for saffron, which is the only spice to be measured by the carat, for it is worth its weight in gold.

HOW IT GROWS

Native to Persia and Asia Minor, the *Crocus sativus* is cultivated in Iran and Turkey, where it still grows wild. The best and most fragrant saffron is reputed to come from the sunny plateau of central Iran. Saffron is contained in the orange-red stigmas of this perennial bulb, which flowers for only two weeks in October. The pretty lavender flowers are picked by hand in the early hours of the morning, before they wilt under the sun, and the delicate stigmas are skillfully prised out of each one and dried. Each crocus bulb produces only one or two flowers and each flower contains three stigmas, so it takes a staggering number of flowers—roughly 80,000—to obtain one pound of dried saffron.

APPEARANCE AND TASTE

The dried stigmas appear in a tangle of wiry threads, about 1 inch long, the texture of straw. The overall color is burnt orange with tinges of red and yellow. The deeper the color, the better the quality. It is mildly pungent and delicately perfumed, with a slightly bitter taste. The threads turn tomato-red when soaked in water and impart a glorious yellow color.

BUYING AND STORING

The dried threads are sealed in containers to prevent them from bleaching. As they are so expensive, they are sold in small quantities. This doesn't matter, though, as only two pinches are required for any one dish. Saffron needs to be stored away from direct light and the color, flavor, and fragrance deteriorate on keeping. Ground saffron is also available, but it is really useful only for color, as it is easily adulterated and has virtually no fragrance or flavor.

Baskets of freshly picked crocus flowers

MEDICINAL USES

Medicinally, saffron was regarded as a tonic for the heart and melancholy, and a cure for fevers. It is also believed to be an aphrodisiac, while a hint of saffron in bed is reputed to have a soporific effect.

CULINARY USES

Saffron's primary role in the Middle East is a culinary one. Yellow being a happy color, saffron dishes are often reserved for festive occasions. The threads can be added directly to a dish or soaked in warm water to extract their color and fragrance. For some cakes and breads, the threads are ground to a fine powder with a little sugar. Throughout the Middle East, saffron is used to color and flavor savory rice dishes, milk puddings, and a delicious, creamy ice cream. The Turks make a saffron rice pudding called *zerde*, usually served at weddings, and the Iranians have *shollehzard*, also a saffron-flavored rice pudding, which is served on the

Liquid saffron

anniversary of the death of a member of Prophet Muhammad's family. Saffron is used throughout the Middle East, but it is used most in Iran, where it is added to many savory and sweet dishes.

Desserts do not play a big role in the cuisine of Iran; fresh fruit is preferred instead, followed by coffee and sweetmeats. The milk-based puddings and rice desserts are generally reserved for raising spirits during bereavement or for inducing an appetite in an ill person. The following rice pudding is traditionally served to commemorate the martyrdom of the Prophet's grandson, Imam Hassan—a Shi'ite tradition that is also practiced by many Sunni Muslims. Known as Imam Hüseyin to the Turks, the same occasion is marked by serving the grain and dried fruit dessert aşure (p109).

SHOLLEHZARD
(SAFFRON RICE PUDDING)

Serves 6–8
Preparation time 5 minutes
Cooking time approximately 45 minutes

⅔ cup pudding rice, washed and drained
Roughly 8 cups water
¾ cup sugar
2 pinches saffron threads, ground with a little sugar and soaked in 1–2 teaspoons tepid water
2 tablespoons rose water
2 tablespoons sunflower oil
Ground cinnamon
Pistachio slivers

Put the rice in a pan with the water and bring it to a boil. Reduce the heat and simmer, until the rice is very soft, about 25 minutes.

Stir in the sugar, saffron, and rose water, and continue to simmer until the sugar has dissolved.

Stir in the oil and simmer for a few more minutes, then tip the rice into a serving bowl or individual bowls. Leave to cool and set, then decorate with ground cinnamon and pistachio slivers, if you like.

In southern Iraq, Al Iraq, the main date- and rice-growing region of the country, the word for rice is timman. The plain steamed rice is similar to the chelow of neighboring Iran and the rice dishes are like the Iranian polow, but the distinctly spicy flavors are reminiscent of the Arabian Gulf.

Timman z'affaran

TIMMAN Z'AFFARAN
(IRAQI SAFFRON RICE)

Serves 5–6
Preparation time 25 minutes
Cooking time approximately 45 minutes

2 pinches saffron threads
½ teaspoon sugar
2 tablespoons rose water
3¾ cups beef or chicken stock
2½ cups long-grain rice, washed and soaked in cold water for about 20 minutes
2 tablespoons clarified butter (ghee)
¾ cup blanched almonds
1 onion, chopped
1 cup ground beef
1–2 teaspoons baharat (p162)
2 tablespoons golden raisins
Salt

Grind the saffron threads with the sugar, add the rose water, and leave to steep to extract the color.

Pour the stock into a heavy-based pan, bring it to a boil, and stir in the saffron. Drain the rice and toss it into the stock with some salt (if the stock is well seasoned, omit the salt). Reduce the heat and simmer, uncovered, for about 15 minutes, until almost all the water has been absorbed.

Meanwhile, heat the clarified butter and stir in the almonds. Cook until golden brown, then remove from the pan.

Add the onion to the pan and fry until it begins to color. Stir in the ground beef and cook until well browned. Add the baharat and golden raisins, cook for 1 minute, then season with salt.

Tip the meat mixture onto the rice and carefully fold it in until they are well mixed. Cover the pan with a clean dishtowel, followed by the lid, turn off the heat, and leave the rice to steam for about 20 minutes. Pile the rice onto a serving dish and garnish with the golden almonds.

CUMIN

(KAMMUN) *Cuminum cyminum*

Cumin seeds

Cumin has been grown in Egypt, Arabia, and the Mediterranean regions since ancient times. In the Bible there are references to the harvested plant being threshed to extract the seeds. The Romans used cumin frequently, often as a substitute for pepper. And Pliny's remark on the spice speaks for itself: "When one is tired of all seasonings, cumin remains welcome."

HOW IT GROWS

Cumin is the seed-like fruit of a pretty, little, annual herb of the parsley family, thought to be native to the Nile Valley. The plant grows to about 1 foot high, with small flowers that range from white or pink to mauve.

APPEARANCE AND TASTE

Cumin seeds are camel-colored with a greenish tinge. They are small and elongated, about ¼ inch long, and look very similar to caraway seeds. They are slightly bitter, with a distinctive warm taste and aroma that are deliciously enhanced when the seeds are roasted. Less common is the black cumin seed, which is known as "black cumin," a name also attributed to the unrelated nigella seed.

BUYING AND STORING

Whole cumin seeds are often sold with tiny flecks of dried stalk left from the threshing and drying process. When you open a new package, they should have a distinctive, spicy aroma. They keep well in an airtight container, stored in a cool dry place away from the light. The ready-ground spice loses its flavor quickly, so it's best to grind your own.

MEDICINAL USES

Cumin is regarded as a dependable cure for gastro-intestinal complaints. A hot infusion with the seeds is drunk to aid the digestion and to calm flatulent colic.

Ground cumin

CULINARY USES

As the belief that cumin calms flatulence is widespread in the Middle East, it is added to many pulse dishes, such as the Egyptian *ful medames*. It is also used in a variety of meat, vegetable, egg, and rice dishes. It is the principal flavoring in *maqaniq* and *sujuk* (two slightly different air-dried sausages made with ground lamb or beef and spices), and it is used in the fenugreek and red pepper paste that coats the air-dried beef filet called *pastırma* in Turkey and *basterma* in Syria and Lebanon (p198). Ground cumin is also one of the main spices in the Arab spice mixture *baharat* (p162), and the Iranian spice mixture *advieh* (p169). And, along with spices like coriander, it is used in some bread doughs, like the medieval savory bracelets, *kahk* (p163).

Hard-boiled eggs are a great favorite on pilgrimages and picnics, and for festivals such as Mulid el Nabi, which celebrates the birth of the Prophet. But they are not just plain hard-boiled eggs; they are flavored with spices, colored with saffron, or cooked gently with onion skins to the ancient recipe *beid hamine*, until the egg yolks are so creamy they melt in the mouth and the whites turn beige. In the following

Sujuk (sucuk in Turkish) hanging in the market, Istanbul

medieval recipe from Egypt, which is as popular in the home as it is on the street, the hard-boiled eggs are fried quickly in olive oil and then dipped in cumin or mixed spices.

BAID MUTAJJAN
(FRIED HARD-BOILED EGGS WITH CUMIN)

Serves 3–6
Preparation time 10 minutes
Cooking time 4–5 minutes

2 teaspoons ground cumin
2 teaspoons ground coriander
1 scant teaspoon ground cinnamon
6 freshly hard-boiled eggs
3 tablespoons olive oil
Salt

Mix the spices together with some salt. Peel the eggs while still warm and heat the oil in a skillet.

Fry the eggs lightly, rolling them around in the pan to make sure they are evenly coated, then dip them immediately into the spices. Eat while still warm.

The cured, horseshoe-shaped sausages hanging in the markets and charcuteries of the Middle East are generally made from beef or lamb and heavily spiced with garlic, red chili pepper, and cumin. They are delicious sliced and grilled, or cooked with beans in a stew. The following Anatolian dish is traditionally made in an earthenware pot, a *güveç*, and left to cook slowly in the ashes of a fire or the cooling bread ovens. More conventionally, it can be made on top of the stove or in the oven. Turkish *sucuk* and Arab *sujuk* and *maqaniq* are available in some Middle Eastern stores.

GÜVEÇTE SUCUK

(SPICY SAUSAGE WITH BLACK-EYED PEAS)

Serves 4–6
Preparation time 20 minutes
   (+ 6 hours' soaking)
Cooking time approximately 45
   minutes

*1–2 tablespoons clarified butter
   (ghee)*
1 onion, halved and sliced
2–3 cloves garlic, roughly chopped
1 teaspoon sugar
1 teaspoon cumin seeds
1 teaspoon coriander seeds
1 cumin-spiced sucuk, *sliced*

*⅓ cup black-eyed peas, soaked for
   6 hours*
*5–6 tomatoes, peeled and
   chopped*
*Salt and freshly ground black
   pepper*
*A bunch of fresh flat-leaf parsley
   or cilantro, chopped*

In a heavy-based pan, melt the clarified butter (or ghee) and stir in the onion, garlic, and sugar. When they begin to color, stir in the seeds, followed by the sliced *sucuk*.

Cook for 1–2 minutes to release some of the flavors from the *sucuk*, then stir in the beans and tomatoes. Pour in enough water to just cover the beans, put on the lid, and simmer for about 30 minutes, until the beans are tender and the liquid has reduced. Alternatively, cook it in the oven (at 350°F) for 30–40 minutes.

Season to taste and toss in the fresh herbs.

Güveçte sucuk

CARDAMOM

(HAIL) *Elettaria cardamomum*

Cardamom pods

Known as the "queen of spices," black pepper being the "king," cardamom is one of the most ancient of all spices, used by the early Egyptians and the ancient Greeks and Romans. With a long history as a prized article of trade, cardamom reached Europe through the old caravan routes. It was of such value that cardamom seeds were sent to family and friends as an invitation to a wedding ceremony. Even today, in the Middle East cardamom is the third most expensive spice after saffron and vanilla.

HOW IT GROWS

Cardamom is the dried fruit of a perennial herb that grows up to 16 feet tall. It belongs to the ginger family and is indigenous to southern India. The fruits, which are oblong, are picked before they are ripe and then cured by drying until they become hard and a woody green color.

APPEARANCE AND TASTE

There are a variety of cardamom pods but the most commonly used in the Middle East are the ribbed, diamond-shaped, wood-green ones and the white ones, which are just green ones that have been bleached. Each fruit, or pod, contains cells that hold as many as twenty small pungent black or dark brown seeds. When crushed or chewed, these seeds have a distinct, warming aroma with a lingering, almost bittersweet, eucalyptus-like taste.

BUYING AND STORING

Look for whole, unbroken, green pods to get the freshest, aromatic seeds, which should be black or very dark brown. The pods keep well in an airtight container in a cool, dry place, but ground cardamom loses its flavor very quickly, so it's better to grind your own.

Fragrant advieh with rose petals

MEDICINAL USES

An infusion of cardamom pods in hot water is drunk to soothe sore heads and stomach disorders. The seeds are also chewed to relieve heartburn and to freshen the breath.

CULINARY USES

In some parts of the Arab world the seeds are used solely as a digestive or as a flavoring in coffee. In Iran the pods are often infused in tea and coffee. When whole pods are added to a dish for flavoring, they are not meant to be eaten—the husk-like shell is tough and indigestible. The seeds are used for flavoring some cookies and pastries, such as the chickpea shortbreads, *nân-e nokhodchi*, and the almond pastries, *ghotâb*, from Iran. They are used in some desserts and sweetmeats, such as *al-salooq* from the Arabian Gulf. Mixed with other spices, they are added to meat stews, particularly the Yemeni dishes *akuw'a* (p156), oxtail stew, and *kirshuh*, liver and kidney stew. The traditional Iranian spice mixture *advieh*, which varies considerably from the Persian Gulf to the Caspian Sea, always

Sweetmeat stall, Yemen

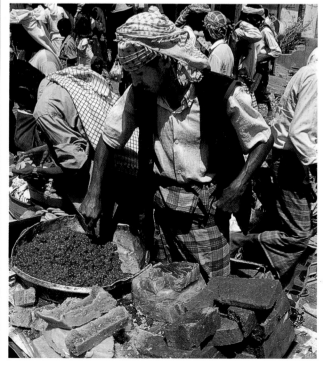

includes cardamom seeds. A basic *advieh* recipe will include roughly equal amounts of cumin seeds, caraway, cardamom, cinnamon, and coriander, all ground to a powder with turmeric. For a mild *advieh*, some people add a lot of cinnamon to the mixture; for a fragrant *advieh*, saffron, dried rose petals, and pistachios might be added; and for a hearty *advieh*, the addition of black pepper and cloves to a greater amount of cumin, coriander, and turmeric gives it a spicy kick, more akin to a mild Indian *garam masala*. Cardamom seeds are also used in the Yemeni spice mixture *hawayij* (p156), a blend of pepper, caraway, cardamom, and turmeric.

Fiery flavors are characteristic of Yemeni cooking. Hot chili pastes and spicy dips, popular from sunrise to sunset, are made in every household. *Zhug* is both a paste added to soups and stews, and a dip for bread. Only a little amount is required at a time.

ZHUG
(HOT CARDAMOM AND GARLIC RELISH)

Makes 1 small jar
Preparation time 20 minutes
(+ 1 hour's soaking)
Cooking time 10 minutes

4 dried red chilies, soaked in water for 1 hour
1 whole head of garlic, peeled and roughly chopped
The seeds of 4 cardamom pods
1 teaspoon caraway seeds
1 teaspoon black peppercorns
½ teaspoon salt
A bunch of fresh cilantro leaves, roughly chopped

Drain the chilies and cut off the stems. Using a mortar and pestle, pound the softened chilies to a puree with the garlic.

Grind the cardamom seeds, caraway and peppercorns to a coarse powder and add it to the pureed chili and garlic. Pound it with the salt and fresh cilantro until it resembles a coarse puree.

Tip the mixture into a small pan with about ¼ cup water. Simmer uncovered for about 10 minutes, then leave to cool.

Spoon the relish into a jar, seal it, and keep it in the refrigerator, ready to use.

A guest in an Arab home is treated like a king, offered coffee or tea, dates, sweetmeats, syrupy pastries, and digestive spices, including cardamom. The guest is not left for a moment without being offered something. The following pastries, shaped like crescent moons as a symbol of Islam, are just one of many sweetmeats offered with coffee.

AL-SALOOQ
(DEEP-FRIED CARDAMOM PASTRIES)

Serves 6
Preparation time 30 minutes
Cooking time approximately 20 minutes

4 cups flour
1 teaspoon baking powder
1 teaspoon ground cardamom
½ cup melted butter or sunflower oil
½ cup milk, boiled and left to cool
Sunflower oil for deep-frying
Confectioners' sugar.

Sift the flour, baking powder, and ground cardamom into a bowl.

Add the melted butter and, using a wooden spoon, mix into the flour until it is crumbly. Pour in the cooled milk and mix to a soft dough. Knead until smooth.

Take walnut-size lumps of dough in your hands, roll them into fat fingers, and shape them into crescent moons.

Heat enough oil for deep-frying in a pan and fry the crescent moons, in batches, until they are golden brown. Drain them on paper towels and toss them in confectioners' sugar.

Al-salooq

BAY LEAF

(WARAQ AL GAR) *Laurus nobilis*

Also known as sweet bay or sweet laurel, the bay leaf is thought to have originally come from Asia Minor. The ancient Greeks and Romans used bay leaves to crown warriors, athletes, and poets, hence the term "poet laureate." In Persian, the name for bay leaf is *barg-e boo*, which means "leaf of fragrance."

Dried bay leaves

HOW IT GROWS

The tree belongs to the family *Lauraceae*, which also includes cinnamon and avocado. It is a small tree with glossy, grass-green leaves and waxy, creamy blossoms.

APPEARANCE AND TASTE

Fresh bay leaves are shiny, slightly waxy, spear-shaped, and the color of freshly cut grass. They are slightly bitter and should be used sparingly with fish or meat. The dried, khaki-colored leaves, on the other hand, are quite spicy without any trace of bitterness.

BUYING AND STORING

The fresh leaves will keep for a few days in a plastic bag in the refrigerator, but it is best to dry them, or buy them already dried, and store them in an airtight container in a cool, dark place. They keep well for about six months and then they start to lose their flavor.

CULINARY USES

Fresh bay leaves can be used in soups and stews if they are shredded before use, but generally it is the dried leaves that are used most. Whole or crushed, they are added to fish dishes, stews, soups, meat and poultry stocks, and marinades. For heavy lamb dishes, the leaves are crushed and fried with the meat to cut the fat and the strong muttony flavor and odor. In Turkey the dried leaves are steeped and simmered in tea with dried figs and sugar.

In the Middle East almost every part of the sheep is consumed. The head is usually rubbed with spices and onion juice and then roasted, or it is boiled in a simple broth, which is often used in the traditional *fatta* (p 34) dishes. Your butcher should be able to prepare the head for you—you can ask him to keep the eyes, if you like.

RAS KHAROUF
(SHEEP HEAD SOUP)

Serves 4
Preparation time 10 minutes (+ 2 hours' soaking time)
Cooking time 2 hours

1 sheep head, skinned, with the brain removed
1 onion, quartered
Roughly 6 peppercorns
3–4 bay leaves
2 dried limes, pierced
Salt

Using a sharp knife, cut the chin muscles on both cheeks and separate the head from the jaw (you could ask a butcher to do this). Wash the head well and soak for 2 hours in salted water, changing the water once or twice.

Place the head, onion, bay leaves, peppercorns, and limes in a deep pan and cover with just enough water. Bring to a boil, remove any foam, and cook for about 2 hours, until the meat comes away easily from the bone.

Lift the head out onto a board, remove all bones, and slice the meat and chop the tongue. Strain the stock, return it to the pan, then season it with salt. Add the meat and tongue, and serve hot.

Bay tree

Tajin samak

Baking it whole in the oven is one of the most popular ways of cooking fish in the Middle East. Almost any fish will do, rubbed in olive oil or clarified butter, or marinated in onion juice, and baked with bay leaves, thyme, oregano, or garlic. The clarified butter, crispy roast garlic, and bay leaves give the following dish a lovely flavor.

TAJIN SAMAK
(FISH BAKED WITH BAY LEAVES)

Serves 2–4
Preparation time 10 minutes
Cooking time approximately 45 minutes

1 whole fish, such as trout, sea bass, red mullet, weighing about 3 pounds, gutted and washed
1–2 tablespoons clarified butter, melted
½ teaspoon cumin seeds
2 cloves garlic, chopped
4–5 bay leaves
Salt
Lemon wedges to serve

Preheat the oven to 300°F.

Make a few incisions in the skin of the fish, rub it in salt, and place it in a baking dish.

Melt the clarified butter with the cumin seeds, garlic, and a few crushed bay leaves. Pour it over the fish and tuck the remaining bay leaves around it.

Bake the fish for about 45 minutes, or until it is ready, and serve hot with lemon to squeeze over it.

MINT

(NAANA) *Mentha*

Mint

Mint was grown by the Romans, who pickled it in vinegar. Similarly, a medieval Arab dressing was made with dried mint, aromatic herbs, saffron, and vinegar. And the Ottomans, who categorized herbs and vegetables as "warming" or "cooling" to the blood, regarded mint as warming. With its refreshing and digestive qualities, mint is one of the most popular herbs in the Middle East. There are many varieties, with different strengths and flavors, but, apart from spearmint, which is used primarily in tea, most of the mint grown in the Middle East is interchangeable. The Arabic name for mint, *naana*, means "gift of Allah."

Herb seller with bundles of mint

HOW IT GROWS

Mint is a perennial herb that grows easily, both wild and cultivated, in temperate and cool climates. It is a bushy plant and can grow up to 2 feet in height.

APPEARANCE AND TASTE

Fresh mint leaves come in different shades of green. Some are tough, scalloped, textured, and hairy, others are smooth and papery. Some are big and oval, others long and pointed. Some are sweet and minty, others peppery, fruity, or like spearmint. Whatever the variety, all should have a clean, strong, minty aroma of their own. Dried mint is usually dark green or grass-green in color with a more subtle fragrance.

BUYING AND STORING

Mint is sold fresh and dried, but, undoubtedly, the fresh is far superior. Dried mint loses its flavor quickly and is better stored in vinegar than in an airtight container. Fresh mint can be kept for a few days in a plastic bag in the refrigerator or with the stems immersed in a glass of water.

MEDICINAL USES

A soothing herb, mint is often used in infusions to ease sore throats, bronchitis, nausea, and stomach disorders. Mint oil is used in throat lozenges, in ointments for weary limbs, and as the fresh flavor in many toothpastes.

CULINARY USES

Fresh mint is one of the most pleasing and useful herbs. In many parts of the Middle East, bowls of fresh mint leaves are passed around during or after a meal to freshen the breath or to aid the digestion after a heavy feast. The leaves are also infused in boiling water to make a soothing tisane. Fresh and dried mint leaves are often added to yogurt to make numerous, delectable *mezze* dishes, such as the Turkish haydari, a simple dip consisting of yogurt, garlic, and mint, and the cool, refreshing yogurt drink abdug (p 43—ayran in Turkey). In Iran the leaves are used to make sharbat-e sekanjebeen, a vinegar and sugar syrup flavored with mint, which is used as the basis of a refreshing drink.

Throughout the Middle East mint is added liberally to simple vegetable, pulse, and grain salads, such as *tabbouleh*. It is one of the preferred herbs for many rice dishes and, along with parsley, it is added to the various regional "gypsy," "shepherd," and "country" salads, which usually consist of chilies, onions, cucumbers, and tomatoes. As a "warming" herb, it is often combined with dill and used to flavor cheese-filled pastries and to balance "cooling" vegetables such as zucchini, marrows, and fava beans. In Turkey fresh or dried mint is used to flavor bowls of *cacık*, a

Mint bush

Dried mint

dish of yogurt and cucumber, which is often served as a refreshing accompaniment to meat dishes, or as a chilled soup. A similar dish called *mâst-o khiyâr* (p 215) is made in Iran, only there it is more exotic, with the addition of chopped walnuts, golden raisins, chives, and rose petals. Also in Iran, mint is added with parsley to the stews from the province of Mazandaran, such as *khoresht-e reevâs*, a delightful lamb stew with rhubarb. And, in the same way that melted butter and red pepper are poured over some dishes in Turkey, a condiment called *na'nâ dâgh*, which consists of dried mint stirred into melted butter or ghee, is poured over winter soups in Iran.

High up in the mountains of eastern Anatolia sits the little town of Bingöl, meaning "a thousand lakes," after which this dish is named. The delicious combination of raw, fried, or steamed carrot with yogurt is found in every pocket of Turkey, but the addition of the pomegranate seeds and mint, representing the thousand lakes, places this *mezze* recipe in Bingöl.

BİNGÖL CACIK
(CARROT AND YOGURT SALAD WITH POMEGRANATE AND MINT)

Serves 4 (as part of *mezze* spread)
Preparation time 15 minutes
Cooking time –

2½ cups thick yogurt
2 cloves garlic, crushed
3 carrots, peeled and grated
Seeds of 1 pomegranate
A bunch of fresh mint leaves, finely chopped
Salt and freshly ground black pepper

Beat the yogurt in a bowl with the garlic. Beat in the carrots with most of the pomegranate seeds and mint.

Season to taste and spoon the salad into a serving bowl or individual bowls.

Sprinkle with the remaining pomegranate seeds and chopped mint leaves.

The word for rhubarb in Farsi is *reevâs*, which stems from the old Persian word *reev*, meaning "a shining light." Believed to cleanse the blood and purify the system, rhubarb has been used in Iranian cooking since ancient times. In Safavid times the plant was used to thicken lamb and vegetable stews, but today finely chopped mint and parsley give substance to such dishes. This pretty pink and green stew is traditionally served to aid the digestion.

KHORESHT-E REEVÂS
(RHUBARB STEW WITH MINT AND PARSLEY)

Serves 4–6
Preparation time 25 minutes
Cooking time approximately 1½ hours

2–3 tablespoons olive oil
2 onions, halved and sliced
1 pound lean lamb, trimmed and cubed
A big bunch of fresh mint, finely chopped
A big bunch of fresh flat-leaf parsley, finely chopped
Salt and freshly ground black pepper
Roughly 2 pounds rhubarb, trimmed and chopped into 1-inch lengths

Heat the oil in a heavy-based pan and fry the onions until they are golden. Add the meat and brown it on all sides, then pour in enough water to just cover. Put on the lid and simmer gently for about 30 minutes.

In a separate pan, fry the chopped herbs in a little extra olive oil, tossing them all the time so that they release their flavor but don't burn. Add the herbs to the meat and continue to simmer for 40–50 minutes, until the meat is tender.

Season the dish, then add the rhubarb, cooking it for a few minutes so that it is hot through but not soft and mushy. Serve immediately with plain rice.

Khoresht-e reevâs

NIGELLA

(HABBAT AL-BARAKAH) *Nigella sativa*

Nigella

Native to western Asia and the Mediterranean region of the Middle East, this little black seed is sometimes mistakenly known as black cumin or black onion seed, although it has nothing to do with either and doesn't taste a bit like them. In Arabic the nigella seed is known under two names: *habbat al-sauda*, meaning "black seed," and *habbat al-barakah*, which means "seed of grace." In Farsi it is *siâhdâneh*, which also means "black seed," and in Turkish it is known as *çöreotu*, as it is most commonly associated with *çörek*, a sweet bun sprinkled with nigella seeds, eaten during the Sweet Festival immediately after Ramazan (Ramadan in Arabic).

HOW IT GROWS

The *Nigella sativa* plant is a close relative of *Nigella damascena*, or love-in-the-mist, whose seeds can also be used as a condiment. It is a hardy annual herb that grows wild on the forest floors and is also cultivated for its seeds. It grows to about 2 feet in height and has dense, feathery foliage and bluish-white flowers that form seed capsules. These have to be collected before they are ripe, otherwise the pods will burst open and scatter the seeds. The pods are dried whole and then crushed to release the seeds.

APPEARANCE AND TASTE

Nigella seeds look like tiny, charcoal teardrops. They are very aromatic and have a slightly bitter, peppery flavor with a light floral hint. It is one of the distinct tastes and smells on bread in the Middle East.

BUYING AND STORING

The seeds are usually sold whole. They can be easily found in Middle Eastern, Indian, and whole-food stores. They keep well in an airtight container in a cool, dry place.

CULINARY USES

Nigella seeds are used primarily for sprinkling on crackers, breads, and buns, such as the Turkish *çörek*. They are used for flavoring vinegar, particularly in Iran, where their distinctive flavor features in pickles and preserves such as *torshi-ye leeteh*, a pickled relish made with vegetables and herbs, and *torshi-ye meeveh*, a blend of pickled fruit and vegetables. They are sometimes roasted and crushed and added to yogurt or onion-juice marinades for lamb. They are used in some simple Armenian salads made with root vegetables such as radishes and carrots. In some parts of the Middle East nigella seeds are sprinkled over the everyday white cheeses and they are a feature of the Lebanese *hallumi*.

Potato salads vary from region to region, but generally they are first cooked in oil and spices and then left to cool. Although this recipe is from the Arabian Gulf, it is similar to dishes in Egypt and Iraq.

SALATAT BATATA
(ARABIAN POTATO SALAD)

Serves 4–6
Preparation time 25 minutes
Cooking time 15 minutes

6–8 medium new potatoes, boiled with their skins on until tender but firm
2 large onions, halved and finely sliced
3–4 tablespoons olive oil or sunflower oil
2 cloves garlic, crushed
1 tablespoon nigella seeds
½ teaspoon ground coriander
½ teaspoon ground cumin
1 teaspoon ground turmeric
1 teaspoon ground chili
Juice of 1 lime + extra for serving
Salt and freshly ground black pepper

Peel the cooked potatoes and cut them into bite-size pieces.

In a heavy-based pan, soften the onions in the oil but don't brown them. Add the garlic and nigella seeds and cook for 1 minute, then stir in the spices. Reduce the heat, add the potatoes, and toss them the pan, making sure they are well-coated with oil and spices. Season to taste and spoon the mixture into a dish. Leave to cool, add the lime juice, and serve with lime wedges.

A beautiful and fragile Nigella flower

Turp salatası

The following dish is Armenian. It is light and refreshing, designed to be eaten with grilled kabobs. The long white radishes, also called "mouli," are used for this salad, but carrots and celery root work well too.

TURP SALATASI
(RADISH SALAD WITH NIGELLA)

Serves 4–6
Preparation time 25–30 minutes
Cooking time –

4 white radishes, peeled and grated
2 teaspoons nigella seeds
2 tablespoons olive oil
Juice of 1 lime or lemon
1 small bunch of fresh parsley or cilantro, finely chopped (optional)
Salt

Put the grated radish into a bowl. Add the nigella seeds and add the oil and lime juice. Sprinkle with salt and mix well.

Leave to sit for about 15 minutes to let the flavors mingle, then mix it again. Toss in the herbs, if you like, and serve.

BASIL

(REYHAN) *Ocimum basilicum*

Green basil

Apart from in Iran, basil is not used widely in the Middle East. The old belief that the plant breeds scorpions may account for its scant use. However, the aromatic, pungent green leaves are often chewed as an appetizer and a breath freshener, or are simply passed around in a bowl as an accompaniment to a meat dish.

HOW IT GROWS

Originally native to India, the green-leafed plant is cultivated in Iran and some parts of the Mediterranean region. It is a pretty plant with a lovely smell and small, purple-tinged white flowers at the top of each stalk. A smaller-leafed, purple variety, which grows wild in the Mediterranean region, is used more widely in the Middle East.

APPEARANCE AND TASTE

The leaves of sweet basil should be soft and bright green with a lovely, pungent smell, particularly when you tear them with your fingers. The wild purple basil, which has a slightly spicy flavor, is similar to the cultivated dark, opal basil, but it has smaller leaves and is quite vibrant in color.

Purple basil

BUYING AND STORING

Always look for fresh, soft leaves with a strong scent. Once the leaves go limp, they lose their flavor. Fresh leaves can be kept in plastic bags in the refrigerator for a day or two. They can also be preserved in oil or vinegar to impart their strong flavor. Basil loses its flavor when dried.

CULINARY USES

Both the green and purple varieties are used to flavor stews, kabobs, and salads. It is one of the preferred herbs to flavor eggplant, often included in the popular stuffed pickled eggplant. In Iran the fresh, pungent leaves are pounded with pistachios to make a kind of pesto, served with the thin noodles, *reshteh* (p125). Also in Iran, the sweet basil seeds are used to make a fragrant syrup, the basis of a refreshing sherbet drink. In Iraq basil is added to the ubiquitous yogurt drink *abdug* (p 43—*ayran* in Turkey), which is generally flavored with mint in other parts of the Middle East.

Yogurt dips flavored with herbs make popular *mezze* dishes. The following recipe is from Iran, but variations of it pop up all over the Middle East.

POLOOR
(YOGURT AND CHEESE DIP WITH HERBS)

Serves 2–4
Preparation time 5 minutes
Cooking time —

1 cup white cheese (feta)
½ cup thick, strained yogurt
A mixed bunch of fresh basil, mint, parsley, and dill
Salt (optional)

Mash the cheese in a bowl and blend it with the yogurt.

Wash the herbs and pat them dry, then chop them finely and beat into the yogurt and cheese.

Season with salt, if necessary, and serve with crusty or flat bread as a dip or spread.

This fragrant Persian dish is traditionally made at No Rooz, the spring festival, with the first fresh herbs of the year. The rice symbolizes bounty, and the dish is often served with an herb omelet, the eggs symbolizing birth, or with lightly fried fish, which symbolize freshness.

SABZI POLOW
(RICE WITH FRESH HERBS)

Serves 4
Preparation time 10 minutes
    (+ 3 hours' soaking of
    the rice)
Cooking time 35–40 minutes

1 tablespoon salt
2½ cups long-grain rice, well rinsed and soaked in salted water for 3 hours
Roughly 5 tablespoons sunflower oil

A big bunch of fresh basil, parsley, mint, dill, chives, and cilantro, finely chopped

1 clove garlic, finely chopped

1 teaspoon ground fenugreek

2 pinches of saffron threads

Sugar

2 tablespoons clarified butter (ghee)

In a deep pan, bring about 9 cups of water to a boil with 1 tablespoon of salt. Drain the rice and tip it into the boiling water for 2–3 minutes. Test to see if it is al dente, then drain it and rinse with lukewarm water.

Heat the sunflower oil in a heavy-based pan and sprinkle a layer of rice across the bottom, followed by a layer of herbs, garlic, and fenugreek. Repeat two or three times, finishing with a layer of rice, piled into a conical shape.

Using the handle of a wooden spoon, poke a few holes through the rice to the bottom. Cover the pan with a clean dishtowel, followed by the lid—lift any trailing flaps of towel over the lid. Keep the pan over a high heat for 1–2 minutes to make it steam, then reduce the heat to very low and leave it to steam for about 30 minutes.

Using a small mortar and pestle, grind the saffron to a powder with a tiny sprinkling of sugar, then stir in 1 tablespoon of boiling water. Put 2–3 spoonfuls of the cooked rice in a bowl, add the liquid saffron, and mix together.

Toss the rest of the rice lightly and tip it onto a serving dish, creating a mound. Sprinkle the saffron rice over it, then quickly melt the clarified butter and pour it all over the rice. Serve immediately.

Sabzi polow

ORCHID ROOT

(SAHLAB) *Orchis mascula*

Orchid roots

Orchid roots have long been thought to have aphrodisiac qualities and it is easy to see why. The root is testicle-shaped, hence the name *orchis*, meaning "testicle" in Greek. The Arabic for the root is *thalab* (fox), originating from *khusya th-thalb*, which translates as "fox's testicle." The orchid roots are ground to a powder that plays an important role as a gelatinous thickening agent in a unique ice cream and in a hot winter drink believed to be nutritious for children.

HOW IT GROWS

The roots come from various members of the orchid family—namely *Orchis latifolca*, *Orchis militaris*, *Orchis morio,* and *Orchis mascula*. These orchid plants grow in the temperate climates of the Middle East.

APPEARANCE AND TASTE

The small, dried roots are hard and bulb-shaped. They are slightly yellowish or chalky white. Often they are sold on strings, like long, beaded necklaces. The roots are ground into a fine, white, almost silky, odorless powder, also called *sahlab* (*salep* in Turkey). When blended with milk, it has a very subtle taste.

BUYING AND STORING

The dried roots, which are sold in the markets in the Middle East, are expensive and difficult to find outside the region. Ground orchid root, which is also expensive, is available in some Middle Eastern stores, but make sure you don't buy "instant *sahlab*," which is a mixture of cornstarch and orchid root used to make an inferior drink. Pure orchid root powder will keep for only a few months in an airtight container.

Sahlab

CULINARY USES

The ground orchid root, *sahlab,* is used more for its properties as a gelatinous thickening agent than for its taste. Principally, it is used in a thick, hot, sweet, milky drink, topped with a sprinkling of cinnamon, which is particularly popular in Turkey, where it is made in big brass or copper urns. And in Iran, Syria, Lebanon, and Turkey it is used to make a snowy-white ice cream, giving it a pleasing elastic consistency. As the creamy ice cream is spooned out, it seems to stretch.

This is a lovely, thick winter drink, made with milk and flavored with cinnamon. It is particularly popular in Istanbul and Bursa, where tea-rooms display the large copper urns in which the *salep* is made. It is also a popular drink in the ski resort Uludağ, above Bursa.

SALEP
(ORCHID ROOT DRINK)

Serves 3–4
Preparation time –
Cooking time approximately 10 minutes

1 tablespoon salep
2½ cups milk
2 tablespoons sugar
Ground cinnamon

Mix the *salep* to a loose paste with a little of the milk.

Heat the rest of the milk with the sugar in a heavy-based saucepan, stirring all the time. Just as it is about to boil, reduce the heat, and stir a little of the hot milk into the slaked *salep* paste, then tip the *salep* into the pan.

Stir vigorously until the mixture thickens, then pour it into individual cups. Sprinkle each one with cinnamon, and drink while it's piping hot.

Thickened with *sahlab* and flavored with *mastic* and orange-flower water, this snow-white ice cream is popular in the Middle East, particularly with the older generation, for whom ice cream was a special treat. Traditionally, the ice-cream sellers made it in large barrel-shaped cylinders, stirring it with a long, rotating pole around the hollow center, which was filled with ice. Nowadays most ice creams are made commercially and there are many to choose from, but traditional ice-cream sellers can still be seen in the streets of Cairo, Damascus, and Istanbul. In the regions that were once part of the Ottoman Empire, a creamy version of this classic ice cream is known as *dondurma kaymak*, from the Turkish *kaymaklı dondurma*. In Iran, a similar ice cream is called *bastani sa'labi.*

BUZA AL-HALIB
(SNOW-WHITE ICE CREAM)

Serves 6–8
Preparation time 2 minutes
Cooking time approximately
  25 minutes

3 tablespoons sahlab
5 cups milk
1 cup sugar

Salep

1 small piece mastic (the size of
  half a fingernail), pounded with
  ½ teaspoon sugar
1 tablespoon orange-flower water
Pistachio nuts

Mix the *sahlab* to a loose paste
with a little of the milk. Put the
rest of the milk in a heavy-based
pan with the sugar and bring it to
a boil, stirring all the time.

Reduce the heat, add some of
the hot milk to the *sahlab* paste,
and tip the *sahlab* into the milk,
stirring vigorously. Add the
ground mastic and keep stirring
vigorously until it has dissolved.

Simmer the mixture gently for
about 15 minutes, stirring from
time to time, until it is thick. Beat
in the orange-flower water and
pour the mixture into a bowl or
dish for the freezer.

Leave it to cool, then cover and
freeze, beating it at intervals to
break up the crystals. (Or pour
the cooled mixture into an ice-
cream maker and freeze
according to the instructions.)

When ready to serve, spoon the
ice cream into bowls and sprinkle
with chopped pistachio nuts.

PARSLEY

(BAQDOUNIS) *Petroselinum crispum*

Parsley—the flat-leaf variety—is probably the most popular of all herbs in the Middle East. It is sold like big bunches of flowers. Used liberally in cooking throughout the region, it is also served on its own to eat with bread, to cut the spice, to cleanse the palate, to sharpen the appetite, or to freshen the breath. In Roman times, recipes often called for the seeds as well as leaves but nowadays only the leaves are used.

Fresh parsley

HOW IT GROWS

The parsley plant is related to celery and is native to the Mediterranean region. It is a fairly hardy plant and grows wild or cultivated in most places.

APPEARANCE AND TASTE

Flat-leaf parsley looks a bit like cilantro, although it has stiffer stems. It is usually a darker green than the curly variety and is packed with that distinctive parsley aroma and taste, which are really released only when the leaves are chopped.

BUYING AND STORING

The fresh leaves and stems should be quite crisp and look fresh. They will last for a few days in a plastic bag in the refrigerator, or with the stems dipped in a glass of water. Dried parsley is a waste of time: it smells and tastes like dried grass.

CULINARY USES

Roughly chopped leaves and stalks are added by the handful to numerous salads, such as the Arab *fattush* and the Turkish *çoban salatası*, and to soups, stews, rice dishes, and numerous meatball dishes. The leaves, dressed with a little lemon juice, are even sometimes offered as a salad by themselves. In Iran, parsley is one of the main herbs used in egg dishes, such as *kookoo-ye sabzi*; combined with mint, it is used to thicken the sauce of traditional stews, such as *khoresht-e reevâs* (p173), from the province of Mazandaran. In the Ottoman kitchens it was the favored herb for meatballs and for meat stuffings. It is used in vast quantities in the Arab cracked wheat salad *tabbouleh* (*tabbuleh*), and in the Turkish version, *kısır*. The strong, garlicky dips and sauces made with crushed nuts or tahini are often lightened with chopped parsley. And stalks of leafy parsley are used to garnish most dishes, especially grilled meats and fish.

Traditionally a mountain dish from the eastern Mediterranean, *tabbouleh* (*tabbuleh*) has become one of the most popular Middle Eastern salads, served as a *mezze* dish or with grilled meat. It is believed to have originated from *safsuf*, a meatless stuffing for vine leaves. In the villages it is still sometimes served with tender vine leaves to scoop it up. And in Turkey a similar dish, *kısır*, is served in vine or lettuce leaves.

The quantities and ingredients vary, but a traditional tabbouleh is always packed with parsley.

TABBOULEH
(BULGUR SALAD WITH MINT AND PARSLEY)

Serves 6
Preparation time 35 minutes
Cooking time –

1½ cups fine-grain bulgur
1–2 red onions or 6 scallions, finely chopped
2–3 large tomatoes, skinned and finely chopped
A huge bunch of flat-leaf parsley, chopped
A bunch of fresh mint, chopped
Roughly ½ cup olive oil
Juice of 2 lemons
Salt and freshly ground black pepper

Rinse the bulgur and soak it in cold water for about 30 minutes, until it is soft but chewy. Drain it thoroughly and tip it into a large bowl with the onions, tomatoes, and herbs.

Pour in the olive oil and lemon juice, season generously, and mix it thoroughly. Adjust the flavors to your taste and serve, with vine or lettuce leaves if you like.

Flat-leaf parsley plant

Like the *fatta* (p 34) dishes, this salad was most probably conceived as a way of using up stale bread—the Arabic word *fattush* refers to the act of breaking or crumbling bread. Traditionally a peasant salad from Syria, it has become fashionable in the main cities of Egypt, Lebanon, and Jordan, where it is usually made with toasted pita bread rather than stale bread. In Turkey there is a similar peasant salad called *çoban salatası*, meaning "shepherd's salad," which sometimes omits the bread. The ingredients may vary a little from family to family, but the salad always contains lots of parsley. Fresh pomegranate seeds or ground *sumac* are sometimes sprinkled over it.

FATTUSH
(SYRIAN BREAD SALAD)

Serves 4–6
Preparation time 20–25 minutes
Cooking time —

1 onion, halved and sliced
1 cucumber, peeled, halved lengthwise, and sliced
3 tomatoes, peeled and chopped
1 sweet pepper, halved and sliced
2 cloves garlic, chopped
A bunch flat-leaf parsley, chopped
A small bunch mint, chopped
1 pita bread
4–5 tablespoons olive oil
Juice of 1 lemon
Salt and ground black pepper
A little sumac

Put the onion, cucumber, tomatoes, pepper, and garlic in a bowl with the chopped herbs.

Open the pita bread, toast it until crisp, then break it into little pieces and add to the bowl.

Toss in the olive oil and lemon juice, season to taste, adding more olive oil or lemon juice if necessary, and serve, sprinkled with a little ground sumac.

Tabbouleh

181

ALLSPICE

(BAHAR HILU) *Pimenta dioica*

Spanish explorers came across allspice in Jamaica at the beginning of the sixteenth century. From there it would have found its way to the center of the Ottoman Empire in the same way that other goods from the New World reached Constantinople, as a result of the Spanish–Ottoman alliance. Although used throughout the Middle East, it is most used in Turkey, where it is known as *yeni bahar*, meaning "new spice," or *dolma bahar*, indicating that it is one of the main spices used in stuffed dishes. In other parts of the Middle East, the spice mixture *baharat* (p162) is often used instead.

Ground allspice

HOW IT GROWS

Allspice is the dried unripe berry of the tropical tree *Pimenta dioica*, which is cultivated mainly in Jamaica, hence its other name, "Jamaican pepper." The handsome, tall, aromatic tree has small white flowers.

APPEARANCE AND TASTE

The unripe berries are round and green. When they dry, they become hard and turn a reddish-brown, similar in appearance to a large peppercorn. The ground spice is a dark rust color. The flavor resembles a mixture of cloves, nutmeg, and cinnamon, which is why it is called "allspice" in English. Most of its flavor is in the oil, which is composed mainly of eugenol, the main element in cloves, and it can be substituted for cloves in some recipes.

Allspice berries

Baskets of dried fruit, herbs, and spices

BUYING AND STORING

As always with spices, it is best to buy the whole berries and grind them yourself when you need them. They keep well in an airtight container in a cool, dark place.

CULINARY USES

The berries are used whole in pickles and marinades. In Iran and Turkey the crushed or ground berries are used in rice dishes and in the aromatic rice fillings for many stuffed fruit, vegetable, poultry, and seafood dishes. Allspice is also used in some lamb, chicken, and game dishes, such as *tavşan yahnisi* (p 204), a spicy rabbit stew, and in some cakes and desserts.

The Persians created some wonderful dishes combining fruit and meat, many of which are popular throughout the Middle East today. The following recipe is used for both quince and apples. The Turks make a similar dish, called *elma dizmesi*, using rice instead of split peas.

DOLMEH SIB

(APPLES STUFFED WITH GROUND MEAT AND YELLOW SPLIT PEAS)

Serves 6
Preparation time 20–25 minutes (+ 25 minutes' cooking of split peas)
Cooking time approximately 50 minutes

½ cup yellow split peas, rinsed
1 onion, finely chopped
1 tablespoon olive oil
1 cup ground beef
½ teaspoon ground allspice
½ teaspoon ground cinnamon
A small bunch of of fresh dill, chopped
6 large tart apples, washed
2 tablespoons white wine vinegar
1 tablespoon sugar
Salt and freshly ground black pepper

Preheat the oven to 350°F.

Put the split peas into a pan, cover with plenty of water, and boil them for about 25 minutes, until they are soft. Drain and refresh them.

Sauté the onion in the olive oil until it begins to color, then stir in the meat. Cook for 1–2 minutes until the meat has changed color, then stir in the spices, dill, and cooked split peas. Season with salt and pepper and remove from the heat.

Core the apples, making sure you leave about ½ inch at the bottom. Hollow out some of the fruit to make room for the filling, chop it, and add it to the meat and split-pea mixture. Stir well, then use the mixture to stuff the apples. Place the apples side by side in a baking dish, dab a bit of butter on top of each one, and pour about 1 cups of water into the dish. Cover with foil and bake for 25–30 minutes.

Heat the vinegar and sugar in a pan with roughly ¼ cup water, and pour it over and around the apples. Continue to bake for a further 15–20 minutes, until the apples are nicely tender. Serve hot or cold.

The following recipe is an Istanbul specialty that is particularly popular as a *mezze* dish in restaurants and at makeshift stalls in the streets. Families chug up and down the Bosphorus and along the edges of the Sea of Marmara in old wooden boats, and dive for the big mussels in the rocks. The catch is usually destined to be tossed in a beer batter and deep-fried, as for *midye tavasi*, or stuffed with an aromatic rice and eaten cold.

MİDYE DOLMASI
(STUFFED MUSSELS)

Serves 6
Preparation time roughly 1 hour
Cooking time 15 minutes

Roughly 24 large fresh mussels
2–3 tablespoons olive oil
2 onions, finely chopped
2 tablespoons pine nuts
2 tablespoons dried currants, soaked in water for 15 minutes
1 teaspoon ground allspice
½ teaspoon ground cinnamon
2 teaspoons tomato paste
Heaping ⅔ cup short-grain rice, rinsed and soaked in water for about 15 minutes
A bunch of fresh dill and parsley, finely chopped
Salt and freshly ground black pepper
Lemon wedges to serve

Put the mussels into a bowl of cold water and discard any that open.

Heat the oil in a pan and stir in the onions and pine nuts. Fry them until they begin to color, then stir in the dried currants, spices, and tomato paste, followed by the rice.

Cover with just enough water, season with salt and pepper, and bring to a boil. Reduce the heat and simmer for 10–15 minutes, until the water is absorbed and the rice is cooked but still firm. Leave the rice to cool in the pan, then add the herbs and, using a fork, gently toss.

Place a colander or steamer in a large pan and pour in enough water for steaming. Then, using a sharp knife, carefully pry the mussels open widely enough to spoon some of the rice into them. Close the shells and pack them tightly into the steamer. Place a plate weighed down with a stone on top of them.

Cover the pan, steam the mussels for about 15 minutes, then leave them to cool. Serve cold with wedges of lemon to squeeze over them.

Midye dolması

ANISEED

(YANSOON) *Pimpinella anisum*

Aniseed is a native of the Levant. The culinary uses of this aromatic seed date as far back as the pharaohs of Egypt and classical Rome. It has long been used as a digestive and diuretic, often in the form of tea, which is also considered to be soporific. The seeds are chewed on their own as a breath freshener and they are particularly popular coated in sugar and given to children as a treat.

HOW IT GROWS

Dill, fennel, caraway, and cumin are all botanical relatives of aniseed. The plant grows to about 2 feet in height and has clusters of yellow white flowers at the top.

APPEARANCE AND TASTE

The leaves and the seeds have an unmistakable bittersweet, warming smell and taste. The small seeds are pale brown and ribbed, often sold among tiny bits of husk and stalk. The seeds can be dry-roasted to produce a strong, sweet, aromatic flavor.

BUYING AND STORING

Fresh or dried aniseed leaves are available in some Middle Eastern markets, but they lose their flavor and aroma very quickly. The seeds also lose flavor quite quickly and need to be stored in an airtight container and used within months. As for ground aniseed, it loses flavor rapidly, so it's best to buy the seeds and grind them yourself as you need them.

CULINARY USES

The fresh and dried leaves are occasionally added to a fish soup or stew, or they are infused to make an aromatic tea to aid the digestion. Combined with other spices, the seeds are used to make a soothing tisane and to flavor some breads, cookies, and cakes. Aniseed marries beautifully with dried figs, and it flavors the ceremonial rice pudding *meghlie*, served to visitors at the birth of a son. It is also the principal flavoring in the Turkish *rakı*, and in *arak* from Syria, Lebanon, and Jordan. Both *rakı* and *arak* are distilled from grapes and diluted with ice and water, which turns the alcohol cloudy. They are drunk with *mezze* or fish.

Middle Eastern jams and preserves are heavenly— aromatic and spicy. Often using whole or large chunks of fruit and vegetables, they are deliciously syrupy, designed to be dribbled over bread, white cheese, or thick yogurt.

TEEN BI SUKKAR
(DRIED FIG JAM WITH ANISEED AND PINE NUTS)

Makes roughly 6½ cups
Preparation time 10 minutes
Cooking time roughly 30 minutes

2 cups water
2 cups sugar
1 tablespoon lemon juice
Roughly 7 cups coarsely chopped dried figs
3–4 fresh rose geranium leaves
1 teaspoon ground aniseed
3 tablespoons pine nuts
A tiny piece of mastic (p186— ¼ teaspoon), ground with a little sugar

Put the water, sugar, and lemon juice into a large pan and bring to a boil, stirring all the time. Reduce the heat and simmer for about 5 minutes.

Stir in the figs and geranium leaves and continue to simmer gently for about 15 minutes, until the figs are tender.

Add the aniseed and pine nuts, simmer for a further 5 minutes, then stir in the mastic. Leave to

Rakı

cool in the pan, then spoon the preserve into sterilized jars and store in a cool, dry place.

In Syria and Lebanon the following rice pudding was traditionally made to celebrate the birth of a son. A drummer, followed by villagers playing reed flutes, would lead well-wishers to the family's door, and large amounts of *meghlie* would be made to serve the flow of visitors. The arrival of a newborn daughter was not usually met with such ceremony, although a humble offering of *meghlie* tea (or *miglee*) was occasionally served to visitors. Nowadays, daughters, who are often referred to as "the flower of

Aniseed

the house," are usually cherished as much as sons, so in many Arab communities this spicy rice pudding is made to celebrate the birth of any child.

MEGHLIE
(RICE PUDDING WITH ANISEED)

Serves 8–10
Preparation time 35 minutes
Cooking time approximately 25 minutes

1 piece of fresh ginger (about 1 inch long), peeled and grated
6½ cups water
¼ cup ground rice or rice flour
Roughly ½ cup sugar
1 teaspoon ground aniseed
1 teaspoon ground caraway seed
1 teaspoon ground cinnamon
½ teaspoon ground cloves
A handful of chopped blanched almonds, toasted pine nuts, or pistachios for the top
Grated fresh coconut

Put the ginger into a small pan with half the water and bring it to a boil. Reduce the heat, cover the pan, and simmer for about 25 minutes. Strain the ginger water—a basic *meghlie* tea—into a bowl and leave it to cool.

In a bowl, mix the ground rice to a loose paste with the cooled ginger water. Add the sugar and spices and mix well.

In a heavy-based saucepan, bring the remaining water to a boil. Gradually add the ground rice mixture, stirring vigorously, with a wooden spoon. Bring the mixture to a boil again, then reduce the heat and simmer gently, stirring from time to time, for about 45 minutes, until it thickens and coats the back of the spoon.

Pour the rice pudding into individual bowls, leave it to cool, then cover and chill. Just before serving, sprinkle with a few nuts and some grated coconut.

Meghlie

MASTIC

(MASTAKA) *Pistacia lentiscus*

This aromatic gum is obtained from the *Pistacia lentiscus,* a tree that grows wild in the Mediterranean region. Mastic has such a strong taste of the tree that it was used as a spice in medieval Islamic stews. Today it is rarely used as a spice in savory dishes but is coveted for the chewy twang and delicious resinous flavor it imparts to sweet dishes and breads. Softened with a little candle wax, it is sold as chewing gum. It should not be confused with gum arabic, the resin of acacia trees, which is used as glue.

HOW IT GROWS

The *Pistacia lentiscus* is a small, bushy, evergreen tree that grows wild on the hillsides of Lebanon, Jordan, Syria, and Turkey. To obtain the mastic, a vertical cut is made on the thin trunk, from which a teardrop of the clear, sticky resin will exude. Some of the blobs of resin are scraped off with a knife, others have to be collected from the ground, where ants may have stuck to them.

APPEARANCE AND TASTE

Mastic is sold in the form of hard, transparent crystals, sometimes complete with ants.

The crystals should smell of the tree, an aroma that is intensified when they are crushed. For cooking. the crystals must first be pulverized with a little sugar in a mortar and pestle. In its natural form, mastic is chewed for pleasure like chewing gum. It has a fresh, resinous aroma and taste.

BUYING AND STORING

Two grades of mastic are available: the perfect, clear crystals, which have been scraped off the tree and are, therefore, more expensive; and the cheaper ones, which have been collected off the ground and may contain some passing wildlife. In my experience, they taste the same and store well in airtight containers away from direct sunlight, which turns them yellow over time.

CULINARY USES

With its rich resinous flavor and chewy texture, mastic is fabulous stuff. In Turkey it is what gives a punch to the famous snowy-white, chewy ice cream and the glorious milk pudding from the Ottoman kitchens. It is occasionally added to *rakı* to give it an interesting, chewy dimension. There is also a mastic-flavored Turkish Delight. In Egypt it is still added to some stews and, in some parts of the Middle East, it is added to some sweet bread doughs for flavor, as well as to make them more elastic.

Mastic is sometimes added to the potent rakı

Mastic

The following deep-fried fritters, which vary in shape and size in the different regions, are usually associated with religious feasting, such as the breaking of the fast of Ramadan. In Turkey they are believed to represent the Prophet's seal and are served during the celebrations of Kandil, when the minarets are illuminated throughout the country. They are delicious flavored with mastic and *rakı,* and soaked in a honey or lemon syrup.

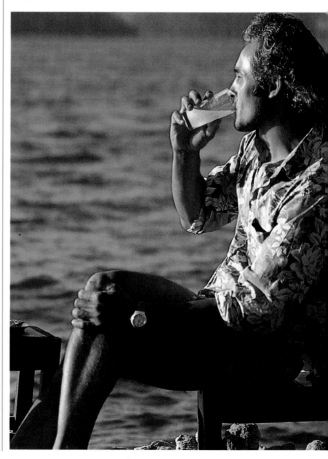

SARAY LOKMASI
(MASTIC-FLAVORED PUFFS IN HONEY)

Serves 6
Preparation time approximately
   5 hours
Cooking time 20 minutes

For the batter:
1 teaspoon active dry yeast
Scant 1 cup lukewarm water
2 cups strong all-purpose flour
A good pinch salt
1 mastic crystal, ground with 1
   teaspoon sugar
2–3 tablespoons rakı

For the syrup:
½ cup sugar
½ cup water
About ¼ cup honey of your choice

Sunflower oil for deep-frying
Ground cinnamon or nutmeg for
   sprinkling

Dissolve the yeast in a little
lukewarm water.

In a large bowl, sift the flour
with the salt. Make a well in the
middle and pour in the yeast,
mastic, *rakı,* and some of the
water. Use a wooden spoon to
draw in the flour from the sides
and gradually add the rest of
the water until you have a
smooth, loose batter.

Cover the bowl with a damp
dishtowel and leave to stand for
4–6 hours until the batter
thickens and becomes quite
elastic.

To make the syrup, put the
sugar and water into a heavy-
based saucepan and bring to a
boil, stirring all the time. Reduce
the heat, stir in the honey, and
simmer for 10 minutes. Put
aside.

When the batter is ready, heat
enough oil in a shallow, or
curved, pan for deep-frying.
Drop little spoonfuls (you might

Muhallabia

find it easier to use two spoons,
one for scooping up the elastic
batter, the other for scraping it
off that spoon) into the oil and
watch them puff up and rise to
the surface. Fry in batches until
golden brown, remove with a
perforated spoon, and drain on
paper towels.

Pop the puffs onto a serving
dish, heat the syrup, and pour it
over them. Use a spoon to coat
them well in the syrup and serve
warm or at room temperature
sprinkled with a little ground
cinnamon or nutmeg.

This classic milk pudding,
common throughout the Middle
East, can be made as plain or as
grand as you like. Served plain,
it is usually sprinkled with
confectioners' sugar. For a
more elaborate presentation, it

is served floating in rose water,
decorated with fresh or
crystallized petals. Some people
decorate the pudding with
almonds and pistachios, others
flavor it with chocolate or
vanilla, but to my mind the
most exquisite of all is the
taste of mastic.

MUHALLABIA
(MASTIC-FLAVORED MILK PUDDING)

Serves 4–6
Preparation time 5 minutes
Cooking time 35–40 minutes

¼ cup rice flour
3¾ cups milk
½ cup sugar
1 piece of mastic (the size of a
   fingernail), pounded with 1
   teaspoon sugar
Confectioners' sugar

In a small bowl, mix the rice
flour to a loose paste with a
little of the milk and put it aside.

Put the rest of the milk into a
saucepan with the sugar and
bring it to a boil, stirring all
the time.

Stir a little of the hot milk into
the rice flour, then tip the rice
flour into the pan. Stirring
vigorously, bring the liquid back
to a boil, then add the mastic.
Reduce the heat and simmer
gently for 25–30 minutes,
stirring from time to time, until
it thickens.

Pour the mixture into a serving
bowl, or individual bowls, and
leave to cool and form a skin
on top.

Chill before serving and sprinkle
with a little confectioners' sugar.

SUMAC

(SUMAK) *Rhus coriaria*

Sumac berries

Long before the arrival of lemons in the Middle East, sumac and the juice of sour pomegranates were the only souring agents, and still are in parts of Syria and northern Iraq where lemons are rare. Sumac was used by the Romans and is mentioned in medieval Arab cookbooks. Mixed with water, ground sumac was believed to aid digestion and prevent diarrhea, but now, in Lebanon, Syria, Turkey, and Iran, it is commonly used as a condiment for grilled fish and kabobs.

HOW IT GROWS

Various species of the genus *Rhus* grow wild in the Middle East and Mediterranean regions, but it is the fruits of the *Rhus coriaria* that are used in Middle Eastern cooking. The shrub grows in the wild and bears dark red berries, which are dried for use.

APPEARANCE AND TASTE

The hard, dried berries are brick-red, tinged with purple, with a lemony, woody taste. They can be used whole, crushed, or ground into a coarse powder.

BUYING AND STORING

Whole or ground berries are available in Middle Eastern stores and some whole-food stores. The whole berries keep for months in an airtight container but the ground berries tend to lose color and flavor quite quickly.

Ground sumac

CULINARY USES

Sumac is used to give a citrus lift to some salads, such as *fattush* (p181), to *pilafs*, eggs, *kibbeh* (p126), flat breads, and to grilled fish and meat. It is one of the key flavorings in the Palestinian country dish *musakhan*, which consists of chicken sautéed in olive oil, spices, and lemon juice, then stuffed into pita bread. The crushed berries can be steeped in water to extract their flavor and the strained liquid can then be drunk or used like lemon juice in a variety of dishes. Ground sumac is sprinkled on soups and grilled meat, and is also one of the spices in the Arabic spice mix *zaatar* (p196), which includes sesame seeds, salt, and thyme. In some restaurants and kabob houses in the Middle East, sumac will be one of the condiments on the table, along with dried mint, oregano or thyme, and Middle Eastern red pepper (p152) or paprika, for sprinkling on soups and kabobs.

These excellent Arab-style pizzas make a wonderful snack as well as a meal. Called *lahmacun* in Turkish and *missahatz* by the Armenians, they are enjoyed by all. The Armenians were at one time responsible for the bread and pastry trade in Syria and Lebanon, and they are still known for their delicious *lahma bi ajeen*. Generally, they are made very thin and served with chopped parsley, sumac, and lemon to squeeze over them. If they are bought in the street, they are usually rolled up and eaten in the hands.

LAHMA BI AJEEN
(SAVORY FLAT BREADS)

Serves 4–8 people (depending on size and how greedy people are!)
Preparation time approximately 3 hours
Cooking time 8–10 minutes for each batch

For the dough:
1 cake compresed fresh yeast or 1 teaspoon active dry yeast
½ teaspoon sugar
Roughly 1¼ cups lukewarm water
4 cups strong white flour
½ teaspoon salt
2 tablespoons sunflower or olive oil

For the filling:
2 tablespoons olive oil
2 onions, finely chopped
2 cloves garlic, finely chopped
2 cups ground lamb
2 tomatoes, peeled, finely chopped, and drained
2 teaspoons tomato paste
1 teaspoon sugar
1–2 teaspoons Middle Eastern red pepper (p152)
Juice of ½ lemon
A small bunch of flat-leaf parsley, finely chopped
Salt

For the top:
1–2 tablespoons sumac
A small bunch of flat-leaf parsley, roughly chopped
1 lemon, cut into wedges

First, dissolve the yeast with the sugar in a little of the lukewarm water.

Sift the flour with the salt into a big bowl and make a well in the center. Pour the yeast, the rest of the water, and the oil into the well, then, using your hands, draw in the flour and work the mixture into a dough.

Turn the dough onto a floured surface and knead it for about 10 minutes, until it is smooth and elastic. Put a few drops of oil into the base of the bowl and roll the dough in it. Cover the bowl with a damp dishtowel and leave the dough to rise for about 2 hours, until it has doubled in size.

Meanwhile, preheat the oven to 475°F.

Heat the oil in a skillet and soften the onions and garlic. Turn off the heat before they brown, leaving them to cool in the pan.

In a bowl, mix the ground lamb, the tomatoes, and the tomato paste. Add the sugar, red pepper, lemon juice, parsley, and salt, and knead the mixture with your hands. Drain the onions and garlic of oil and add them to the mixture, kneading well.

When the dough has risen, punch it down and divide into 8 balls, or lots of walnut-size ones. On a floured surface, roll each ball into a thin, flat circle or oval, stretching it a little with your hands. Spread the meat filling generously in a smooth layer on each flat dough, right up to the edges, and transfer them to lightly greased baking sheets.

Pop them into the oven for about 8–10 minutes, depending on the size of the flat dough. (If cooking in batches, the oven temperature may drop—try not to let it go below 450°F.) The meat should be cooked but the flat bread should remain soft enough to roll up.

Sprinkle each one with sumac and parsley, and a squeeze of lemon juice if you like, and eat it flat off a plate, or roll it up and eat it with your hands.

Lahma bi ajeen

A Palestinian country dish, *musakhan* is popular in Jordan, where a large proportion of the population is Palestinian. The chicken, flavored with sumac and other spices, is traditionally baked on thick, spongy *tabun* bread, which is similar to Turkish *pide*; ordinary pita bread is often used as a substitute.

MUSAKHAN
(PALESTINIAN BREAD WITH CHICKEN AND SUMAC)

Serves 4 as a meal, 8 as a snack
Preparation time 10 minutes
Cooking time 25–30 minutes

3 tablespoons olive oil and a little butter
3–4 onions, chopped
1 pound boneless chicken breasts, cut into bite-size pieces
2 teaspoons ground sumac
1 teaspoon ground cinnamon
½ teaspoon ground cardamom
Juice of 1 lime
Salt and ground black pepper
4 pita breads, halved to form 8 pockets

Preheat the oven to 350°F.

Heat the oil and butter in a heavy-based pan and stir in the onions.

Cook until they just begin to color, then add the chicken and sumac. Cook for a few minutes to sear the chicken, then reduce the heat and stir in the spices and lime juice. Cook gently for about 10 minutes until the chicken is tender.

Season to taste, then fill the pita pockets with the chicken mixture. Arrange them on a baking sheet and pop them in the oven for about 10 minutes.

Serve with strained yogurt, either spooned into the pocket or on top, and a salad.

ROSE

(WARD) *Rosa*

Dried roses in spice store

The origins and uses of the rose can be traced back to ancient Egypt, Persia, and Babylon. In the days before soap, the Egyptians bathed in water scented with rose petals, as a perfumed body was believed to give sensual pleasure. The Romans, who associated the rose with Venus, scented their water and wine with roses and celebrated their victories by scattering rose petals in the streets. By the ninth century the Persians were making wine from rose petals and distilling rose water on a large scale. However, the discovery of rose water has been attributed to the eleventh-century Persian physician Ibn Sina, known as Avicenna in the West, as it was in his time that the scented water was used as a food flavoring in the sumptuous Arab dishes. During the Ottoman period it became one of the favorite flavorings of the palace kitchens, where it was used in many syrupy pastries and milk puddings. As the Ottoman Empire expanded, roses were introduced to Bulgaria, where the Valley of the Roses is famous for its roses and rose products.

HOW IT GROWS

There are numerous species and hybrids that have edible petals and from which rose water can be made. The most common types used for culinary purposes in the Middle East are *Rosa centifolia* (cabbage rose), *Rosa damascena* (damask rose), and *Rosa moschata* (musk rose). They grow well in Azerbaijan and around the desert city of Kashan in Iran, and they grow in the lake district of central Anatolia and in the plains and hillsides around Isparta in Turkey. The roses are planted in January and don't produce a crop of flowers until their third year, but the plants live for twenty to thirty years. The flowers are gathered in the early morning before they are exposed to the hot sun and lose their essential oils.

APPEARANCE AND TASTE

Most of the rose petals used for culinary purposes are candy pink, lilac, or red. They must be in full bloom and richly scented to impart their sweet smell to a dish. Fresh rose petals can be used for culinary purposes but generally they are dried first. Rose water is colorless and has a light, fresh smell of roses.

BUYING AND STORING

If you have your own garden, you can harvest petals from your own roses, otherwise you will have to choose fresh, fragrant roses from a flower store and dry them yourself. Bags of dried rose petals are available in Middle Eastern stores. Rose water and rose oil are sold in whole-food and Indian stores, as well as Middle Eastern stores. The petals will lose their fragrance over time, as they do in pot-pourri, if they are not kept in an airtight container. Rose water will last for a couple of years and the oil will keep no longer than five years.

OTHER USES

Attar of roses (from Persian *atr*), also known as otto of roses or rose oil, is made by soaking or steaming the petals to extract their fragrance. Attar of roses distilled from *Rosa damascena* is an essential oil used in many fine perfumes. It takes three to four tons of fresh rose petals to produce 2¼ pounds of oil, which makes its value comparable to its weight in gold. Turkey produces 60 percent of the world's attar of roses, and it also produces a refreshing, fragrant rose cologne.

Rose- and lemon-flavored Turkish Delight

CULINARY USES

To capture their delightful, sweet fragrance, rose petals have been infused in sugar, wine, honey, oil, vinegar, syrup, milk, and water since ancient times. In Iran and Turkey rose petals are used to make a heavenly scented jam and a refreshing floral sorbet. In those parts of the Middle East influenced by the Ottoman Empire, rose water is used to flavor chilled fruit and nut compotes, such as *khoshaf* (p145), and traditional milk puddings, such as *muhallabia* (p187). It flavors the plain or milky syrups used in sweet pastries, such as the Turkish *güllaç*, made with starch wafers and most commonly associated with Ramadan, and in sweet dishes such as *belila* (p126), a Jewish grain dessert served in Sephardic communities to commemorate happy occasions, such as the cutting of a baby's first tooth. It is also used to flavor *aşure* (p109), which, according to legend, was made with all the grains, fruit, and nuts on Noah's Ark when supplies ran low, and it is the favorite flavoring in the famous Turkish Delight *güllü lokum*. In Iran the dried petals or dried rosebuds are added to a mild version of the spice mixture *advieh* (p169) to give it a fragrant lift. And in Azerbaijan the dried petals are ground to a powder to give a fragrant lift to some sweet and savory rice dishes, and to sprinkle over chicken. The fruits (rose hips) are occasionally used for tea or for flavoring syrup.

This exquisite, scented jam is one of the ancient delights of the Middle East. Packed with delicate rose petals and runny like thick syrup, it is delicious spooned on bread or over *ataif*

Gül reçeli

(p143), the Middle Eastern pancakes. Any scented rose petals will do, even the old-fashioned cottage garden rose. Sometimes rose petals are soaked in lime water, or slaked lime, to render them almost transparent before adding them to the syrup.

GÜL REÇELI
(ROSE PETAL JAM)

Makes approximately 3 cups jam
Preparation time 5 minutes
Cooking time 40 minutes

1 pound fresh or dried, scented
   pink or lilac rose petals
1¼ cups water
2 cups sugar
Juice of 1 lemon

Trim the petals, rinse them if necessary, and drain them.

Pour the water into a deep, heavy-based pan, add the petals, and bring it to a boil. Strain the petals, put them aside, and pour the rose-scented water back into the pan.

Stir in the sugar and bring the water to a boil, stirring all the time. Reduce the heat and simmer for about 10 minutes.

Stir in the lemon juice and the rose petals and simmer for a further 10–15 minutes, until the syrup thickens. Leave the jam to cool in the pan, then spoon it into sterilized jars.

Confectionery plays a big part in the social life of the Middle East. Special candies are eaten on religious holidays and festive days, and are distributed at celebrations such as births, weddings, and circumcisions. In the home, sweet pastries or cakes are offered to guests with tea, coffee, or a cool sherbet drink. Guest don't come empty-handed either, arriving with wrapped boxes of sweet pastries such as baklava (p137) or Turkish Delight, *lokum*. Rose-flavored Turkish Delight is one of the all-time favorites, often tinged pink with a little red food coloring. Homemade Turkish Delight is much softer than its commercially made cousin and melts deliciously in the mouth.

GÜLLÜ LOKUM
(ROSE-FLAVORED TURKISH DELIGHT)

Makes 30–35 pieces
Preparation time 5 minutes
Cooking time approximately
   2 hours

3 cups sugar
2½ cups water
¾ cup cornstarch (+ extra for
   lining the mold)
2–3 tablespoons rose water
Confectioners' sugar

Line a 7–8-inch square mold with a piece of cheesecloth covered with a layer of cornstarch.

Put the sugar and water into a heavy-based pan and bring it to a boil, stirring all the time. Put the cornstarch into another pan with about 1 cup of water. Mix it well and bring it to a boil, stirring all the time until it is smooth and creamy.

Gradually add the cornstarch mixture to the hot syrup, stirring vigorously to prevent lumps from forming. Keep stirring while you bring the mixture to a boil, then reduce the heat to very low. Cook, uncovered, for about 1½ hours, stirring frequently to prevent sticking and caramelizing. The mixture should be so thick, it barely drips off the spoon.

Add the rose water and a few drops coloring if you wish, then test the mixture by dropping a little into a cup of cold water to see if it forms a soft gelatin.

Pour the mixture into the mold and leave it to cool and set. Spread a thick layer of confectioners' sugar on a flat surface and invert the *lokum* onto it. Remove the cheesecloth, brush off the excess cornstarch, then cut the block into small squares. Roll each one in the confectioners' sugar until it is well coated.

CLOVE

(MASAMIR QARANFUL) *Syzygium aromaticum*

The name clove derives from the Latin *clavus*, meaning "nail," which is also reflected in the Arabic, *masamir qaranful*, which translates as "nails of clove." Used in China as early as the third century BC, cloves are thought to have originated in the Moluccas, the Spice Islands. The Dutch, who occupied the islands in 1605, cultivated cloves and controlled the monopoly until the French smuggled seeds to Mauritius, from where the spice reached Madagascar and Tanzania. Cloves first entered the Middle East from India through Egypt, and made their way to the Mediterranean regions.

HOW IT GROWS

Cloves are the dried, unopened flowerbud of a small evergreen tree that belongs to the myrtle family and grows only in tropical, maritime climates, so it thrives in Indonesia, Madagascar, and Tanzania. It flowers twice a year and the fully grown, unopened buds, which grow in clusters, are harvested by hand just at the moment they develop a pink flush. When the buds have been picked, they are dried in the sun until they become woody and turn brown. It is the four petals of the flower, with the stamens inside, that form the nail-like head of the clove.

APPEARANCE AND TASTE

The shape of the clove is similar to a small nail, which is reflected in the Arabic name, as well as in French, Spanish, and Portuguese. Freshly dried cloves should be dark brown with a strong, almost sharp, bitter taste on the tongue when chewed on their own. They leave the mouth feeling quite warm and numb, as well as refreshed. It is the eugenol, which is also present in cinnamon, that gives cloves their distinctive flavor.

BUYING AND STORING

Look for whole cloves that are definitely brown, not gray or dusty. If they have been dried recently, they will be slightly oily when you press or crush them. Whole cloves keep well if stored in dry, airtight containers, but ground cloves lose their flavor quickly, so it is best to grind them when you need to.

CULINARY USES

Whole cloves are used to flavor some rice dishes, festive cookies, desserts, and jams, such as the Turkish plum-tomato jam. They are also used to cut the fat in heavy meat stews, and to purify the meat in some variety-meat dishes, such as the Turkish dish of stewed brains, *beyin salatısı*, and the Arab dish of calf's feet and chickpeas, *kawareh bi hummus*, found all over the Middle East. Whole cloves are also infused with cinnamon, ginger, and aniseed to make the Arab spiced drink *miglee (meghlie)*, which is served to visitors when a baby is born. Cloves feature in the Arab spice mixture *baharat* (p162), which also includes black pepper corns, coriander seeds, cinnamon, cumin, cardamom, nutmeg, and paprika. With their cleansing, spicy aroma and sensation, whole cloves are often chewed to freshen the breath after strong tastes such as garlic and mint.

The cooked feet of lambs and calves are very popular in the Middle East. Traditional soups and stews are made with them when an animal is slaughtered, particularly during Eid-el-Kurban, the festival to mark the near-sacrifice of Isma'il (p 69). The calf's feet in the following dish, which is enjoyed in the Balkans, Portugal, and Spain too, are sometimes replaced by pig's feet in some Christian communities.

KAWAREH BI HUMMUS

(CALF'S FEET WITH CHICKPEAS)

Serves 4
Preparation time 20 minutes (+ 8 hours' soaking)
Cooking time approximately 4 hours

2–3 tablespoons clarified butter (ghee), or olive oil with a little butter
2 calf's feet, thoroughly cleaned and blanched in boiling water
1 heaping cup chickpeas, soaked for 8 hours, or overnight, and drained
1–2 teaspoons ground turmeric
6 whole cloves
2 dried bay leaves
4 eggs, well scrubbed
Salt and freshly ground black pepper

Heat the clarified butter, or oil, in a heavy-based pan and brown the feet all over.

Add the chickpeas, turmeric, cloves, and bay leaves, and cover with water. Season with salt and pepper, and carefully slip in the whole eggs.

Bring the liquid to a boil, then turn the heat down very low and simmer for 3–4 hours, adding more water if necessary, until the meat is almost falling off the bones. Cut the meat off the bones, if you like, and serve hot with flat bread and pickles.

Whole cloves

This delightful jam comes from Turkey, where the plum tomatoes are first dipped into a lime-water solution to stabilize the firm texture. It is more of a conserve than a jam, ideal for spooning onto bread or yogurt. To prepare the tomatoes, submerge them in boiling water for a few seconds, then plunge them into a bowl of cold water, and peel.

DOMATES REÇELİ
(PLUM-TOMATO AND ALMOND JAM)

Makes 3–4 jars
Preparation time 15–20 minutes
Cooking time approximately 30 minutes

4 pounds firm plum tomatoes, peeled
About 1¼ cups water
4 cups sugar
1¼ cups whole, blanched almonds
8–10 whole cloves

If the tomatoes vary in size, halve some of the larger ones, but keep most of them whole.

Put the water and sugar into a pan and bring it to a boil, stirring all the time.

Add the tomatoes and boil vigorously for a few minutes, skimming some of the foam off the top. Reduce the heat and simmer for 5 minutes, then stir in the blanched almonds and cloves.

Bring back to a boil, then simmer for 10–15 minutes, until the syrup coats the back of a spoon. Turn off the heat and leave to cool completely. Spoon the jam into sterilized jars and store in a cool place.

Domates reçeli

TAMARIND

(TAMER HINDI) *Tamarindus indica*

Native to tropical Africa, the large evergreen tamarind tree spread to India in

Tamarind pods

prehistoric times and now grows in the tropical and subtropical regions of the world. It would have been the Arabs who first brought tamarind across the Persian Gulf from India, influencing the cooking of the southeast of Iran, the Gulf region, and Egypt. Some of the best recipes using tamarind are found in the coastal regions of the Gulf, where it is often married with fenugreek, turmeric, or curry powder in delicious fish dishes, echoing the flavors of India. Reflecting its origins, the Arabic for tamarind means "Indian date."

HOW IT GROWS

With strong, bending branches and an extensive root system, the tree can survive in dry soil and high winds. The cinnamon-colored pods, which are the fruit of the tree, grow in clusters and contain very small beans, which are surrounded by a sour, fruity pulp. When the pods have fully ripened, it is the pulp that is extracted for culinary use.

APPEARANCE AND TASTE

The bean-shaped pods and small seeds are inedible, but the fresh tamarind fruit pulp, which is light brown, is dried and compressed into sticky blocks that look like a mass of fruit, fibers, and seeds. It is also pressed and strained to make a smooth, concentrated paste. Both the blocks and paste are dark, almost black, a color similar to dried dates, and have a taste akin to a sour prune.

BUYING AND STORING

Fresh tamarind pods are available only in some Asian markets, but both the blocks of compressed tamarind pulp and the jars or tubs of paste are available in Middle Eastern, Asian, and whole-food stores. They both keep for a long time but, once opened, the block should be stored in an airtight container; the paste keeps better in the refrigerator. A prepared syrup, ready to be diluted as a drink, can also be found in some of the same stores.

CULINARY USES

The tamarind pulp needs to be soaked in water, then strained to extract the dark brown juice. The concentrated paste can be diluted with hot water or added directly to a dish, often balanced by sugar or honey to give a sweet–sour flavor. A teaspoon of the concentrated paste, sweetened with sugar and diluted with boiling water, is sometimes served as a drink. Tamarind syrup is also added to dishes for its sweet–sour flavor and it is used to make an instant, refreshing drink by just adding chilled water. Tamarind is used for its unique flavor in a number of meat and vegetable dishes. It works very well as a sauce with stuffed or sautéed onions, leeks, potatoes, and eggplants, or in a dressing for shellfish. In Iran and the Gulf region it is a popular flavor in fish and shellfish dishes.

This delicious dish from the Persian Gulf represents a history of trade between the Arabs and Indians who stopped off at the Persian ports. It is one of many such dishes from that area using local fish and large shrimp.

GHALIYEH MÂHI

(FISH STEW WITH TAMARIND AND GARLIC)

Serves 6
Preparation time 20–25 minutes
Cooking time 45 minutes

½ cup tamarind pulp, soaked in 1½ cups water for about 15 minutes
2 tablespoons all-purpose flour
2 tablespoons olive oil
1 teaspoon curry powder
1 teaspoon ground fenugreek
½ teaspoon ground turmeric
½ teaspoon red chili powder
3–4 cloves garlic, chopped
A big bunch of flat-leaf parsley, chopped
2¼ pounds fresh white fish, such as porgy or haddock, cut into steaks
Salt

Squeeze the tamarind paste in your fingers to separate the pulp from the seeds and stalks, then strain the pulp and reserve the tamarind water.

Brown the flour in a heavy-based pan. Add a little oil and stir in the curry powder, turmeric, chili powder, and fenugreek, working them into a paste.

Add the garlic and parsley and toss them in the pan for a few minutes, making sure that the spices don't burn. Stir in the tamarind water, cover the pan, and simmer gently for 15–20 minutes.

Slip in the fish steaks and simmer for a further 15–20 minutes, until the fish is tender. Season with salt and serve with rice.

As you travel inland, tamarind tends to be combined with vegetables in sweet-and-sour dishes, a taste that Arabs have enjoyed since medieval times. The preferred vegetables are leek, eggplant, and onion, which are sometimes stuffed before being cooked in tamarind juice. The following simple dish can be made with small onions, shallots, scallions trimmed down to the white stalk and bulb, or leeks.

BASAL BI TAMER HINDI
(SWEET-AND-SOUR ONIONS WITH TAMARIND)

Serves 4–6
Preparation time 15 minutes
Cooking time 25–30 minutes

2–3 tablespoons olive oil
1 pound small onions or shallots, peeled and left whole
1 tablespoon tamarind paste
1 tablespoon sugar
Salt
A small bunch of fresh cilantro, finely chopped

Heat the oil in a heavy-based flat pan and add the onions. Toss them in the pan until they are golden brown all over.

Stir in the tamarind and sugar with enough water to cover the base of the pan and create a sauce, then reduce the heat and put on a lid.

Simmer gently until the onions are soft and the sauce has reduced. Season with salt, sprinkle with cilantro, and serve hot or cold.

Basal bi tamer hindi

THYME

(ZAATAR) *Thymus vulgaris*

Thyme grows wild in the hills and Mediterranean regions of the Middle East, where it is also known as "mountain oregano" because of its similar appearance and aroma. Although there are many types of thyme, there is one (*Thymus capitatus*) that is particularly associated with the Middle East. In Arabic it is called *zaatar farsi*, meaning "Persian thyme," and it this species that is usually used in the spice mixture *zaatar*.

Fresh thyme

HOW IT GROWS

Thyme is a hardy and aromatic plant with small lilac flowers that produce a lovely pungent honey. The leaves are usually picked and dried in the sun. *T. capitatus* (Middle Eastern thyme) is one of the species that provides us with oregano and marjoram.

APPEARANCE AND TASTE

Fresh thyme has a lovely, warm, dry, and spicy aroma, which is intensified when it grows under a hot sun. The thin stems are quite woody and the small, green leaves are usually oval and pointed, or rounded, covered in minute hairs. The herb tastes exactly as it smells: warm, dry, and aromatic. Thyme dries well, turning a darker shade of green but retaining its flavor and aroma.

BUYING AND STORING

Fresh thyme is available in most supermarkets and keeps quite well in plastic bags in the refrigerator. The best dried thyme comes from the Middle East, as the leaves are picked from wild plants and dried in the sun. It's available in Middle Eastern and whole-food stores and should be stored in an airtight container.

CULINARY USES

Zaatar (or *za'atar/zahtar*) is the Arabic name for wild thyme and also the name for the Arab spice mixture that consists of dried wild thyme, ground sumac, salt, and occasionally toasted sesame seeds. In the markets and streets this spice mixture is sold in paper cones, ready to dip hot, fresh bread into. Thyme is the herb used in the ancient dish *mefarka*, a cold dish of ground meat and fava beans that is popular in Jewish communities. Used in much the same way as oregano, which is popular in Turkey, Azerbaijan, and other parts of northwest Iran, thyme is sprinkled on bread, white cheese, fish, tomatoes, thick yogurt, and fried eggs. It can be mixed to a paste with olive oil and spread on bread dough before it is baked, to make *fatayer bi zahtar*. Dried thyme is also used to make an aromatic tea that is believed to be an aphrodisiac. Fresh thyme, which is thought to aid the digestion, is used to flavor game and heavy lamb dishes containing sheep tail fat.

Dried thyme and dried oregano

A dish of ancient origin, *mefarka* is prepared by Jews on feast days, often for the men returning from the synagogue. It is an unusual, aromatic dish that is served cold.

MEFARKA
(FAVA BEANS WITH GROUND BEEF AND THYME)

Serve 4–6
Preparation time 15 minutes
Cooking time 25–30 minutes

1 pound fresh fava beans, shelled
1 teaspoon dried thyme
3 tablespoons olive oil
1½ cups lean ground beef
1 teaspoon baharat (p162)
2 eggs
Juice of ½ lemon
Salt and pepper

Put the fava beans into a pan with the thyme, some salt and pepper, and 1 tablespoon of olive oil mixed with about ⅔ cup of water. Simmer gently, topping up with a little more water as it is absorbed, until the beans are tender.

Meanwhile, heat the remaining olive oil in a heavy-based pan and add the beef. Stir in the spice mixture and add enough water to just cover the meat. Simmer until the meat is cooked but still moist, and season to taste with *baharat*.

Zaatar

Add the beans to the pan and mix well with the beef, crushing the mixture lightly with a fork. Break the eggs into the pan and stir them into the mixture until they have set.

Turn the contents of the pan onto a serving dish and leave to cool. Taste to check the flavors, adding more salt or thyme if necessary, and serve with a splash of lemon juice.

These little spice breads are popular breakfast and snack food, sold in cafés, in bakeries, and on the street.

FATAYER BI ZAATAR
(THYME AND SUMAC BREADS)

Makes 20
Preparation time approximately 2½ hours
Cooking time 10 minutes for each batch

For the dough:
1 cake compressed fresh yeast or 1 teaspoon active dry yeast
½ teaspoon sugar
1¼ cups lukewarm water
4 cups strong white flour
½ teaspoon salt
2 tablespoons olive oil

For the paste:
¼ cup dried thyme
2 tablespoons ground sumac
¼ cup olive oil
Salt

Fatayer bi zaatar

Dissolve the yeast with the sugar in a little of the water, until it foams. Sift the flour with the salt in a big bowl and make a well in the center. Pour in the yeast, the rest of the water, and the oil. Draw in the flour from the sides and work the mixture into a dough.

Turn the dough onto a lightly floured surface and knead for about 10 minutes, until it is smooth and elastic. Pour a few drops of oil into the base of the bowl and roll the dough in it. Cover with a damp distowel and leave the dough to rise for about 2 hours, until it has doubled in size.

Meanwhile, preheat the oven to 450°F.

In a bowl, mix together the thyme, sumac, olive oil, and salt to form a paste.

When the dough has risen, punch it down and divide it into roughly 20 pieces. Flatten the pieces out in the palm of your hand, stretching them with your fingers. Place them on lightly greased baking sheets and, using your fingers, spread some of the paste evenly over each one.

Pop them in the oven for about 10 minutes, until lightly browned. Serve hot or at room temperature.

Fenugreek seeds

FENUGREEK

(HILBEH) *Trigonella foenumgraecum*

The botanical name of fenugreek means "Greek hay," as the plant used to be cultivated in the Mediterranean region for animal fodder, although the seeds were reserved for medicinal purposes. The ancient Egyptians were known to plaster their bodies in a paste made from ground fenugreek seeds to reduce fever. Fenugreek greens are a staple food in Yemen and the seeds, which are rich in vitamins and sugar, are used in a number of Arab dishes. Ground fenugreek, which is more often associated with commercial Indian curry powder, features in the cooking of the Arabian Gulf.

The best *pastırma* is said to be made by the Armenians, who have been involved in its manufacture since the height of the Ottoman Empire. Finely sliced, this dry, flavorsome delicacy is often served as *mezze* along with olives and white cheese, or it is cooked with spinach, eggs, or beans. The following Anatolian peasant dish, in which the *pastırma* lends its deliciously pungent flavor and aroma to the other ingredients, is traditionally cooked in a flat earthenware dish, or curved tile, called a *kiremit*. Turkish *pastırma* and Arab *basterma/bastırma* are available in some Middle Eastern stores.

Pastırma (or basterma in Arabic)

HOW IT GROWS

Related to clover, fenugreek is cultivated in the Mediterranean region, Yemen, and Egypt. It is an annual plant that grows to about 2 feet tall. The oval leaves grow in clusters, with slender pods that contain the seeds.

APPEARANCE AND TASTE

Fenugreek seeds are like small, golden pebbles. They are extremely bitter to taste and need to be dry-roasted to bring out their warm, spicy, celery-like aroma, which is both pleasant and pungent. Ground fenugreek should be the color of golden sand.

BUYING AND STORING

Whole seeds and ground fenugreek are available in most Middle Eastern and Indian stores. Sometimes the fresh and dried leaves are available too. The seeds store well in an airtight container and are easy to roast and crush or grind to a powder.

MEDICINAL AND OTHER USES

Ancient herbalists believed that fenugreek reduced fever and aided digestion. In the eleventh century the Persian physician Ibn Sina (Avicenna) recommended fenugreek for diabetes. Today, too, fenugreek is used in medicines for diabetics and in the manufacture of some oral contraceptives. Crushed or ground fenugreek yields a yellow dye, which is used in fabrics and to color wool for carpet-making.

Ground fenugreek

CULINARY USES

Fenugreek greens are cooked like spinach in Yemen. In the Arab kitchen, the seeds are often used to flavor spinach, vegetable stews, lentils, and a sweet rice dish called *shola-e-olba*. The seeds are also used in pickling. Ground fenugreek is used in some sauces for meat, poultry, and fish, and in the fenugreek dip *hilbeh*, which is popular in Yemen and the Arabian Gulf. Ground fenugreek is also the principal flavoring in *çemen*, the red pepper and garlic paste that coats *pastırma*, the Turkish air-dried filet of beef (called *basterma/bastırma* in the Arab world). The fresh leaves, seeds, and powder also give some of the Iranian and eastern Anatolian herb omelets and vegetable stews their distinctive flavor and pungency.

KIREMİTTE PASTIRMA

(*PASTIRMA* BAKED WITH ONIONS AND PEPPERS)

Serves 4–6
Preparation time 15 minutes
Cooking time 45 minutes

8 ounces finely sliced *pastırma*, cut into small pieces
2 bell peppers, roughly chopped
2 onions, roughly chopped
2 cloves garlic, roughly chopped
Olive oil
Salt and freshly ground black pepper
A small bunch of fresh flat-leaf parsley or cilantro, chopped

Preheat the oven to 400°F.

Put the *pastırma*, peppers, onions, and garlic into a shallow baking dish and drizzle with a generous amount of olive oil. Cover the dish with foil and pop it in the oven for about 25 minutes.

Remove the foil and return the dish to the oven for 20 minutes.

Season the mixture and toss in the fresh herbs. Serve hot with flat bread.

Kiremitte pastırma

The flavor of fenugreek is one of the distinctive features of the cooking of Yemen and the Arabian Gulf. *Hilbeh*, a paste made with fenugreek seeds and fresh cilantro, is one of the household condiments, like *zhug* (p169), that is used as a dip for bread or added to stews. Bound with choppedf fresh tomatoes, it is served as a *mezze* dish, also called *hilbeh*.

HILBEH
(FENUGREEK RELISH)

Serves 4
Preparation time about 25 minutes (+ 18 hours' soaking)
Cooking time —

* *2 teaspoons fenugreek seeds, soaked in water for about 18 hours until they have softened and formed a gelatin-like coating, drained*
* *2 cloves garlic, chopped*
* *1 fresh chili, chopped*
* *A good-sized bunch of fresh cilantro, chopped*
* *2–3 big tomatoes, peeled and very finely chopped*
* *½ teaspoon sugar*
* *Juice of ½ lemon*
* *Salt*

Using a mortar and pestle, grind the fenugreek seeds, garlic, chili, and cilantro to a coarse paste. Tip it into a bowl and bind it with the tomatoes.

Beat in the sugar and lemon juice and add salt to taste. Serve with flat bread to scoop it up.

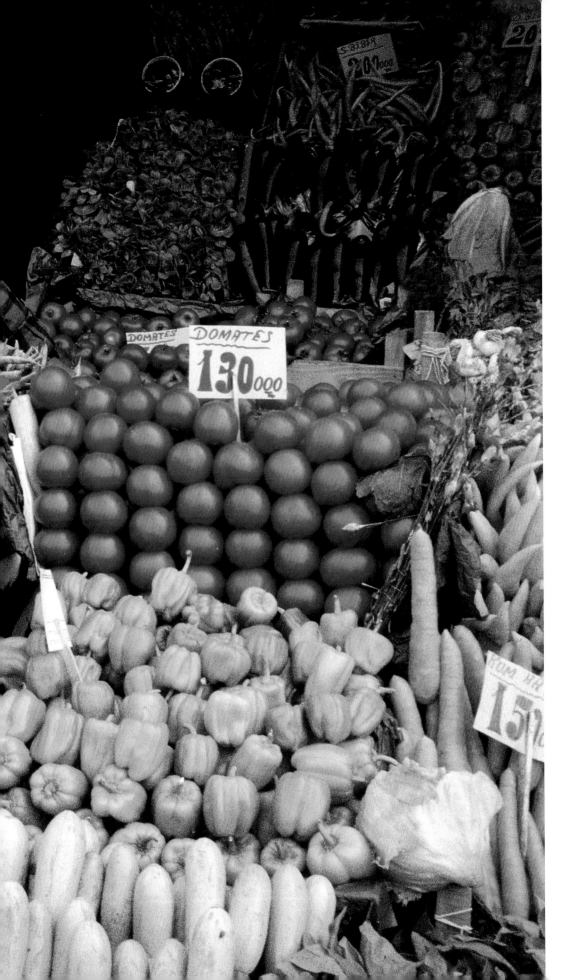

VEGETABLES

ONION

(BASAL) *Allium cepa*

Onions

Originally native to central Asia, various members of the onion family have been cultivated and eaten since prehistoric times. They appeared in the tomb paintings of ancient Egypt, and onion bulbs were placed inside the bandages of mummies to encourage the dead to breathe again. In the Bible (Numbers 11:5) the Israelites are said to have longed for onions and garlic in the wilderness. In ancient Greece and Rome, onions were eaten by the common people and shunned by the nobility because of their lingering, pungent smell. Like garlic, onions gave men courage and strength but bad breath too. The Prophet Muhammad is said to have liked eating onions but disliked their odor, so he asked people not to smell of onion or garlic when they came to the mosque. Today in the Middle East, onions are used liberally and daily, raw and cooked. In Iran fried onions play such an important role that it's said a girl is ready for marriage when she can make her onions crispy and golden.

HOW IT GROWS

Different varieties of onion grow in the Middle East—some are harvested in the spring, others in the autumn, so they are always available. Scallions and the long, thick onion tops are also popular. Scallions, named after the ancient Palestinian port of Ascalon, are grown as salad onions.

APPEARANCE AND TASTE

The most common varieties of onion in the Middle East are the big, round, white-skinned ones, which are mild in taste; the elongated pinky-gold or purple ones, which are sweet and strong with a pinkish flesh; and the pale golden-skinned ones, which can be quite strong. The scallions are quite sweet and juicy, usually munched on like a celery rib, and the onion tops are quite sharp-tasting, like leeks, so they are often mellowed in butter or cooked in an Arab *eggah* (p219).

BUYING AND STORING

All onions should be hard and firm when bought. Don't buy them if they are soft or sprouting little green shoots. In theory, onions should store well through the winter if they are kept in a cool, dry place.

CULINARY USES

As a simple *mezze* dish to be eaten with bread, onions are sometimes chopped and mixed with fresh, sour pomegranate seeds and a squeeze of lemon juice, or marinated in a little vinegar and chopped fresh mint. One of their principal roles in Middle Eastern cooking is in the form of onion juice, used as a marinade for grilled fish or lamb, such as the Turkish dish *çöp şiş*. (p 73). To make onion juice, the onions are grated or chopped to a pulp, sprinkled with salt, and left to weep. The pulp is then pressed through a strainer to extract the juice.

Freshly harvested onions drying on a mesh top

Onion and tomato seller at a vegetable market, southern Turkey

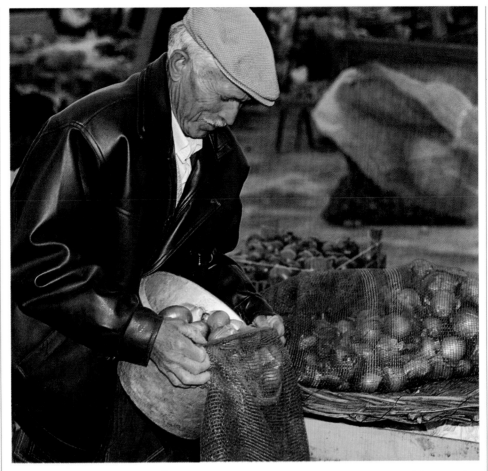

Raw onions often form part of a salad, such as the Syrian and Turkish ones made with oranges, lemons, onions, and olives, or the gypsy and peasant ones made with fresh herbs and onions, often with a little crumbled cheese tossed through them. They are also used in numerous bean salads, and the bulgur and herb salads tabbouleh (p180) and *kısır*, so popular in Turkey, Syria, and Lebanon. The large, sweeter onions are often hollowed out, stuffed with a meat or rice filling, and baked. Whole sweet onions are also baked in their skins, often in the bread ovens or ashes of a fire, and then the mellow, cooked flesh is roughly chopped and dressed with olive oil, lemon juice, and parsley. The smaller onions are often cooked whole in stews or grilled in kabobs. And the little button or pearl onions are delicious cooked in a sweet-and-sour dish with golden raisins and mint.

Onions are chopped or sliced and added to stews, such as the Turkish *yahni* dishes, and to soups, particularly the Iranian soup *eshkeneh*, an onion and egg soup with broken, dried bread, said to have been fed to the Ashkani foot soldiers during King Arsaces' reign. Crispy, fried onions are an important component of many Iranian dishes, where they are used for flavor, for thickening sauces, for stuffings, and for a garnish.

Scallions are mostly eaten raw in salads, and the long, fresh onion tops are popular fried in butter and cooked in a type of omelet. Onion seed, *shamar* in Arabic, is often mixed with sesame seeds and sprinkled on bread and on the bracelet-shaped *kahk* (p163).

Such is the stigma of onions that some Muslims stay clear of them on Fridays, the day of prayer at the mosque. But there is a saying that "he who eats onions for forty-one days will become a *hadji* [pilgrim] to Mecca." As Mecca is in Saudi Arabia, here is a delicious onion dish from there.

MAHSHI BASAL
(SAUDI ARABIAN STUFFED ONIONS)

Serves 4
Preparation time 35–40 minutes
Cooking time 1¼ hours

2 large onions, peeled and left whole
1 cup lean ground lamb
½ cup long-grain rice, washed and drained
2 teaspoons tomato paste
1 teaspoon ground cinnamon
A small bunch of fresh parsley, finely chopped
2 tablespoons olive oil
1–2 tablespoons vinegar
1 teaspoon sugar
Salt and freshly ground black pepper

Bring a pan of water to a boil. Using a sharp knife, make a cut in each onion from top to bottom down one side, then place them in the boiling water for about 10 minutes, until they are soft and begin to unwrap. Drain and refresh the onions, then separate each layer.

Put the ground lamb in a bowl and knead it for 1–2 minutes, slapping it down into the bowl. Add the rice, tomato paste, cinnamon, parsley, and some salt and pepper, and knead for about 10 minutes to make sure it is well mixed.

Place roughly 1 tablespoon of the filling into the hollow of each onion layer, and roll it up tightly.

Put the stuffed onions in a wide, heavy-based pan, packed together closely. Add the olive oil, vinegar, a sprinkling of sugar, and enough water to just cover. Put the lid on and cook gently for about 50 minutes, until the rice and meat are well cooked.

Meanwhile, preheat the oven to 400°F.

When the stuffed onions are cooked, quickly transfer them to a baking sheet and put them in the oven for about 15 minutes to dry them out a little and wrinkle them. Serve hot with lemon to squeeze over them.

Wild game, such as rabbit, hare, and deer, has featured in Middle Eastern recipes since medieval times but nowadays it is seldom found in the cities. In the rural areas, where people can rarely afford to buy meat, wild rabbit and other creatures often end up in a stew. The following Turkish recipe, one of the few to use wine, is for a tasty hunter's stew, served on a winter's day with lots of bread to mop up the aromatic juices. The word *yahni* in Turkish always denotes a stew made with onions.

TAVŞAN YAHNİSİ
(AROMATIC RABBIT STEW WITH ONIONS, GOLDEN RAISINS, AND FIGS)

Serves 2–3
Preparation time 20 minutes

Cooking time approximately 1¼ hours

2–3 tablespoons clarified butter (ghee)
1 rabbit, cleaned and cut into 4 or 6 portions
10 shallots or small onions, peeled and left whole
6–8 cloves garlic, peeled and left whole
6–8 allspice berries, crushed
4–6 cloves
1 cinnamon stick
1 whole dried chili or 1 teaspoon roasted Middle Eastern red pepper (p152)
2 tablespoons golden raisins
A handful of dried figs, halved
1 tablespoon honey
A sprinkling of fresh or dried thyme
1 tablespoon red or white wine vinegar
Roughly 1 cup red wine

Heat the clarified butter in a wide, heavy-based pan. Add the rabbit, brown the meat on all sides, and transfer it to a dish.

Add the shallots, garlic, spices, and chili to the pan and cook for a few minutes, until the shallots and garlic begin to color. Stir in the golden raisins, figs, honey, and thyme, and return the rabbit to the pan.

Quickly, pour in the vinegar to deglaze the pan, then pour in the wine. Bring the liquid to a boil, then reduce the heat, cover the pan, and simmer gently for about 1 hour, until the rabbit is tender. Serve immediately with lots of bread.

Selling freshly cut onion tops, Eastern Turkey

Robust, traditional soups, padded out with dried or stale bread, are generally regarded as peasant fare but have become fashionable in the cities of the Middle East too. According to legend, this soup dates back to the ancient Persian Arsacid dynasty, the Ashkanians. Like *işkembe çorbası* (p208), the traditional Turkish tripe soup, *eshkeneh* is usually served with vinegar or pickled vegetables.

ESHKENEH
(PERSIAN ONION SOUP)

Serves 6
Preparation time 10 minutes
Cooking time 1 hour and 10 minutes

3 onions, sliced
1–2 tablespoons clarified butter, or 1 tablespoon olive oil with a little butter
2 tablespoons all-purpose flour
1 tablespoon dried fenugreek leaves
1 teaspoon turmeric
Roughly 9 cups chicken stock or water
3 eggs, beaten
Dried or stale flat breads, broken into pieces
Salt and freshly ground black pepper

In a deep, heavy-based pan, cook the onions in the clarified butter until golden brown.

Stir in the flour, dried fenugreek leaves, and turmeric, and pour in the stock. Bring the liquid to a boil, stirring all the time, then reduce the heat and simmer for about 1 hour.

Season the soup to taste. Just before serving, bring the soup back to a boil and stir in the beaten eggs.

Toss in the pieces of stale bread and serve immediately with a splash of vinegar or pickled vegetables and fresh bread.

Tavşan yahnisi

GARLIC

(TOM) *Allium sativum*

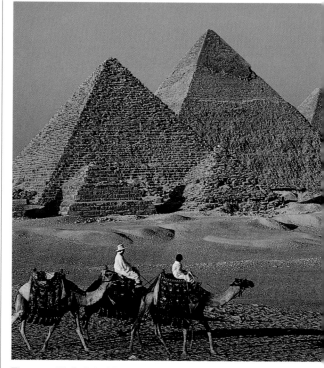

The pyramids, built by laborers whose strength was fortified with garlic

Garlic, which is one of the most powerfully flavored vegetables, probably originated in central Asia or the eastern Mediterranean. It was an important ingredient in the diet of the ancient Egyptians, helping to keep up the strength of the laborers as they built the Great Pyramid, and it was left as an offering in the tombs. As they began their exodus, the Israelites looked back longingly at the garlic of Egypt (Numbers 11:5). The ancient Greeks and Romans also regarded garlic as a strengthening food, good for soldiers and oarsmen but not necessarily for the nobility. Horace, the Roman poet, complained that the smell from garlic could make one's lover refuse a kiss and move over to the far side of the bed. In most regions of the Middle East, where garlic is used fairly liberally, bowls of fresh parsley or basil and mint are passed around to sweeten the breath. In Iran garlic is really used only in the dishes of the coastal regions, and in the Ottoman palace dishes of Istanbul it is used with a light touch. Because of its pungency and the "magical" powers attributed to it, strings of garlic are hung in doorways to ward off the evil eye.

Garlic heads

HOW IT GROWS

A variety of wild and cultivated garlic grows in the Middle East. It is a hardy, perennial herb from the onion family and easy to grow. With long, reed-like leaves, garlic resembles the onion above the ground but, unlike the onion, the harvested bulb, or head, is divided into segments.

APPEARANCE AND TASTE

Garlic is an onion-shaped bulb, made up of individual moon-shaped segments. The bulb is encased in a white or a pinky-purple papery sheath, as is each creamy-colored segment, called a "clove." Bulbs and their cloves vary in size and strength. Generally, fresh garlic, or wet garlic, is milder in flavor than the ubiquitous dried heads of garlic, which are generally pungent and quite sharp. A larger variety of garlic, *Allium ampeloprasum*, aptly named elephant garlic or Levant garlic, after its place of origin, has a much milder flavor, so it is often baked whole in its skin, threaded whole onto kabobs, or sliced raw and added to salads and flat-bread fillings.

BUYING AND STORING

Dried heads of garlic can be found almost everywhere, all year. Look for plump, firm heads with bright, healthy-looking sheaths. They are often sold individually or on strings. Fresh garlic, which is usually sold on the stalk, is available in the spring and the autumn. Both fresh and dried garlic keep well if stored in a dry, cool place.

MEDICINAL AND OTHER USES

Pickled garlic

CULINARY USES

Garlic seller, United Arab Emirates

Garlic is such a useful ingredient, it is used as an herb, a condiment, a vegetable, and even as a treat on its own, tossed into the ashes of a fire and left to soften to a mellow cream. It is popular pickled, preserved whole or in individual cloves, and it is added to other pickled foods for flavor. Its strong flavor puts a punch in the nut-based *tarator* sauce, a popular accompaniment to fish and shellfish in Turkey, Syria, Lebanon, and Egypt. It is often crushed and rubbed over small fish and poultry, such as red mullet and quails, before they are grilled or fried, and it is an essential part of the hot, spicy sauce in the Arab fish dish *samak harra*. It is used in a number of spice mixtures, such as the North African *harissa* (p155), which makes an appearance in some parts of the

Garlic is the "bulb of life." It has been used medicinally, or therapeutically since ancient times. It is rich in minerals, including high amounts of sulfur compounds, and is famous for its antibacterial, antifungal, antirheumatic and antithrombotic qualities. Because of the antiseptic qualities, strings of garlic are hung around children's necks to guard them during epidemics of infectious diseases. Garlic is also rich in vitamins B1 and C, and it contains iron and calcium.

Middle East, and the fiery Yemeni paste *zhug* (p169).

In Iran its role is sparse, but it is essential in the Caspian fava bean stew *khoresht Gol dar*

Chaman. Numerous meat, vegetable, and poultry stews, marinades, meatballs, and egg dishes include a clove or two of garlic. *Mezze* dips, such as hummus and the Turkish *ezme* dishes, are flavored with garlic. Garlic cloves are stuffed into green olives or marinated and crushed with them. Whole heads of garlic are grilled with sheep tail fat in eastern Anatolia, as in the famous kabobs from Amasya and Tokat. But perhaps its most unique role, and definitely my favorite way of eating garlic, is in the sublime combination of yogurt and garlic, so often served with grilled or fried vegetables, or bound with them when they are pounded or grated, particularly in the *meze* dishes of Turkey.

Tying garlic

A lesser-known feature of the Middle Eastern kitchen is the number (and variety) of egg dishes. Whether they are cooked in their shells to an ancient recipe, *beid hamine*, bound with vegetables and fried in an Arab *eggah*, or simply fried with garlic, *beid bi tom*, they can be transformed from the ugly duckling into the swan—a street snack to an elegant dish at an elaborate feast.

BEID BI TOM
(FRIED EGGS WITH GARLIC)

Serves 3–6
Preparation time 5 minutes
Cooking time 5–10 minutes

6 eggs
2 tablespoons butter
3 cloves garlic, crushed with salt
1 teaspoon ground sumac (p188)
A pinch dried mint
Salt

Break the eggs into a bowl. Melt the butter in a large skillet and stir in the garlic and sumac. As soon as the garlic begins to color, carefully slip in the eggs. Fry gently and sprinkle with the dried mint.

Cover the pan for 1–2 minutes to help the eggs set, then serve them lightly sprinkled with salt.

Associated with *Kurban Bayramı*, when every part of the sacrificed sheep is used, this Turkish soup is also a great favorite for late-night workers, travelers, and drinkers, as it is renowned for its sobering qualities. A particular feature of this very traditional soup is the sharp, tangy accompaniment of garlic-flavored vinegar and garlicky pickled vegetables.

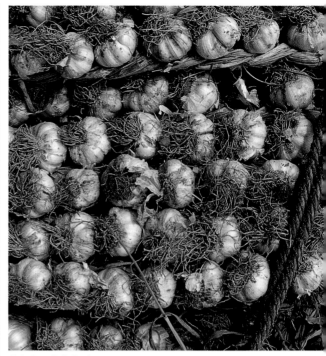

Dried garlic in baskets

İŞKEMBE ÇORBASI
(TRIPE SOUP)

Serves 4–6
Preparation time 30 minutes
Cooking time 20 minutes

8 ounces lamb tripe, well washed
5 cups water
1 tablespoon clarified butter
2 tablespoons all-purpose flour
1 egg yolk
Juice of lemon
Salt and freshly ground black pepper

To serve:
2-3 cloves garlic, crushed
¼ cup white-wine vinegar
Salt
Sharp, garlicky pickles (p 55) or pickled garlic

For the top:
2 tablespoons ordinary butter
1 teaspoon flaked Middle Eastern red pepper (p152)

Put the tripe into a pan and cover it with water. Bring it to a boil, skim off any foam from the top, and continue to boil for 20–25 minutes, until the tripe is tender. Drain and reserve the cooking liquid, then cut the tripe into fine slices.

Melt the clarified butter in a deep heavy-based pan. Stir in the flour to make a roux and pour in the cooking liquid, stirring until it thickens a little. Add the tripe and simmer gently for about 15 minutes.

In a bowl beat the egg yolk with the lemon juice. Add a little of the hot soup to it, then tip it into the pan, stirring vigorously to make sure it is well blended. Season the soup to taste and keep it simmering gently while you make the final preparations.

In a bowl, stir the crushed garlic with a little salt into the vinegar and set it aside. In a small pan, melt the butter and stir in the red pepper. Pour the soup into individual bowls, spoon a little of the spiked butter into each one, and serve with the garlicky vinegar and pickles.

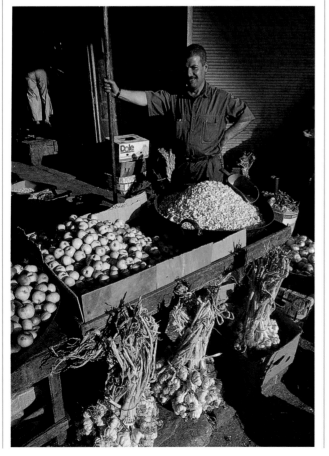

Fruit, nut, and garlic stall, Syria

This is a wonderful garlicky sauce, popular in Egypt, Syria, Lebanon, and Turkey. It can be used as a dip, but it is more commonly used as a sauce for fish and shellfish, particularly in the Arab dish *samak tarator*. This is a large baked fish, such as sea bass, garnished with fried nuts and black olives. In the Turkish dish *midye tavası*, mussels deep-fried in a beer batter are added. The sauce is usually made with walnuts, almonds, or pine nuts, and the quantity of garlic used varies from hand to hand.

TARATOR
(GARLIC AND NUT SAUCE)

Serves 4 as a dip or sauce
Preparation time 20 minutes if pounding by hand (2 minutes in the mixer)
Cooking time –

1 head garlic, peeled and crushed to a pulp
3–4 slices day-old or stale bread, soaked in water and then squeezed out
Juice of 1 lemon
½ cup roughly ground walnuts
4–5 tablespoons olive oil
Salt and freshly ground black pepper

Using a large mortar and pestle, pound the garlic, bread, lemon juice, and walnuts to a pulp, adding the olive oil gradually, as you would to make mayonnaise. Beat the mixture until it is a thick puree. Alternatively, whiz the ingredients in an electric mixer, still adding the oil gradually.

Add salt and pepper to taste, and garnish with crushed nuts or parsley.

Tarator

CAPSICUM PEPPER

(FILFIL HILU) Capsicum annum

Immature capsicum peppers

Like hot red peppers, tomatoes, and potatoes, the plump, bell-shaped capsicum entered the Middle East in the sixteenth century, when the Ottomans and the Spanish dominated the political stage, resulting in a great deal of trade with the New World.

Red capsicum

Another name for this mild capsicum fruit is pimento. There is also a delightful bright green, long, tapering pepper that comes from the same family and is called *çarliston biber* in Turkish, which may indicate its place of origin. In the Mediterranean regions of the Middle East, the red bell peppers are ground to a pulp with a few hot peppers, olive oil, and salt. This pulp is then spread out in shallow pans and left to dry in the sun until it resembles a thick paste. Buckets of this paste are often sold in the markets. Dried red peppers are often ground to a powder, which we know as paprika.

Paprika

HOW IT GROWS

All capsicums are native to the Americas and are related to the tomato and potato. Despite its botanical name, it is a perennial plant in its native habitat; everywhere else it is an annual plant that bears fruit within a couple of months of sowing.

APPEARANCE AND TASTE

The large sweet peppers of the Middle East range in color from a deep olive green to bright red and yellow. All are slightly sweet, crunchy, and juicy. Immature green peppers are picked when they are small, light green, and thin-skinned, as they are slightly piquant and ideal for stuffing. The long, green *çarliston* peppers are delicately perfumed and can be quite fiery.

BUYING AND STORING

All fresh peppers should feel hard and crisp and have glossy skins. Unless you are planning to dry them, fresh peppers should be used within ten days, before they start to become soft, dull, and wrinkly. Red pepper paste and paprika are available in Middle Eastern stores and some supermarkets. Both keep quite well in a cool, dry place.

CULINARY USES

Peppers, particularly the *çarliston* variety, are added to salads or they are grilled and peeled, then tossed in olive oil and lemon juice, or fried and served with garlicky yogurt. Peppers are often stuffed with a meat or rice filling and baked or poached. In Iran the filling is

Sacks of red capsicum peppers at a depot, Turkey

Çarliston peppers

sometimes made with yellow split peas. In Turkey, Syria, and Lebanon, the young, thin-skinned peppers are stuffed and served cold with an aromatic rice filling. Chunks of pepper are often threaded onto skewers for meat, chicken, or fish kabobs, or they are cooked with vegetables such as eggplants and tomatoes in dishes that are served hot or cold. All peppers are popular pickled, whole or stuffed.

Like eggplants, red peppers are hollowed out and left to dry in the sun. Then they are hung on strings and used through the winter to stuff or to add to stews. The red pepper paste is used to flavor dips, sauces, stews, meatballs, and stuffings. It is also spread on bread with olive oil, crushed garlic, or chopped onions and parsley as a snack. A similar paste can be made by chopping roast peppers to a pulp with a few hot red peppers, or by whizzing them to a puree in a food processor, then heating the puree with olive oil and salt in a saucepan and leaving it to simmer until it has reduced to a paste. Like the slightly hot Middle Eastern ground red pepper (p152), paprika is sprinkled liberally on smooth *mezze* dishes, such as *hummus*, and on kabobs. It is also one of the ingredients in the Arab spice mix *baharat* (p162).

This salad is from northern Cyprus and, given the history of the island, it could be of Greek origin. However, the refreshing combination of grilled peppers and soft, juicy fruit is quite common in the Mediterranean regions of southern Turkey, Syria, and Lebanon. Peaches, melons, and plums are all delicious with the soft grilled or roast sweet bell peppers.

KIBRIS SALATASI
(GRILLED PEPPER AND PEACH SALAD)

Serves 3–4
Preparation time 25 minutes
Cooking time –

2 red bell peppers
2 large ripe peaches, peeled and pitted
2 tablespoons olive oil
Juice of 1 lime
Salt

Place the peppers over charcoal, directly over a gas flame, or in a conventional broiler. Keep turning them until they buckle and blister all over. Pop them into a plastic bag to sweat for a few minutes, then hold them under running cold water and peel off the skin.

Halve the peppers lengthwise, remove the stalks and seeds, and cut the peppers into thick slices. Slice the peaches into similar-size pieces, then place them and the peppers in a shallow bowl.

Pour in the olive oil and lime juice, season with salt, and toss lightly before serving.

Stuffed peppers are one of the most popular dishes throughout the Middle East. They are a particular favorite in the Mediterranean regions, where the immature, thin-skinned peppers are often filled with an aromatic rice and served cold as a *mezze* dish. They are also often stuffed with a ground meat filling and served hot, usually accompanied by stuffed tomatoes, stuffed zucchini, and stuffed eggplants.

MAHSHI FILFIL HILU
(STUFFED GREEN PEPPERS)

Serves 4
Preparation time 40 minutes
Cooking time 30–40 minutes

6–8 small green bell peppers
2 tablespoons olive oil
1 onion, finely chopped
½ teaspoon sugar, + some to sprinkle
3 tablespoons pine nuts
2 tablespoons dried currants
1–2 teaspoons dried mint
1 teaspoon ground cinnamon
½ teaspoon ground allspice
1 cup short-grain rice, washed and drained
2–3 tomatoes
Juice of a lemon mixed with ¼ cup olive oil
Salt and freshly ground black pepper
2 lemons cut into wedges

Cut the stalks off the green peppers and remove the seeds and pith. Wash the peppers inside and out, and set aside.

In a heavy-based pan, heat 2 tablespoons of olive oil and stir in the onion and ½ teaspoon of sugar. As the onion begins to color, stir in the pine nuts and dried currants. When the currants plump up and the nuts begin to brown, stir in the mint. Add the cinnamon and allspice, followed by the rice, and pour in enough water to just cover. Stir in salt and pepper, bring the water to a boil, and simmer until the water has been absorbed.

Cut the sides off the tomatoes to make lids for the peppers. Spoon some of the rice mixture into each pepper, fit them with the tomato lids, and place them upright, side by side, in a heavy-based pan.

Mix roughly 1 cup of water into the olive oil and lemon juice mixture, and pour over the peppers. Sprinkle with a little sugar, cover the pan, and cook gently for approximately 30 minutes, until the peppers are tender.

Leave to cool in the pan. Serve cold with wedges of lemon to squeeze over them.

Mahshi filfil hilu

MELOKHIA

(MELOKHIA) *Corchorus olitorius*

The leaves of the melokhia plant are eaten as a vegetable in parts of the Middle East, North Africa, the Caribbean, and Southeast Asia, but it is in Egypt that they have the greatest culinary importance. In fact, one of Egypt's national dishes is an ancient peasant soup called *melokhia*. Prepared in exactly the same way as depicted in some of the pharaonic tomb paintings, the soup is made almost daily by the peasant women, who carry large pots of it on their heads to the men working in the fields. The word *melokhia* means mallow in Arabic, and the vegetable is often referred to as Jew's mallow.

Field workers tilling the soil, Cairo, Egypt

Dried melokhia

HOW IT GROWS

Related to the mallow, melokhia belongs to the same genus as the jute plant, which is grown all over the world as a source of fiber. In the summer, most Egyptian peasants reserve a small patch of ground to grow melokhia.

APPEARANCE AND TASTE

The leaves of the plant are dark green with serrated edges. They taste a bit like sorrel and, in a similar way to okra, they impart a mucilaginous quality to the dish.

BUYING AND STORING

In the markets of the Middle East, the leaves are sold fresh. They are also dried for storing, which is how they are usually sold outside the Middle East.

CULINARY USES

Generally, melokhia leaves are cooked and eaten like spinach or purslane, another leafy, mucilaginous vegetable. In Egypt, where they are used the most, the leaves are made into the glutinous, peasant soup called *melokhia*, which in medieval times was much more of a meal because fried meatballs were added to it. In Syria and Lebanon, the Egyptian *melokhia* soup is very thick and is made with chicken stock. It is then used as a sauce for the chicken that has been boiled for the stock and is served with rice.

This is such a popular soup among the hard-working Egyptian peasants that some of them eat it at midday and again in the evening. As it is eaten so often, the leaves are usually cooked in a simple vegetable stock, water in which other vegetables have been boiled. In this recipe I am using dried melokhia leaves; if you can find fresh leaves, they need to be washed and dried first, then chopped to a pulp, added to a boiling stock, and cooked for about 10 minutes.

MELOKHIA
(EGYPTIAN MELOKHIA SOUP)

Serves 4–6
Preparation time 20 minutes'
  soaking
Cooking time 30 minutes

Melokhia

1 pound dried melokhia leaves
5 cups vegetable or chicken stock
2 cloves garlic
1 tablespoon clarified butter
  (ghee)
1–2 teaspoons ground coriander
1 scant teaspoon ground red
  pepper
Salt and ground black pepper

Crush the dried melokhia leaves with your hands and soak them in a little boiled water until they have doubled in bulk.

Heat the stock in a large saucepan and bring it a boil. Stir in the melokhia and boil for about 25 minutes.

Crush the garlic with a little salt and fry it in the ghee. When it begins to brown, stir in the coriander and ground red pepper, and mix to a paste.

Stir this paste into the soup and simmer for a few minutes. Add salt and pepperto taste and serve hot.

CUCUMBER

(KHIYAR) *Cucumis sativus*

The cucumber, which probably originated in India, is one of the oldest cultivated vegetables. It has been known in the Middle East, since classical times. As they are 96 percent water, fresh cucumbers are very refreshing. In fact, their most important role in the Middle East is to quench the thirst. Street sellers peel and salt them for thirsty passersby in hot weather.

Cucumbers

HOW IT GROWS

A member of the squash family, the cucumber is cultivated throughout the Middle East, both indoors and outdoors. It is in season from March to December.

APPEARANCE AND TASTE

Middle Eastern cucumbers can be short and stubby, almost seedless, with slightly pimply skins, or long and slender with smooth skins. Most are sweet and juicy, but some, like their ancestors, are quite bitter and require salting before use. There are also tiny cucumbers, which are used for pickling.

Left: Growing cucumbers in the desert, Egypt

Right: Cucumber seller, Gaza Strip

BUYING AND STORING

When buying cucumbers, the main thing to look out for is that they are firm to the touch. They store well in warm and cool places, but they will turn to water if you freeze them. The Middle Eastern cucumbers can be found in some Indian and Italian stores as well as in Middle Eastern outlets.

CULINARY USES

Peeled, salted strips of fresh cucumber are a delight, often served as a *mezze*. They are added to salads for their refreshing bite, usually married with warming herbs such as dill, mint, and parsley, and dressed with lemon juice or orange-flower water. In Egypt diced cucumber is added to a mixture of onion, lemon juice, olive oil, and a crumbly white cheese, like feta, to make the wonderful dish *michoteta*. Throughout the Middle East, cucumber is combined with yogurt in a light salad, such as the Iranian *mâst-o khiyâr*, an extremely decorative and delicious dish with walnuts and golden raisins. Similarly, cucumber and yogurt are combined in the Turkish dish *cacık*, which can be served as a chilled soup, as a *mezze* dish, or as an accompaniment to meat or *pilafs*.

Occasionally, cucumbers are added to summer stews in place of eggplants or zucchini, and they are sometimes added to the famous Lebanese and Syrian dish of bulgur and herbs, tabbouleh (p181). In Turkey and Iran they are tossed with pomegranate seeds in a simple, juicy salad. In Iran, they are also soaked in lime water for a few days, until they are transparent, and then boiled with sugar to make a delicious, delicate-looking jam, *morabbâ-ye balang*.

Dips made with mashed or pulped ingredients are some of the most popular *mezze* dishes, ideal for scooping up with flat bread. The following Egyptian dish, made with crumbly white cheese, is sometimes served as an accompaniment to the great national favorite, *ful medames* (p116). A similar *mezze* dish, called *peynir ezmesi*, is popular in Turkey.

Mâst-o khiyâr

MICHOTETA
(CHEESE AND CUCUMBER SALAD)

Serves 3–4 as part of *mezze* spread
Preparation time 15 minutes
Cooking time –

1½ cups crumbly white cheese (or feta)
2 tablespoons olive oil
Juice of 1 lemon
1 red onion, finely chopped
1 small cucumber (½ a large one), peeled and diced
Salt and freshly ground black pepper
A few mint leaves, finely chopped

Using a fork, mash the cheese in a bowl, then work in the olive oil and lemon juice. Mix in the onion and cucumber, and season.

Spoon into a serving bowl, drizzle with a little olive oil, and sprinkle with fresh mint.

Yogurt and cucumber are a very refreshing combination. On this theme, the two dishes that stand out are *cacık*, a Turkish dish enjoyed all over the Middle East, and *mâst-o khiyar*, the following Iranian dish, which is characteristically exotic and flamboyant with its garnish of dried rose petals.

MÂST-O KHIYÂR
(YOGURT AND CUCMBER SALAD WITH WALNUTS AND GOLDEN RAISINS)

Serves 4 as part of *mezze* spread
Preparation time 20 minutes
Cooking time –

1 long cucumber, peeled, seeded, and finely chopped
1 cup thick, strained yogurt
2–3 tablespoons halved golden raisins
1–2 tablespoons coarsely chopped walnuts
A small bunch of chives, finely chopped
A small bunch of fresh dill and mint, finely chopped
Salt and freshly ground black pepper
A few dried rose petals
2 pinches dried mint

Sprinkle the cucumber with salt to draw out the water.

Beat the strained yogurt in a bowl, and stir in the golden raisins, walnuts, chives, dill, and mint. Add the weeping cucumber and season to taste.

Chill for 1 hour before serving, and garnish with the rose petals and dried mint.

PUMPKIN

(QAR'AT) *Cucurbita pepo*

The pumpkin is another vegetable that came to the Middle East from the New World. Perhaps more than any other vegetable, the pumpkin is linked with the cuisines of various peoples rather than countries. The Armenians and the Kurds, in particular, are known for their sumptuous pumpkin dishes. Invariably, the pumpkin is flavored with strong, aromatic spices such as cinnamon and cloves, and it is sweetened with honey or golden raisins.

HOW IT GROWS

Pumpkins are the gourd-like fruits of an annual plant that grows in temperate and tropical climates. From the same genus as the melon, it is a rapid-growing plant that spreads itself wildly along the ground, producing large fruits that expand at a fast rate.

APPEARANCE AND TASTE

Middle Eastern pumpkins are generally orange in color, large, and round or oval. Eaten when they are fully ripe, their bright orange or yellow flesh is fibrous and delicately perfumed when cooked. Generally, the more vibrant the color, the tastier the pumpkin, but the larger the pumpkin, the less flavorsome it is.

Pumpkins

Shelled pumpkin seeds

BUYING AND STORING

Pumpkins come in all sizes, so buy what you need. Go for taut, medium-size or squat pumpkins. Stored in a cool, dry place, they should keep for a couple of months. Peeled pumpkin wrapped in plastic wrap keeps in the refrigerator for a week to ten days.

CULINARY USES

Pumpkins are used in both savory and sweet dishes. Cooked pumpkin is used as a filling for some sweet, syrupy pastries and it is mashed with spices, herbs, or onions, and bulgur to fill savory pastries. In Armenian communities cooked pumpkin is often layered with rice in a sweet, spicy, homey dish. The Armenians, the Kurds, the Turks, and the Jews all have their own version of a syrupy pumpkin jam or preserve; a thick, hearty pumpkin soup; and whole pumpkins stuffed with an aromatic lamb, rice, and pine-nut filling. The Turks and the Kurds poach cubes of pumpkin in syrup to make the sumptuous, golden, winter dessert *bal kabağı tatlısı* or *shirini*. And, like melon seeds, roasted and salted pumpkin seeds make a popular snack.

In Turkey the following winter dessert is called *bal kabağı tatlısı*, but in other parts of the Middle East it is known as *shirini*, a classic Kurdish specialty. Although the Kurds are Muslims, they are not Arabs, and possess their own language, customs, and dishes. One of the most famous Kurds in history was Saladin, who became the sultan of Egypt and Syria in the twelfth century.

SHIRINI
(PUMPKIN POACHED IN SYRUP)

Serves 4–6
Preparation time 20 minutes
Cooking time approximately 2 hours

2 cups sugar
1 cup water
Juice of ½ lemon
3–4 whole cloves
2 pounds peeled pumpkin, cut into 2-inch cubes or rectangula blocks

Put the sugar, water, and lemo juice into a heavy-based pan, a bring to a boil, stirring all the time until the sugar has dissolved. Toss in the cloves an add the pumpkin pieces, then cover the pan and bring the liquid back to a boil.

Reduce the heat and leave the pumpkin pieces to poach gentl turning them over from time t time until they are tender and gleaming—depending on the size of your pumpkin pieces, th should take 1½–2 hours. Leave the pumpkin to cool in the pa then place the pieces on a dis and spoon the syrup over ther Serve chilled, or at room temperature, with clotted crea

Pumpkin seeds

Throughout their history the Armenians have been invaded, conquered, and dispersed. In the pre-Ottoman era, when Byzantium was at its peak, many Armenians were based in Constantinople, where their culinary culture merged with that of the city and the Greek community to create a cuisine that would later influence the Turks. Still residing in Istanbul and beyond, the Armenian communities, being Christian, drink wine and eat pork, unlike their Muslim neighbors. This recipe is for one of their homey dishes, usually served with pork.

ERMENİ PİLAVI
(ARMENIAN RICE WITH PUMPKIN, CINNAMON, AND HONEY)

Serves 4–6
Preparation time 35–40 minutes
Cooking time 30 minutes

Roughly 1½ pounds peeled pumpkin, finely sliced
1 tablespoon clarified butter (ghee)
1 onion, chopped
1 teaspoon sugar
2 tablespoons golden raisins
1 teaspoon cardamom seeds
1 teaspoon ground cinnamon
1¼ cups long-grain rice, washed and drained
¼ cup tablespoons honey
2 tablespoons ordinary butterSalt and freshly ground black pepper

"Turk's Turban" pumpkins

Preheat oven to 400°F

Bring a pan of water to a boil. Add the pumpkin slices and cook for 2 minutes, then drain and refresh under cold water, and set aside.

In a heavy-based pan, melt the clarified butter and stir in the onion with the sugar. When the onion begins to color, add the golden raisins and cardamom seeds, and then the cinnamon. Stir in the rice and pour in enough water to just cover. Stir in salt and pepper, and bring the water to a boil, then reduce the heat and simmer until it has been absorbed.

Meanwhile, melt the honey in a pan and grease an ovenproof dish with a generous amount of the butter. Dribble some of the honey into the base, then line it with half the pumpkin slices, overlapping each other. Dribble a little more honey over the slices and tip the rice on top. Arrange the remaining pumpkin slices, and press down firmly over the rice.

Return the pan of honey to the heat, melt the rest of the butter in it, and pour over the pumpkin. Place the dish in the oven for about 30 minutes, until the pumpkin is tender and slightly caramelized. Serve hot with roast or grilled meat.

Shirini

ZUCCHINI

(KOUSA) *Cucurbita pepo*

Zucchini in flower

Zucchini are an offspring of the vegetable marrow, which has been used in Mediterranean cooking for a long time. The wealthy Romans indulged in outrageous feasts that featured the tongues of flamingos and nightingales and vast quantities of vegetable marrows. The Byzantine emperors enjoyed vegetable marrows stewed with grape juice, a dish that Mehmet the Conqueror served at banquets in the fifteenth century. In the parts of the Middle East where culinary trends were influenced by the Ottomans, vegetable marrows are still believed to be cooling to the blood, so they are balanced by warming herbs such as dill and mint.

HOW IT GROWS

The vegetable marrow is a squash, a member of the *Cucurbita* family, which is a creeping plant with serrated leaves, large, papery, yellow flowers, and an elongated fruit. When picked young and slim (4–8 inches long), they are known as zucchini.

APPEARANCE AND TASTE

Very fresh, tender zucchini should have a delicate, almost perfumed flavor. They can be eaten raw or lightly cooked. They shouldn't be watery.

BUYING AND STORING

Look for the bright green, slim and firm zucchini, preferably with a flower still attached—they really will be fresh. Zucchini have a tendency to become limp and rubbery quite quickly, even if they are kept in a cool, dry place, so don't store them for long.

CULINARY USES

As zucchini have such a delicate flavor, they should be lightly cooked. Raw, grilled, lightly steamed, or fried young zucchini are often added to salads, such as the Turkish dish *bostancı*, with lamb's lettuce, or they are lightly fried with golden raisins, roast pine nuts, and a little lemon juice. They are delicious steamed and served with a *tarator* sauce made with crushed hazelnuts (p133) or pine nuts. In the fashion of all stuffed vegetable dishes, *mahshi khodar* (*dolma* in Turkey, *dolmeh* in Iran), they are often filled with aromatic rice or bulgur, or a ground lamb and rice mixture, and then poached or baked. At the beginning of the season, the zucchini flowers as well are stuffed with similar fillings. There is an ancient dish, which may have Persian origins, that calls for zucchini to be filled with rice and ground lamb, then layered in a pan with soaked, dried apricots. Like carrots and eggplants, zucchini are fried, or deep-fried in batter, and served with yogurt, particularly in Turkey. Zucchini are also grated and fried and added to an egg and cheese mixture to make lovely, light patties. They can also be combined with cheese and egg in savory pastries, or baked with cheese and egg. On the egg and cheese theme, they are a popular vegetable in the Arab *eggah* (Persian *kookoo*) dishes, which are a bit like thick Spanish omelets, packed with flavor. Cooked with tomatoes and dill, they appear in a number of vegetable, pulse, and meat stews, in which they are interchangeable with eggplant. Similarly, steamed or fried zucchini or eggplant is added to ground meat to make tasty meatballs. And a mock *İmam bayıldı* (p 51) using zucchini has become popular in recent years. In Iraq there is a special dish called *koubba helwa*, (p79), which is a type of *kibbeh* in a semolina shell cooked in a tomato and zucchini sauce. In Turkey zucchini are used make a delightful *helva*, flavored with cardamom, which has echoes of Iran and India.

Throughout the Middle East, the roasted and salted seeds of mature vegetable marrows are a nutritious and tasty snack—but the seeds of zucchini are far too small, of course.

Zucchini

Vegetable stall with cucumbers and zucchini

The Arab omelet *eggah* is thick, firm and full of character. It can be made on top of the stove or in the oven, and is eaten hot or cold, cut into rectangular portions. Often packed with ingredients, the most common *eggah* dishes include fava beans, eggplant, leek, spinach, ground meat, and chicken.

EGGAH BI EISH WA KOUSA

(ARAB BREAD AND ZUCCHINI OMELET)

Serves 6
Preparation time 25–30 minutes
Cooking time 25 minutes

2–3 zucchini, sliced
1 onion, sliced
2–3 tablespoons ordinary or clarified butter
A small bunch of fresh mint, chopped
6 eggs
3 slices bread, crusts removed, soaked in a little milk
Salt and freshly ground black pepper

Sprinkle the zucchini with a little salt to draw out the water, rinse them, and pat dry.

In a heavy-based pan, soften the onion in half the butter, then add the zucchini. Fry until soft and golden, and stir in the mint. Leave to cool.

Beat the eggs in a bowl. Squeeze the bread dry and crumble it into the beaten eggs. Add the zucchini and onions, and season with salt and pepper.

Heat the rest of the butter in a heavy-based skillet. Tip the egg mixture into the hot butter and cook gently over a low heat until the eggs are set. Cover the pan with a large plate and invert it, so that the *eggah* lands on the plate upside down, then carefully slip it back into the pan to brown the other side. Flip the eggah onto a serving dish and cut it into segments, like a cake.

Generally, vegetable stews are made with a little meat, but in the hot months a meatless stew is often favored. In rural communities these stews are cooked in earthenware pots that are placed in the cooling bread ovens to bake. A summer stew will always include zucchini, eggplant, and peppers, to which beans and artichokes are sometimes added, and plenty of herbs.

KHUDRA BIL FURN

(MIXED VEGETABLE STEW)

Serves 6
Preparation time 25 minutes
Cooking time approximately 1 hour

3–4 zucchini, cut into slices roughly 1 inch wide
2 long, slim eggplants, or 1 fat one, quartered lengthwise, then cut into 1-inch chunks
2 green or red bell peppers, stalks and seeds removed, cut into similar-size pieces
2–3 onions, peeled and quartered
4 tomatoes, peeled
4 cloves garlic, finely chopped
1 teaspoon ground fenugreek
1 teaspoon sugar
A bunch of fresh flat-leaf parsley, dill, and mint, chopped
½ cup olive oil
Juice of 1 lemon
Salt and freshly ground black pepper

Preheat the oven to 400°F.

Place the zucchini, eggplant, peppers, and onions in an earthenware pot or oven dish. Chop 3 of the tomatoes and add them to the pot, along with the garlic, fenugreek, sugar, and herbs. Mix it well, then season generously with salt and pepper.

Mix the olive oil and lemon juice together, add enough water to increase the volume to about 1¼ cups, and pour it over the vegetables. Slice the remaining tomato finely and lay the slices over the top of the vegetables (if using a wide oven dish, you will need an extra tomato), then pop the vegetables into the oven for about 1 hour, or until they are tender, stirring them once after the first 30 minutes.

Serve the hot stew either with rice, or as an accompaniment to meat or poultry.

Khudra bil furn

ARTICHOKE

(KHURSHUF) *Cynara scolymus*

Dedicated to Venus and believed to be an aphrodisiac, it was no wonder that the globe artichoke became a regular feature in the diet of wealthy Romans. In fact, Pliny described the vegetable as a luxury fit only for the wealthy and noble. The globe artichoke is just a glorious thistle, a superior version of the ancient cardoon that grows wild in the Mediterranean region, but it is regarded as a delicacy in the Middle East. The old Arabic name for artichoke, *al-khurshuf*, means prickle or thorn.

Artichokes

HOW IT GROWS

The globe artichoke is a tall, majestic plant with serrated leaves; when the purple flowers are in full bloom, it is a splendid sight. The globe artichoke is harvested in the early summer, but there is a cone-shaped, smooth-edged variety that is harvested in the winter. Artichokes are picked to eat before the flower blooms, although some are left to provide seeds for the next year's crop.

APPEARANCE AND TASTE

The globe artichoke is usually spherical and mossy green or purplish. It is made up of sharp-pointed, layered scales that encase the flower and the nectarous calix. In Europe and America people eat the inner part of the scales, but in the Middle East people usually feed the scales to animals and consume only the heart. Full of goodness, the gently cooked heart is delicate and sweet, with a firm but soft texture.

BUYING AND STORING

Artichokes were expensive for the Romans and they still are today. Usually, they are not weighed by the pound, but individually. When selecting them yourself, choose large heads with tightly closed, fresh-looking, juicy scales. They turn brown and dry out very quickly. If you hold them by their thick stems, the heads should nod. If they are stiff, like maracas, then the stem and heart will be woody. Stand fresh artichokes in water, like a bunch of flowers, until you are ready to use them. Frozen prepared hearts are also available in Middle Eastern stores and some supermarkets.

MEDICINAL USES

The artichoke has been used for medicinal purposes since early times, mainly because it contains cynarin, which is understood to be beneficial to the liver. The tonic properties of the artichoke are believed to improve the body's metabolism and a person's complexion, as well as giving an overall feeling of well-being. They are also said to have aphrodisiac qualities.

CULINARY USES

In parts of the Middle East, prepared artichoke hearts are sold in the streets, which makes life easy, as preparing them yourself can take time. After you have removed the stalk, scales, flower, and hairy choke, you

Selling bundles of artichokes

must rub lemon juice over the exposed heart before it discolors, and then plunge it into a bowl of salted cold water with a little lemon juice. In the early summer the hearts are much sought after. They are particularly popular in Turkey and Egypt. They can be stuffed with ground meat and served in an egg and lemon sauce, or they can be stuffed with a mixture of diced carrot and potato, and poached in olive oil and lemon juice. A classic Middle Eastern dish consists of artichoke hearts stuffed with fresh, green fava beans, sometimes with almonds or pine nuts, and poached in olive oil and lemon juice. At their simplest, the hearts are poached alone in olive oil and lemon juice with a little fresh dill for flavoring. The cooked hearts are pounded to a paste with ground meat to make an Egyptian meatball dish. The boiled or steamed hearts, chopped and dressed in olive oil, crushed garlic, and lemon juice, or with preserved lemon, make a lovely salad or *mezze*. And the raw hearts are pickled in oil and lemon juice.

Globe artichokes growing in a field

Of all the Turkish *zeytinyağlı* dishes, this one is king. Cooked gently in olive oil, flavored with lemon and dill, and served cold, it is one of the nicest ways to appreciate the subtle taste and texture of the creamy artichoke hearts.

Zeytinyağlı enginar

ZEYTİNYAĞLI ENGİNAR
(ARTICHOKE HEARTS IN OLIVE OIL)

Serves 4
Preparation time 20–25 minutes
Cooking time roughly 30 minutes

4 fresh globe artichokes, trimmed
   down to the hearts, rubbed with
   lemon juice, and kept in a bowl
   of salted cold water with a little
   lemon juice until ready to use
½ cup olive oil
Juice of ½ a lemon
Roughly ¼ cup water
Salt
A small bunch of dill, chopped
1 lemon, cut into wedges

Place the artichoke hearts in a heavy-based pan with the olive oil, lemon juice, and water. Cover with the lid and poach gently for 15–20 minutes. Add salt to taste and continue to poach for a further 10 minutes, until the hearts are tender. Leave to cool in the pan.

Place them on a serving dish, spoon the cooking liquid over them, sprinkle with the dill, and serve with wedges of lemon to squeeze over them.

In some parts of the Middle East the artichokes are known by the more modern Arabic name, *ardishawki*, and are frequently stuffed with meat or, as in the following Lebanese dish, combined with fava beans.

ARDISHAWKI WA FUL AKHDAR
(ARTICHOKES WITH FAVA BEANS AND ALMONDS)

Serves 4
Preparation time about 30 minutes
Cooking time 35–40 minutes

1 tablespoon all-purpose flour
1¼ cups water
2 teaspoons sugar
Juice of 1 lemon
2 cloves garlic, crushed
A small bunch of dill
2–3 tablespoons olive oil
6–8 fresh globe artichokes,
   trimmed down to the hearts,
   rubbed with lemon juice, and kept
   in a bowl of salted cold water
   with a little lemon juice until
   ready to use
⅔ cup fresh shelled and, if
   necessary, peeled fava beans
½ cup blanched almonds
Salt and ground black pepper

Mix the flour to a loose paste with 2 tablespoons of the water, then pour it and the rest of the water into a heavy-based pan.

Add the sugar, lemon juice, garlic, dill, and about ½ teaspoon salt, and bring the liquid to a boil, stirring all the time so that the flour doesn't become lumpy. Simmer for about 10 minutes, then stir in the olive oil.

Add the artichoke hearts, fava beans, and almonds, and cook gently for about 20 minutes, until they are tender.

Add salt and pepper to taste, and serve hot or cold, with the fava beans and almonds spooned into the cupped hearts.

CARROT

(JAZRA) *Daucus carota*

The carrot is believed to have originated in Afghanistan, where wild red and purple varieties have grown since ancient times. It appeared on the list of aromatic herbs, rather than vegetables, grown in the royal gardens of Babylon in the eighth century BC, indicating that the carrot leaves and seeds, both of which have a carrot flavor, were used instead of the roots. In fact, it took a long time for the carrot root to be cultivated and consumed; there is no mention of the Greeks or Romans eating carrots. When he conquered the Persian Empire, Alexander the Great took the dark purple carrot as one of the spoils of war, but it wasn't until somewhere between the eighth and tenth centuries AD that the carrot traveled westward with the Arabs across the north of Africa and into Spain. One of the earliest descriptions of the carrot was by an Arab writer who talked about a red variety that was tasty and juicy, and a yellow one that had an inferior flavor. At some point on its journey in Western Europe in the seventeenth century, the carrot changed color to orange, and was depicted in the Dutch paintings of the period. Both red and yellow varieties still grow in the Middle East, and purple carrots are cultivated in the south of Turkey.

HOW IT GROWS

The wild carrot still grows in its natural habitat in western Asia, particularly Afghanistan. The cultivated orange carrot grows well throughout the Middle East and keeps for a long time in the soil.

Purple carrots, Turkey

APPEARANCE AND TASTE

Most carrots are orange, due to the presence of beta-carotene. They are long and slim, with tapered ends. Orange carrots contain quite a lot of natural sugar, so they are generally sweet and juicy. The purple and red varieties are slightly sharper in taste, as you would imagine a radish crossed with a carrot might taste.

BUYING AND STORING

The conventional orange carrot should be firm and juicy-looking when fresh, not rubbery or woody. If stored in a cool, dry place, or in sand, carrots keep for a long time.

CULINARY USES

The natural sweetness and vibrant color of the carrot are exploited to the full in the Middle East. Shredded raw or cooked carrot is often added to a *pilaf* or salad for a splash of color. In Iranian rice dishes it is often married with blanched almonds and bitter-orange peel for flavor and texture. A glorious-looking, syrupy jam is made with thinly sliced or shredded carrot in Iran and Turkey. Carrot slices are pickled in salt and vinegar, often with one of its umbelliferous relatives, such as celery or fennel seeds, to accentuate the flavor. Carrots are grated raw and served as a simple salad dressed with lemon juice, and they can be fried in olive oil or deep-fried in batter and served with yogurt as a *mezze*. As you would expect, carrots appear in many stews, soups, pulse dishes, and *pilafs*.

I've eaten this delicious carrot jam in a number of places but only the Persian version uses cardamom seeds. You can shred or slice

Carrots

the carrot into any shape or size you like, but I prefer thin rounds so that it looks like carrot jam rather than orange marmalade. As with most Middle Eastern jams, the consistency is more like a syrupy conserve than a solid, easy-to-spread jam.

MORABBÂ-YE HAVEEJ
(CARROT JAM WITH ORANGE AND CARDAMOM)

Makes enough for 2–3 small jars
Preparation time 30 minutes
Cooking time 20–25 minutes

3 cups sugar
2 cups water
2 pounds carrots, peeled and sliced into fine rounds
Juice of 2 small oranges, and the peel, cut into slivers
Juice of ½ lemon
2 tablespoons rose water
Seeds of 5–6 green cardamom pods
½ cup blanched almonds, cut into slivers

Gently dissolve the sugar in the water in a deep, wide, heavy-based pan and bring the liquid to a boil, stirring all the time.

Stir in the carrots and orange peel and return to a boil. Continue to boil the liquid, stirring from time to time, until it begins to thicken and become syrupy.

Stir in the rose water, orange and lemon juice, cardamom seeds, and almond slivers, and gently boil the syrup for a further 5 minutes, until the carrots are tender and the syrup is just right (test it by spooning a little onto a plate and leaving it to cool—it should be quite thick and dribble slowly, not run, from your finger). Leave the jam to cool completely, then spoon into sterilized jars.

In the summer months, families congregate outdoors as much as possible, eating on balconies, terraces, in gardens, and in any space in the countryside.

Morabbâ-ye haveej

Weekends are peppered with picnics, often consisting of olives, white cheese, fruit, a rice dish, and *kibbeh* or *köfte*. The following Turkish *köfte* are delicious hot or cold, so they are ideal for country picnics.

HAVUÇ KÖFTESİ
(CARROT ROLLS WITH APRICOTS AND PINE NUTS)

Serves 4–6
Preparation time 40 minutes
Cooking time 5–10 minutes

10 medium-sized carrots, peeled, steamed until soft, and drained
2–3 slices day-old bread, rubbed into crumbs
8–10 dried apricots, finely chopped
4 scallions, finely sliced
3 tablespoons pine nuts
2–3 cloves garlic, crushed
1 teaspoon Middle Eastern red pepper (p152) or paprika
A bunch of fresh flat-leaf parsley, mint and dill
1 egg

Salt and ground black pepper
All-purpose flour
Sunflower oil for frying
Some lemon wedges

Put the cooked carrots into a bowl and mash with a fork. Add the rest of the ingredients except the flour, oil, and lemon wedges, and knead well. The mixture should be moist and sticky—if it is too wet and sticky, add extra bread crumbs. Tip a small heap of flour onto a flat surface. Take an apricot-size portion of the mixture in your hands and mold it into a sticky, oblong roll. Dip the roll in the flour to coat it, pat it into shape, and put it on a plate. Repeat with the rest of the mixture.

Heat a thin layer of sunflower oil in a heavy-based skillet. Place the carrot rolls in it and fry over a moderate heat until they are nicely brown on all sides. Drain them on paper towels and serve hot or cold with lemon wedges, or with garlic-flavored yogurt.

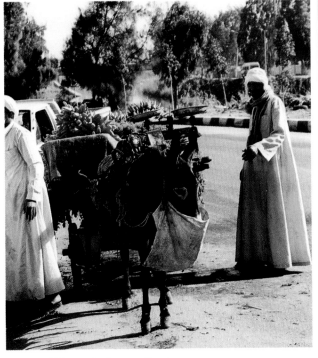

Carrots sold from a donkey cart, Egypt

OKRA

(BAMIA) *Hibiscus esculentus*

Okra is thought to be native to Africa but there is no trace of it in the Middle East until the thirteenth century, when it was recorded growing beside the Nile in Egypt. In some parts of the Middle East immature okra is picked while still small and hung on strings to dry.

Fresh okra

A field of okra

HOW IT GROWS

Another member of the mallow family, the *Hibiscus esculentus* is an annual plant that grows in tropical and subtropical regions. Although they are eaten as a vegetable, okra are the pods of this plant. It is cultivated extensively in Egypt.

APPEARANCE AND TASTE

Generally, the pods are ridged, dark or light green, and long and tapering, hence their other name, "ladies' fingers." However, some varieties are stubby and fat, while others are almost red.

They range in size from about 1 inch to 8 inches. Each pod has compartments filled with seeds and a gummy substance that gives okra its particular character. If left whole and cooked lightly, they remain crunchy and pod-like, but if they are cut before cooking, they become slimy, a texture that some people like. The tiny dried pods are gray-green and quite hairy. When they are added to soups and stews, they impart a tart flavor.

Dried okra

BUYING AND STORING

Fresh green okra should be firm and free of black markings. They are available in Asian stores and in some supermarkets, but don't keep for very long. Dried okra, on the other hand, are available only in Middle Eastern and whole-food stores. They keep for a year in a dry place.

CULINARY USES

When preparing okra, some cooks toss them in lemon juice before cooking so they retain their color. Lightly fried with a little sugar and lemon juice is quite a popular way of cooking fresh okra quickly to eat with rice or as a *mezze* dish; they can also be dipped in batter and deep-fried. They are sometimes used instead of zucchini in the sauce for the Iraqi specialty *koubba helwa* (p 79). And

throughout the Middle East, apart from in Iran, okra are cooked with beef, lamb, or chicken in a stew, or with tomatoes and onions in a simple ragout, sometimes flavored with garlic, sour pomegranate juice, dill, or fresh cilantro. In Iran they are relatively new and don't make an appearance in the traditional dishes, but their Persian name, *bamieh*, is borrowed by sweet pastries that are shaped like okra and bathed in syrup. The dried okra beads are used solely for stews and soups, such as the Anatolian dish *kuru bamya çorbası*.

In parts of the Middle East it is quite common to cook vegetables with a little sugar and lemon juice, especially if the dish is going to be eaten cold. Okra are particularly good done this way, as are leeks, shallots, and eggplants. In this simple Arab recipe the okra are kept whole and eaten like deep-fried anchovies, from head to tail. The whole sweet-and-sour pods are popped into the mouth, complete with stalk, as they are deliciously tender with a crunchy bite to them.

BAMIA
(SWEET-AND-SOUr OKRA)

Serves 4
Preparation time 5 minutes
Cooking time 10–15 minutes

12 ounces fresh okra, washed and
   left whole
Juice of 1 lemon
3 tablespoons olive oil
1 tablespoon sugar
Salt and freshly ground black
   pepper

Put the okra into a bowl and
toss in the lemon juice. Leave
them for 5 minutes, then lift
them out onto a plate, leaving
most of the lemon juice behind.

Heat the olive oil in a wide,
heavy-based pan and add the
okra. Sauté them for about
5 minutes, tossing them gently

about in the pan. Sprinkle with
the sugar and toss them again,
then add the lemon juice.

Season the okra with salt and
pepper, and pour in a little water
to just cover the base of the pan.
Cook for a further 5 minutes,
adding a splash more water if
necessary, until the pan juices are
almost caramelized and the okra
are beautifully tender.

Serve hot, or leave to cool in the
pan and serve cold, dipped in the
sweet-and-sour juices.

**The strings of small, sour-tasting
dried okra hanging in the
markets are usually destined for
a lamb or chicken stew, or for
this traditional Anatolian soup,
which is served to refresh the
palate between courses at
ceremonial feasts.**

KURU BAMYA ÇORBASI
(DRIED OKRA SOUP)

Serves 4–6
Preparation time 10 minutes
Cooking time 50 minutes

¼ cup diced mutton
2 onions, finely chopped
1 teaspoon coriander seeds
1–2 tablespoons sheep tail fat or
   clarified butter (ghee)
2 tablespoons tomato paste
5 cups lamb stock
2 ounces small dried okra
Juice of 1 lemon
Salt and freshly ground black
   pepper

In a heavy-based pan, fry the
meat and onions with the
coriander seeds in the fat or
butter. When they begin to
brown, stir in the tomato paste,

followed by the stock. Bring to a
boil, then reduce the heat and
simmer for about 20 minutes,
until the meat is tender.

Meanwhile, rub the dried okra in
a clean dishtowel to remove the
dust and hairs. Rinse them, toss
them in half the lemon juice, and
place them in a pan. Cover with
just enough water and boil them
for about 10 minutes. Drain and
refresh them, and if they are on
strings, slip them off at this stage,
then add them to the soup with
the rest of the lemon juice.

Bring the soup to a boil once
more, add salt and pepper to
taste, then cover the pan, reduce
the heat, and simmer for a further
15–20 minutes. Serve the soup
hot with bread, or spoon it over
plain rice.

Bamia

TOMATO

(BANADURA) *Lycopersicon lycopersicum*

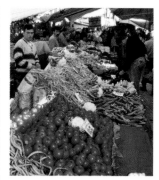

Covered vegetable market, Turkey

In spite of its ubiquitous use, the tomato is relatively new to the Middle East. The Aztec cultivated it long before it ever arrived on the Mediterranean shore, where it was treated with suspicion because it came from the family that contained deadly nightshade. Along with potatoes, corn, and capsicum and chili peppers, tomatoes reached the Ottoman Empire from the New World, via Spain, in the sixteenth century, when Madrid and Constantinople dominated the political stage. Considering how ancient the Middle Eastern culinary tradition is, it is amazing that the influence of this relatively recent fruit is so great in the food of the Middle East. It sits so perfectly in practically every dish, as if it has always been there. The most descriptive name for tomato is the Persian *gojeh farangi*, which means "foreign plum." The flat roofs of rural dwellings throughout the Middle East are used for reducing and thickening fresh tomato pulp in the hot sun, to be used by each household in winter.

Plum tomatoes

Vine tomatoes

HOW IT GROWS

The tomato plant, which is a member of the *Solanaceae* family, to which capsicum peppers, potatoes. and eggplants belong, grows well in a Mediterranean climate, often in poor soil. Generally, the fruit (it is termed a vegetable only because of its culinary use) of the plant is harvested from late summer to early autumn.

APPEARANCE AND TASTE

The tomatoes of the Middle East are usually large and long or fat and round. They range in color from greenish red to brilliant crimson, and because they grow in the right conditions, they are all tasty, juicy, and sweet.

MANUFACTURING

Turkey is one of the biggest producers of tomatoes. Tons of fresh tomatoes are exported every year. Many are preserved in cans or turned into a commercial tomato paste, and they are dried for export too.

BUYING AND STORING

Freshly plucked tomatoes that still smell of the vine are the best, but most tomatoes for sale have been kept refrigerated for days. No matter what shape, color or size, choose firm, taut-skinned tomatoes and keep them in a cool place. Tinned tomatoes and tomato paste keep for a long time if unopened. Once opened, they must be used within days. Dried tomatoes keep well in an airtight container or in olive oil.

CULINARY USES

The culinary role of the tomato is infinite. It marries well with herbs, onion, garlic, eggplant, peppers, pulses, grains, meat, and fish. The list goes on. It provides the color, pulp, and juice in many vegetable, meat, and fish stews and soups, such as *âbgoosht* (p115), a substantial working man's lamb soup in Iran. It binds together onions, garlic, and peppers in stuffings and fillings, as in the famous Turkish dish *İmam bayıldı* (p 51), and in *khandrajo*, a Jewish tomato and eggplant filling for pastries. It binds together similar ingredients in egg dishes, such as *menemen* or the Arab *eggah* dishes. Various tomato-based rice dishes, some with herbs, others with potatoes or eggplants, are served with grilled or roast meat and poultry.

The big, juicy, round tomatoes are often baked or poached whole, stuffed with an aromatic rice or ground meat mixture. Slices of tomato provide a moist cap for many other stuffed vegetables, and chunks of tomato are often threaded onto

Weighing carrots and tomatoes

kabobs for a burst of juice. Raw tomatoes are so sweet and refreshing, they are often added to vegetable, grain, or pulse salads. They are pulped and used to make a sauce for *rishta* (noodles, p126), *manti* (an ancient form of pasta), and for some meatballs. Sometimes the sauce is spiced with chili, garlic, coriander, and cumin, with a touch of fruitiness from the sour pomegranate or grape molasses.

Tomato paste is added to stews and pulse and rice dishes, and it binds the spices in the raw meat and bulgur balls called *çiğ köfte* in Turkish and *kibbeh nayya* in Arabic. Tomato paste is also used for the delicious Arab flat breads, *lahma bi ajeen* (p188), which are a bit like a thin pizza with a tasty, ground lamb topping. Unripe green tomatoes are pickled in salt and vinegar, and really ripe, freshly picked tomatoes are often eaten like a fruit to quench the thirst.

One of the characteristics of Yemeni cooking is the use of hot spices. *Zhug* (p169), which is one of the fieriest pastes in the Middle East, and *hilbeh* (p199), a hot fenugreek and cilantro paste, both come from Yemen. Even this simple salad is lit up with a hot chili.

BANADURA SALATA BIL KIZBARA
(TOMATO SALAD WITH CHILI AND CILANTRO)

Serves 4
Preparation time 20 minutes
Cooking time –

6 plump, fresh tomatoes, peeled and coarsely chopped
1 hot green chili, stalk and seeds removed, finely chopped
2 cloves garlic, finely chopped
A bunch of fresh cilantro leaves, finely chopped
A little sugar
2–3 tablespoons olive oil
Juice of ½ lime or lemon
Salt

Put the chopped tomatoes into a bowl.

Add the chili, garlic, and cilantro. Sprinkle with a little sugar and mix it all together.

Pour in the olive oil and lime or lemon juice, season with salt, and toss it again before serving.

Tomato-based stews featuring a single vegetable are common throughout the Middle East. Particularly popular are the ones made with okra, zucchini, green beans, and Jerusalem artichokes. This dish can be served hot or cold as a side dish or on its own with rice.

TARTOUFA
(JERUSALEM ARTICHOKE AND TOMATO STEW)

Serves 3–4
Preparation time 15minutes
Cooking time 35–40 minutes

2–3 tablespoons olive oil
1 onion, finely chopped
1–2 cloves garlic, smashed
1 pound Jerusalem artichokes, washed, peeled, and cut into thumb-length pieces
2–3 tomatoes, peeled and chopped
1 tablespoon tomato paste
1 teaspoon sugar
A small bunch of fresh flat-leaf parsley and dill, chopped
Salt and freshly ground black pepper
1 lemon, cut into wedges

In a heavy-based pan, fry the onion in the olive oil until it begins to brown.

Stir in the garlic, then add the artichokes and cook for 1–2 minutes, rolling them about in the pan.

Add the tomatoes, the tomato paste, sugar, and most of the parsley and dill (reserve some for serving). Pour in just enough water to cover, then simmer gently for about 30 minutes until the artichokes are tender and the sauce has reduced.

Add salt and pepper to taste, sprinkle with the remaining parsley and dill, and serve with lemon to squeeze over it.

Harvesting tomatoes in the Jordan valley

The following Turkish dish is often cooked in ports and bus stations while passengers wait for transport. Large, slightly curved, shallow pans are set over a fire or gas flame, and the dish is cooked in minutes. As street and station food, the eggs are usually scrambled through the tomatoes and peppers, but when the dish is cooked at home, the eggs are often set on top. It is delicious served with a dollop of garlic-flavored yogurt.

MENEMEN
(TOMATOES AND PEPPERS WITH EGGS)

Serves 4
Preparation time 15 minutes
Cooking time approximately 20 minutes

2 onions, sliced
2 green peppers, sliced
2 tablespoons olive oil + a little butter
1 teaspoon Middle Eastern red pepper (p152) or 1 chili, finely sliced
1–2 teaspoons sugar
5–6 tomatoes, peeled and chopped or 1 can of chopped tomatoes
4 eggs
5 tablespoons thick, set yogurt
1–2 cloves garlic, crushed
Salt and freshly ground black pepper

In a wide skillet, fry the onions and green peppers in the olive oil and butter until they take on a bit of color. Then stir in the Middle Eastern red pepper or chili, and add the tomatoes and sugar. Cook for a few minutes until the liquid has reduced.

Season to taste, then crack the eggs over the top of the tomato mixture, positioning them around the pan. Cover and leave to cook gently until the eggs are just cooked.

Meanwhile, beat the yogurt with the garlic in a bowl and season to taste. Serve the *menemen* directly from the pan and enjoy it with the cool yogurt.

EGGPLANT

(BADINJAN) *Solanum melongena*

Originally from India, the eggplant plays such a leading role in the culinary cultures of the Middle East one would think it had always been there, yet it was introduced only in the seventh and eighth centuries. The Arabs fell under its spell when they conquered Iran in the seventh century and adopted the Old Persian name, *badin-gan*, changing the hard "g" to *al-badinjan*. From there, the Arabs spread the eggplant through the rest of the Middle East and North Africa, where it is now considered a staple food, often referred to as "poor man's meat." In Iran it is called "poor man's caviar." The eggplant is also known as *betingan* in parts of the Middle East, and as *patlıcan* in Turkey, where it is considered to be the king of vegetables. As there are said to be two hundred dishes using eggplant in Turkey and they appear so frequently on the table, there is a saying: "*Patlıcansız tarafından olsun!*" ("Let it be from the part without an eggplant"), meaning, "For goodness sake, let's have a change!"

Eggplant jam

HOW IT GROWS

Eggplants need warmth to grow, so the Mediterranean climate suits them well. They are grown throughout the Middle East.

APPEARANCE AND TASTE

There are many different kinds of eggplant. In the Middle East the most common varieties are long and slender, ideal for stuffing, or large and bulbous, which are delicious smoked over a flame or fried. Their shiny skins vary in color from violet to deep purple and blue-black. Eggplants have their own distinct taste, but when they are cooked with spices, herbs, and other ingredients, they absorb the flavors of the dish. Eggplants cooked whole over a naked flame or fire have a sharp, smoky flavor that blends beautifully with yogurt and olive oil.

BUYING AND STORING

Regardless of color or size, fresh eggplants should be firm and glossy. If they are soft, spongy, or turning brown, they are too old. Generally, supermarkets sell fat or thin eggplants, with little variation on color and size. Italian, Greek, Middle Eastern, and Asian stores sell a variety of shapes and sizes, including the tiny eggplants (sometimes from Kenya) that are ideal for jam and the classic Persian stew *khoresht-e bâdenjân*. Fresh eggplants keep for about two weeks stored in a cool, dry place, or in the refrigerator. Dried eggplant shells, used for stuffing and eggplant pickles and jams, are available in some Middle Eastern stores.

Dried eggplant skins

CULINARY USES

Eggplants have a sponge-like ability to soak up oil and cooking juices. Rather than being a drawback, this is one of the delights of eggplants, except when they are fried. To prevent them from absorbing too much oil in the skillet, Middle Eastern cooks soak the sliced or diced eggplants in salted water and then drain them before using. Otherwise, the succulent eggplant should be left to absorb all

Eggplant

the garlicky, tasty goodness of the dish.

Perhaps the most famous eggplant dish in the Middle East is the Turkish İmam bayıldı (p51), the sumptuous stuffed eggplant over which the Imam was said to have fainted with pleasure at the quantity of olive oil used. Eggplants are frequently smoked over a naked flame and then the cooked pulp is used in numerous olive oil- or yogurt-based salads and dips, such as the Turkish patlıcan ezmesi and the great Lebanese and Syrian favorite, baba ghanoush (p 82, also known as moutabal). In Turkey the famous dish Hünkâr beğendi (p 46), meaning "Sultan's delight," consists of the smoked pulp combined with a cheese sauce and served as a bed for meatballs cooked in a tomato sauce. The long, thin varieties are stuffed with an aromatic rice, and the plumper ones are split open and stuffed with meat, as in the Turkish karnıyarık.

Throughout the Middle East, they are fried or grilled and served with plain or garlic-flavored yogurt or a fresh, piquant tomato sauce. They can also be served with a dressing made with olive oil, garlic, and pomegranate or grape molasses. In recipes for which we can also use zucchini, fried eggplant slices or chunks are added to meatballs and patty mixtures and are baked with rishta (p125) in a tomato sauce.

Eggplants are a popular ingredient in bulgur and rice pilafs, such as the Istanbul patlicanlı pilav; in pulse and vegetable dishes, such as the Iranian eggplant and pomegranate stew sheeshandâz, which is just an eggplant fesenjân; in savory pastries, and in lamb stews. They are delicious in an Arab fatta dish, particularly favored in Egypt and Syria, where a bed of toasted pita bread is layered with cooked lamb and fried eggplant, and topped with a garlic and tahini-flavored yogurt. A rather splendid-looking mold of eggplant, lamb, and rice, makloub (maqlubi, p131), meaning "turned over," is Palestinian in origin but can also be found in Jordan, Lebanon, and Syria.

In the south of Turkey, Iran, and Syria, a delicious jam is made with young, small, seedless eggplants, which are dipped in lime water to preserve their color and shape before cooking. Pickled eggplant is also a great favorite, often stuffed with walnuts or peppers and wrapped in celery leaves; sometimes the eggplant slices are wrapped around garlic.

The pulp of smoked, grilled eggplants is mixed with a variety of ingredients throughout the Middle East to create tasty, soothing mezze dishes. The following recipe is particularly popular in Turkey.

PATLICAN EZMESİ
(SMOKED EGGPLANT PUREE)

Serves 4
Preparation time 5 minutes
  + 15 minutes' grilling and
  peeling eggplants
Cooking time –

2 big eggplants
2–3 tablespoons olive oil
2 tablespoons white wine vinegar
3–4 cloves garlic, crushed
4–5 heaping tablespoons creamy
  thick yogurt
Salt and freshly ground black
  pepper

Place the eggplants directly onto a gas flame or, if cooking outdoors, over a charcoal grill. Turn them occasionally until they are well smoked and soft. (If you are using a gas flame the eggplant skin will become charred and papery, whereas the charcoal grill lightens and toughens the skin.)

Take the eggplants by the stalks and hold them under cold running water to gently remove the skin, taking care to leave behind as much of the vegetable as possible. Still holding the eggplants by the stems, gently squeeze the softened pulp to drain off the excess water, then lay them on a board.

Cut off the stems and chop the eggplants to a pulp. Put the pulp into a bowl and beat in the olive oil, vinegar, and garlic, followed by the yogurt, salt, and pepper. (All of these ingredients can be adjusted to your own taste.)

Spoon the mixture onto a serving dish and splash a little olive oil over it to keep it moist. Serve with plenty of fresh bread.

Patlıcan ezmesi

Wherever they conquered, the Arabs introduced the eggplant and its many dishes, like the following classic Persian stew. Many variations of it can be found in the path of the Arab conquests. Traditionally, small whole eggplants and tiny, sour grapes are used for this dish. To substitute, large eggplants can be cut into long strips and golden raisins could be used, but the sourness will come only from unripe grapes.

KHORESHT-E BÂDENJÂN
(PERSIAN EGGPLANT STEW)

Serves 4
Preparation time 15–20 minutes
Cooking time approximately
   1 hour

3–4 tablespoons olive oil (you
   may need more if using strips of
   eggplant, as they will absorb
   more oil)
2¼ pounds small eggplants
1 onion, halved and sliced
8 ounces lamb, trimmed of fat
   and cut into 1-inch cubes
1 teaspoon ground turmeric
2 tablespoons tomato paste
2 tomatoes, peeled and chopped
½ cup small, unripe grapes
Juice of ½ lemon
Salt and freshly ground black
   pepper

Heat the olive oil in a heavy-based pan and fry the whole eggplants until they have softened. (If using long strips of eggplant, fry them until golden.) Remove from the pan and drain on paper towels.

Add the onion to the pan and fry until golden. Add the lamb and brown it on both sides, then stir in the turmeric. Add the tomato paste, chopped tomatoes, sour grapes, and lemon juice, with enough water to cover. Put on the lid and simmer gently for approximately 30 minutes.

Strings of dried eggplants and capsicum peppers for sale

Pop the eggplants back into the pan, add a little water to cover, season with salt and pepper, and simmer for a further 20 minutes, until the meat is tender.

Spoon the stew onto a serving dish, placing the eggplants around the edge with the rest in the middle. Serve hot with rice.

A classic dish from the Ottoman palace kitchens, *karnıyarık* literally translates as "split stomach," referring to the whole eggplants being slit open and filled. The dish can be made with fat or thin eggplants and served hot or cold.

KARNIYARIK
(EGGPLANT STUFFED WITH GROUND LAMB)

Serves 4
Preparation time 25–30 minutes
Cooking time approximately
   1 hour

1 cup ground lamb
1 onion, finely chopped
2 tomatoes, peeled and chopped
1 tablespoon tomato paste
2 tablespoons pine nuts
1 teaspoon ground cinnamon
1 teaspoon ground allspice
A bunch of fresh parsley and dill,
   chopped
4 eggplants, partially peeled like
   the stripes of a zebra and
   soaked in salt water for 1 hour
Sunflower oil
1 tomato, sliced
1 green bell pepper, seeded and
   cut into 4 strips
¼ cup olive oil
Juice of ½ lemon
Roughly ¼ cup water
1 teaspoon sugar
Salt and freshly ground pepper

Preheat the oven to 400°F.

Put the ground lamb in a bowl with the onion, tomatoes, tomato paste, nuts, spices, herbs, salt, and pepper, and mix well. Knead the mixture with your hands, lifting it up and slapping it down into the bowl, until it resembles a paste.

Drain the eggplants and pat dry. Heat some sunflower oil in a shallow pan and roll the eggplants in it until they are lightly browned and softened. Lift the eggplants out of the oil and place them in an ovenproof dish.

Use a knife or tongs to slit each eggplant open down the middle from top to bottom, taking care not to cut through the bottom and to leave the ends intact. Prise each slit open and stuff the eggplants with the meat mixture. Place a slice of tomato at the head of the meat stuffing and a strip of pepper below it, as if it is the stem and the tomato is the flower.

Mix the olive oil, lemon juice, and water with the sugar, and pour over the stuffed eggplants. Cover the dish with foil, pop it in the oven for 20 minutes, then remove the foil and put the dish back in the oven for a further 40 minutes, until the meat and eggplants are very tender and almost all the liquid has gone. Serve hot or cold.

SPINACH

(SABANIKH) *Spinacia oleracea*

Fresh spinach

According to the twelfth-century Arab writer Ibn al-Awam, spinach is the "prince of vegetables." It originated in Persia, where it was cultivated as early as the fourth century AD and was used as an herb. The word spinach derives from the old Persian name, *aspanakh*. After the Arabs had incorporated spinach into their cuisine, it spread across the Middle East and into Europe via the Moorish occupation of Spain. There are medieval recipes of Arab origin that use spinach in sweet dishes, combined with ingredients such as honey, almonds, and spices, but today all the spinach dishes of the Middle East are savory.

HOW IT GROWS

Spinach is a member of the beet family, which grows in temperate climates, often near the sea. It can be grown all year, but it is best picked small while the leaves are still tender.

APPEARANCE AND TASTE

Fresh spinach leaves vary in size and tenderness but all are dark green. When cooked, spinach becomes soft and has a strong flavor, which marries well with spices and creamy substances such as yogurt and soft cheese.

BUYING AND STORING

You have to buy a lot of fresh spinach to make a reasonable-size dish—the leaves reduce greatly when cooked. If you can, buy spinach on the stalk while it's still springy. Fresh spinach doesn't keep for long, but it can be cooked and frozen, or bought frozen, which is useful for soups and stews.

MEDICINAL AND OTHER USES

Spinach has a mild laxative effect. It is rich in vitamins and minerals, and is regarded as a source of iron and calcium. Spinach juice is such a strong green color, it is used as a vegetable dye.

CULINARY USES

Spinach combines well with cheese and eggs in the Arab-style omelet, *eggah*, and in fillings for thin savory pastries and flat breads, such as *fatayer bi sabanikh*, a bread-dough pie filled with a mixture of spinach, raisins, and walnuts. In Iran spinach is layered with rice and meat in a rather grand inverted dish called *tahcheen-o esfenâj*. Throughout the Middle East, spinach is added to *pilafs* and partnered with beans or chickpeas for color and texture, as in *aloo sfenaj*, a Persian dish of black-eyed beans, spinach, and prunes. It forms a thick sauce in a variety of lamb stews with almonds, golden raisins, apricots, and prunes, or with tart yellow plums in the Iranian dish *khoresht-e esfenâj-o aloo*. It is often cooked on its own, softened in a little butter with prunes or almonds, or sautéed with onions and blended with yogurt in the Iranian dish *boorâni-ye esfenâj*, and in a similar Turkish dish, *ispanak ezmesi*. In Iran and the Gulf a piquant, sour-tasting soup is made with spinach and split peas, and in Egypt the yogurt soup *labaneya* can be made with spinach or beet leaves. Chopped spinach is added to meatballs, or it is cooked in an ancient, hearty manner with meatballs and chickpeas, and it also appears with brown lentils in a medieval Persian dish, *shula kalambar*, which was believed to cure the sick.

Masjid-I-Jomeh, Isfahan, Iran

Baskets of spinach in a marketplace

A popular way of cooking spinach in the Middle East is to sauté it with onions or with pine nuts and raisins, toasted almonds or prunes. Simple and delicious, the following recipe is from Iraq.

SABANIKH BI KHAWKH
(SPINACH WITH PRUNES AND TOMATOES)

Serves 3–4
Preparation time 5–10 minutes
Cooking time 10 minutes

12 cups fresh spinach
2 tablespoons olive oil + a little butter
1 onion, halved and sliced
2 tomatoes, peeled and chopped
⅔ cup soft, pitted prunes (soak in water if not soft)
½–1 teaspoon ground coriander
1 scant teaspoon sugar
Salt and freshly ground black pepper

Wash the spinach well and remove any tough-looking leaves or stems. Put it into a pan with just the water remaining on the leaves, cover with the lid, and cook for a few minutes over a low heat, until the leaves soften and droop. Drain off any excess water and chop the spinach coarsely.

Heat the olive oil and butter in a shallow pan, stir in the onion, and fry until golden.

Add the tomatoes, prunes, coriander, and sugar, and cook for a few minutes, until the mixture has reduced a little. Mix in the spinach, season to taste, and serve hot.

According to legend, the origins of the Persian boorâni dishes are attributed to Queen Poorandokht, a monarch of the Sassanian dynasty in AD 626. She was said to be so fond of yogurt dishes that the chefs of the royal

Sabanikh bi khawkh

kitchens created some specifically for her, calling them Poorâni after the Queen herself. Later, the conquering Arabs adopted these dishes, changing the "p" to a "b" to suit their alphabet. The most popular boorâni dish is made with spinach, and variations of it are found throughout the Middle East. Traditionally, it is served as an accompaniment to a main course. In Turkey, where the dish is known by its Persian name in two of the Islamic strongholds, Bursa and Konya, it is served as a meze.

BOORÂNI-YE ESFENÂJ
(SPINACH WITH YOGURT)

Serves 4
Preparation time 5–10 minutes (+ overnight straining of yogurt if necessary)
Cooking time 10–15 minutes

2 tablespoons olive oil + butter
2 onions, halved and sliced
½ teaspoon ground turmeric
2¼ pounds fresh spinach, washed, drained, and chopped
1 cup strained yogurt
Salt and freshly ground pepper

In a heavy-based pan, heat the oil and butter. Stir in the onions and fry until golden. Stir in the turmeric and add the spinach.

Cover the pan and cook gently until the spinach is soft. Mix well and leave to cool.

Beat the strained yogurt in a bowl and add the spinach. Mix well and season to taste.

Serve cold, or chilled, with bread.

GLOSSARY

Advieh An Iranian spice mixture that varies from region to region, sometimes made with pistachio nuts or rose petals, but always including cardamom.

Alya The fat rendered from the podgy tail of the Asian sheep bred in the Middle East. Called *kuyrukyağı* in Turkish and *roghan-e donbeh* in Farsi, it is mainly used in the meat and grain dishes of rural areas.

Arak A clear alcoholic drink distilled from grapes and flavored with aniseed, which turns cloudy when diluted with water. In Turkey, where it is particularly popular with *meze* and fish, it is called *rakı*.

Baharat A ground spice mixture used throughout the Arab world. It varies from region to region, but generally includes black pepper, coriander seeds, cumin, cinnamon, cardamom, cloves, nutmeg, and paprika.

Bastirma Air-dried filet of cured beef in a fenugreek and garlic paste, called *pastırma* in Turkish and sometimes spelled *basterma* in Arabic.

Börek Turkish savory pastries from the Ottoman period. They can be baked, steamed, or fried.

Chelow Persian steamed white rice that is first parboiled.

Dibs A thick molasses from a variety of pressed fruits, used as a sweetener or for its fruity flavor. Called *robb* in Iran and *pekmez* in Turkey.

Dolma Any Turkish dish that is stuffed, such as peppers, tomatoes, zucchini flowers, vine leaves, and baby squid. Even the stuffed taxis in the cities are called *dolmuş*. In Iraq stuffed vegetables are known as *yapraq,* from the Turkish word for leaf, *yaprak*.

Eggah Arab omelets packed full of ingredients, akin to a Spanish omelet. Similar omelets in Iran are called *kookoo*.

Eid-el-Kurban An Islamic festival that marks Ibrahim's near-sacrifice of Isma'il (p69). A sheep is slaughtered and almost every part of it is consumed. In Turkey the same festival is called Kurban Bayramı.

Eishta Thick clotted cream, usually made from water-buffalo milk, known as *gaymar* in Iraq and *kaymak* in Turkey.

Ezme A Turkish *meze* dish of pounded, pulped, or pureed ingredients, often with olive oil or yogurt, that can be scooped up easily with bread.

Fatta A traditional dish of toasted or stale bread soaked in broth. The word *fatta* describes the breaking or crumbling of bread into pieces.

Fesenjân An ancient Persian dish of fowl or fish stewed with walnuts and sour pomegranate juice, known as *fisinjan* in Iraq.

Fila Paper-thin sheets of flat bread dough, used for sweet and savory deep-fried and layered pastries. Similar flat breads are called *yufka* in Turkey and *lavash* in Iran. The thin sheets of dough are called phyllo in America.

Furn A communal oven used for leavened and unleavened breads, called *firin* in Turkish.

Halwa A sweetmeat made with wheat or tahini and nuts or spices, called *helva* in Turkey.

Hawayij A peppery spice mixture from Yemen combining black peppercorns, caraway, cardamom, and turmeric.

Kanaka The small, tin-lined, brass or copper pot with a long handle for brewing coffee, called a *cezve* in Turkish.

Khoresht A thin Persian stew that is traditionally used as a sauce for rice.

Kibbeh Savory balls or patties made with pounded meat and bulgur, a specialty of Lebanon and Syria.

Kishk A dried and fermented mixture of wheat and yogurt used to flavor and thicken stews and soups, known as *tarkhina* in Iraq and *tarhana* in Turkey.

Laban The thick and creamy yogurt made from the milk of cows, sheep, or goats. In Farsi it is *mâst*. The Turkish word is *yoğurt*, from which the English word derives. *Laban* is also a

popular yogurt drink, which is sometimes called *abdug* and is known as *doogh* in Farsi and *ayran* in Turkish. When yogurt is strained to the consistency of cream cheese, it is called *labna* in Arabic.

Lime water Slaked lime powder diluted with water, used for bleaching and preserving young fruits and vegetables in jams.

Mansaf The national dish of Jordan and Arabia, consisting of a whole sheep or baby camel served on a bed of rice.

Mezze Literally translated as a "pleasant taste," *mezze* can be served either as an appetizer to a meal or as a nibble with a drink. The key to *mezze* dishes is to keep the quantities small, the colors vibrant, and the textures and tastes varied. In some parts of the Arab world *mezze* are called *mazza; ,* in Turkey the spelling is *meze*.

Polow A Persian method of cooking rice by parboiling it and then steaming it with vegetables, fruit, nuts, and spices.

Ramadan The ninth month of the Muslim lunar calendar during which the devout fast from sunrise to sunset. It is called Ramazan in Turkey.

Rishta Middle Eastern noodles, which are boiled or baked like pasta. The word derives from the Persian, *reshteh*.

Samna Clarified butter (or ghee), made from the churned milk of sheep, goats, or buffalo. With its distinctive taste and good keeping qualities, it is the preferred cooking fat among the nomadic and peasant communities.

Sujuk Air-dried lamb or beef sausages with lots of spices, particularly cumin. It is called *sucuk* in Turkish.

Tahdeeg The golden-brown crust that forms at the bottom of the rice pot, a traditional feature of Persian rice.

Tahini A thick sesame paste made from crushed sesame seeds, used most in the cuisines of Syria and Lebanon. It is called *tahin* in Turkish and *rashi* in Iran and Iraq.

Tandoor A traditional outdoor clay oven for bread, called a *tandır* in Turkish.

Tarator A nut and garlic sauce commonly served with fish.

Zaatar An Arab spice mixture that includes sesame seeds, sumac, salt, and dried thyme.

Zeytinyağlı Vegetable dishes cooked in olive oil and served cold, a legacy of the Ottoman palace kitchens.

Zhug A fiery paste from Yemen, made with chilies, cardamom, and garlic.

BIBLIOGRAPHY

For further reading on the food and culinary cultures of the Middle East, here's a list of books that proved invaluable to me when researching this one:

Miriam Al Hashimi, *Traditional Arabic Cooking* (Garnet Publishing: 1993)
Ghillie Başan, *Classic Turkish Cookery* (I.B. Tauris: 1997)
Alan Davidson, *The Oxford Companion to Food* (Oxford: 1999)
Halil Inalcık, *The Ottoman Empire* (Phoenix: 1994)
Tess Mallos, *The Complete Middle East Cookbook* (Grub Street: 1995)
Middle East (Lonely Planet, third edition: 2000)
Claudia Roden, *A New Book of Middle Eastern Food* (Penguin Books: 1986)
Margaret Shaida, *The Legendary Cuisine of Persia* (Penguin Books: 1994)
Wilfred Thesiger, *Arabian Sands* (Penguin Books: 1964)
Wilfred Thesiger, *The Marsh Arabs* (Penguin Books: 1967)
Sonia Uvezian, *Recipes and Remembrances from an Eastern Mediterranean Kitchen* (University of Texas Press: 1999)
Sami Zubaida and Richard Tapper (eds), *Culinary Cultures of the Middle East* (I.B. Tauris: 1994)

INDEX

ACKNOWLEDGEMENTS

We would like to thank everyone, here and abroad, who has been involved in this book. It has been a delightfully aromatic journey from beginning to end and we are indebted to many. In particular, we would like to mention Sally Little of the Jordan Tourism Board and Lana Harmaneh in Amman, Bärbel Kirchner of the Government of Dubai, Dubai Department of Tourism and Commerce Marketing, Turkish Airlines (THY) and the Turkish Tourist Board. We would also like to thank the Fry family of Frys of Chelsea for supplying fruit and vegetables for photography, particularly Maureen, who went out of her way to send them to us in our remote location. And Mrs Shahla Suleiman and Lel Scobie in the Department of Islamic and Middle Eastern Studies at Edinburgh University, who gave up their time to assist with some of the Arabic words.

We would like to mention our agent, Giles Gordon, who is always an encouraging voice at the end of the phone. We take our hats off to Kyle Cathie, herself, both for taking us on in the first place and for bearing with us under frustrating circumstances. Georgina Burns worked hard and long, patiently sourcing photographs. And Sheila Davies, the editor, deserves a medal for her mammoth task of laboriously checking details and photographs against the clock. Where others would have torn their hair out, she never lost her charm or her cool.

On a more personal note, we salute Emin and Sibel Iren for all their help on the ground and for extending their warm hospitality in their sumptuous apartment to include our boisterous children. Similarly, Ali and Tess Erginsoy kindly leant us props and dishes but, more importantly, they frequently and uncomplainingly looked after our children. To both sets of friends, we owe a big thank you.

All photography by Jonathan Başan except the following:
Bridgeman Art Library p13, 15 (Rouargue brothers), p138 (Lemoine engraving) & 232; **Garden Picture Library:** Christi Carter p180, Christopher Fairweather p80 (bottom); Lamontagne p97 (bottom), 217; Marie O'Hara p202; **Hayes Archive:** p86 (top), 138, 150, 170, 172, 176 & 221; **Impact Colour Library:** Christopher Bluntzer p39, 69 & 81; Mark Cator p64 & 80 (top); Rupert Conant p25; Alex Dufort p26, 56 & 212; Ben Edwards p23 & 126; Paul Forster p53; Michael Good p33 (top), 38, 49 (top), 60 (bottom) & 168; Mark Henley p16, 18, 72 (top), 86 (bottom), 101 & 208x2; Colin Jones p240; Alan Keohane p11, 14, 17, 19, 22, 30/1, 34 (top), 36, 45, 46x2, 49 (bottom), 51, 62, 65x2, 66, 68, 72 (bottom), 84 (bottom), 93 (top), 190 (top), 214 (bottom left); Toby Key p83 & 84 (top) Robin Laurance p5 & 27; Alain le Garsmeur p52 (top); Wendy Levine p158; W. Louvet/Visa p210; Bill Lyons p107 & 227 (bottom); Farzin Malaki p42, 61 (top), 76 & 121 (top); Gary John Norman p24; Caroline Penn p20, 28, 33 (bottom), 52 (bottom), 61 (bottom), 122, 124, 134, 164, 207 (top) & 219; Dominic Sansoni p148/9; Simon Shepheard p34 (bottom), 71 (bottom), 90 & 206; Paul Simmons p12; Bruce Stephens p214 (bottom right); Pamela Toler p99 (top) & 174; Alexis Wallerstein p224; **Lonely Planet:** Greg Elms p44 (top), 103 (top), 130, 132 (bottom); Eddie Gerald p60; Thomas Hartwell p110/1; Matthew Kurrian p93 (bottom); Chris Mellor p58/9 & 94; Tony Wheeler p117; **Still Picture Library:** Jack Mikrut p8/9